# Psychoanalysis in a New Light

What kind of a science is psychoanalysis? What constitutes its
domain? What truth claims does it maintain? In this unique
and scholarly work concerning the nature of psychoanalysis,
Gunnar Karlsson guides his arguments through phenomenological
thinking which, he claims, can be seen as an alternative to the
recent attempts to cite neuropsychoanalysis as the answer to the
crisis of psychoanalysis. Karlsson criticizes this effort to ground
psychoanalysis in biology and neurology and emphasizes instead the
importance of defining the psychoanalytic domain from the vantage
point of the character of consciousness. His understanding of the
unconscious, the libido and the death drive offer new insights into
the nature of psychoanalysis, and he also illuminates and develops
neglected dimensions such as consciousness and self-consciousness.
Karlsson's approach to psychoanalysis is rigorous yet original, and
this book fills an intellectual gap with implications for both the
theoretical understanding and clinical issues of psychoanalysis.

GUNNAR KARLSSON is Professor in the Department of Education at
Stockholm University. He is also a private practising psychoanalyst.

# Psychoanalysis in a New Light

GUNNAR KARLSSON

CAMBRIDGE
UNIVERSITY PRESS

CAMBRIDGE UNIVERSITY PRESS
Cambridge, New York, Melbourne, Madrid, Cape Town, Singapore,
São Paulo, Delhi, Dubai, Tokyo

Cambridge University Press
The Edinburgh Building, Cambridge CB2 8RU, UK

Published in the United States of America by
Cambridge University Press, New York

www.cambridge.org
Information on this title: www.cambridge.org/9780521122443

Originally published in Swedish as *Psykoanalysen i Ny Belysning*
by Symposion 2004, © Gunnar Karlsson 2004

First published in English by Cambridge University Press 2010 as *Psychoanalysis
in a New Light* © Gunnar Karlsson 2010

English translation © Gunnar Karlsson 2010

First published 2010

Printed in the United Kingdom at the University Press, Cambridge

*A catalogue record for this publication is available from the British Library*

*Library of Congress Cataloguing in Publication data*
Karlsson, Gunnar, 1955–
  Psychoanalysis in a new light / Gunnar Karlsson.
    p.  cm.
  ISBN 978-0-521-19805-9 (hardback)
  1. Psychoanalysis.  I. Title.
  BF173.K357 2010
  150.19′5–dc22
  2010001518

ISBN 978-0-521-19805-9 Hardback
ISBN 978-0-521-12244-3 Paperback

# Contents

# Preface

Know thyself
*Inscription at Delphi*

Don't be ashamed that you are human, be proud!
Within you, vault opens up behind vault ad infinitum.
Never will you be finished, and that's as it ought to be.
*Tomas Tranströmer*
*For the living and the dead*

Psychoanalysis has been pronounced dead a number of times, despite its short history within the scientific field of study. Psychoanalysis has not only been dismissed due to its alleged lack of scientific character. Per Magnus Johansson (1997: 10) provides a sample of some of the other types of accusations that have been made against the psychoanalytic method:

> Psychoanalysis has, during its hundred year old history ...
> among other things, been accused of: pansexualism, encouraging
> sexual frivolity, being a Jewish science, for possibly being more
> suitable to the people of Southern Europe, but hardly applicable
> to those living in Northern Europe. It has also been assumed
> to be suitable to the Nordic population but not the Latin.
> Psychoanalysis has been criticised for exclusively analysing and
> being applicable to upper-class women, and for being captive to
> an oppressive patriarchal system, for being a bourgeois science.
> It has also been criticised for being too time-consuming and
> expensive, for being unscientific and for not having any evident
> therapeutic effect, and even for being harmful and dangerous.

The scientific status of psychoanalysis deserves an in-depth discussion. It is indeed a complex science. I hope that this book can be viewed as a contribution to the discussion of the scientific nature of psychoanalysis. What is its scientific domain? What constitutes this scientific domain? What truth claims does it maintain? These are some of the main topics I will discuss in my book. I have not based my discussion on an evaluation of the scientific and/or therapeutic effectiveness of psychoanalysis. Such research on psychoanalysis is valuable, but has its limits if one wishes to understand the nature of psychoanalysis. The basis of my work has been to examine instead the actual psychoanalytic process (what actually happens in the psychoanalytic interaction between the analysand and the analyst) as a scientific project – that is to say, research project – namely psychoanalytic research. Psychoanalytic research, roughly described, strives towards self-knowledge. I thus wish to discuss the scientific domain, conditions for and character of psychoanalysis/psychoanalytic research.

I have to some extent borrowed from phenomenological philosophy in order to carry out this task. Phenomenology as a philosophical movement is approximately as old as psychoanalysis, founded by the philosopher and mathematician Edmund Husserl (1859–1938). Psychoanalysis and phenomenology belong to the dominating traditions of thought that were developed during the twentieth century. There has been a certain amount of discussion between the two traditions, but these two exciting and sophisticated sciences have not had as much to do with each other as would have been expected. By taking some of the phenomenological ways of thinking into consideration, I believe that psychoanalysis could achieve a more profound self-understanding as a science.

In chapter 1 I will discuss the relationship between phenomenology and psychoanalysis in general. A brief introduction to phenomenology and some of its main concepts will be provided. I will identify a number of points in common that allow for a fruitful interchange between them. In this book, phenomenological philosophy and its theory of knowledge will assist in the understanding of psychoanalysis, its scientific domain and its conditions.

Chapter 2 deals with the issue of how scientific descriptions of the world are preceded by as well as preconditioned by everyday experiences. Husserl has given this prescientific experience of the world the term 'life-world'. The life-world, in other words, is the world we are born into and in which we grow up. The life-world is of epistemological importance to the phenomenologist, as it constitutes the foundation from which sciences can be constructed. The life-world cannot be reduced to purely (natural) scientific descriptions, as the so-called 'naturalistic attitude' seeks to accomplish. The chapter contains a critique of naturalism, the idea that the natural scientific descriptions of the world are descriptions of an objective reality, independent of the subject/man. In the naturalistic attitude, the primordiality of the life-world, both logically and chronologically, is neglected in relation to the natural scientific method of describing the world. Through the use of Husserl's phenomenological reflection, I will argue for the primordiality of the life-world in relation to natural scientific descriptions of the world. The chapter is important for two reasons. Firstly, it clarifies the overarching function of phenomenology in this book. Secondly, the chapter provides background for the critical examination of a neuropsychoanalytic project conducted in the following chapter.

The relationship between psychoanalysis and biology has been debated, and one can find various ideas among psychoanalysts regarding the question of the relevance of natural scientific biology for psychoanalysis and psychoanalytic practice. The question is complex and in chapter 3 I will limit myself to critically examining a neuropsychoanalytic project that encompasses a discussion on the age-old philosophical problem of the relationship between body and mind, as well as the creation of a new discipline: neuropsychoanalysis. Neuropsychoanalysis claims to show a way out of the dead end that traditional (non-neurological) psychoanalysis has supposedly found itself in. My examination of *The brain and the inner world* (Solms and Turnbull 2002), in particular, demonstrates that neuropsychoanalysis suffers from a variety of problems – among others, serious self-contradictions. In accordance with the background of chapter 2, in which I argue in favour of the epistemological priority of the life-world in relationship to the (natural) sciences, neuropsychoanalysis as examined in chapter 3 shows itself to be an example of a naturalistic attitude. According to the naturalistic attitude, one does not do justice to subjectivity or life-world experiences. These have a tendency to be reduced to natural scientific descriptions, in this case clothed as the unconscious.

After examining this (neuro)psychoanalysis, it is deemed urgent to find an appropriate starting point for the examination of the domain of psychoanalysis, not least the unconscious. Chapter 4 contains a discussion on the psychoanalytic conceptualization of the psychical in psychoanalysis and attempts to discuss the conditions for and the character of the unconscious. In my view, it is important that an investigation of what the unconscious is starts where the unconscious reveals itself in clinical practice. This is where the issue of consciousness enters, since the psychoanalytic process begins with the conscious self-understanding of the analysand and moves forward through the use of conscious validations of interpretations made in relation to the unconscious.

In order to understand what the unconscious is, we must understand what essentially characterizes consciousness, and here we can make use of phenomenological analyses of consciousness. In phenomenology, the essence of consciousness is that it is intentional (meaning-bestowing). My thesis, discussed in the chapter, is that the unconscious, in its most radical form, breaks with the synthesizing function of consciousness. The unconscious has a dissolving character and shows itself as something contrary to and foreign in relation to the conscious intending of the ego. I concur with the French psychoanalyst Jean Laplanche's (b.1924) ideas of the unconscious as untamed and wild, as it is expressed in Freud's id (*Das Es*) or Laplanche's own original version of the death drive.

Furthermore, my argument is that the unconscious can only emerge given certain pre-sexual prerequisites, in the form of a self-contained bodily ego. The unconscious can be said to be positioned in between something I call 'the ego's conscious intending' and a rudimentary body-ego experiencing. The thoughts introduced in chapter 4 are developed in the following chapters. Concerning the unconscious and its basically libidinal character, these thoughts are further developed in chapters 5 and 6, and in chapter 7 I return to the ideas concerning the pre-sexual conditions of the unconscious.

In chapter 5, Freud's theory of drives is discussed.[1] Sexuality has played the central role in Freud's theoretical work from the very beginning. The libido or sexual drives can be said to be the core of the unconscious according to Freud. However, sexuality is not everything, and therefore psychoanalytically it should be understood in relation to a counter-force of sexuality – for example, the ego or the ego-/self-preservative drives. In this chapter I attempt to show that Freud's characterization of sexuality differs from the conventional notion of sexuality as a natural condition limited to an adult heterosexual genital relationship. According to Freud, sexuality must be considered in a broader context and infantile sexuality must be taken into account. Furthermore, I argue that the libido concept, or the sexual drives, should not be understood as experienced sexuality, or even as possible to experience. The concept of libido should rather be understood as a theoretical construction, and as such expresses itself most clearly in Freud's economic, energy point of view.

The unconscious in its most radical, constructed character can be captured through the use of different descriptions. We can think of such important concepts as Freud's pleasure principle and its striving towards the immediate discharge of energy; the Nirvana principle, where the energy of the drives aims at a discharge to point zero; or Freud's death drives as Laplanche has interpreted them. Laplanche

---

[1] For Freud's German concept *Trieb*, I have chosen throughout the book to use the word 'drive' rather than 'instinct' (as is often the case in English psychoanalytic texts). However, when quoting English texts – for example, Strachey's translation of Freud's Collected Works – I comply with the text in question, even though this has meant rendering *Trieb* as 'instinct'.

argues that the death drive belongs to sexuality when it functions according to the principle of free energy. Such a description reminds us of Freud's wild and untamed id, which is part of Freud's structural theory. Laplanche means that Freud provides a deeper understanding of the unconscious with the help of the id. My point is that these different ways of seeking to grasp the unconscious are idealized, theoretical constructions.

An important idea presented in chapter 5, which later provides the starting point of chapter 6, is that Freud's view on sexuality is not based solely on his clinical practices. For Freud, the importance of sexuality in psychopathology – and in life in general – had the character of a vision (May 1999), which he attempted to verify in his scientific work during his lifetime. This is an idea that I will explore further and develop in chapter 6, where I argue that Freud's constructed libido (or the sexual drives) is founded in prescientific sexual life-world experiences.

Chapter 6 fulfils an epistemological function in the sense that the psychoanalytic concept of libido is founded in the sexual life-world experiences. The theoretical concept of libido becomes comprehensible by identifying its roots in the life-world experiences and by illuminating the measures/achievements that are required for moving from experienced sexuality to the theoretical construction of libido, which psychoanalysis uses in its project. In this chapter, certain characteristics of the life-world are described phenomenologically, such as how this experience of the life-world 'normally' appears to us, as well as a form of life-world experience that differs from the 'normal' experience of the life-world, namely experiences of injuries and illness. These different types of life-world experiences then function as the ground against which the conscious sexual experience of the life-world can be delineated. It is on the basis of this unique character of the sexual life-world experience that the psychoanalytic concept of libido can be constructed. The libido, or sexual drive, provides psychoanalysis with a perspective from which the subjective life can be understood and explained.

Chapter 7 returns to a theme discussed in chapter 4, namely the psychic achievements that are the conditions for the unconscious system governed by the pleasure principle. The vantage point of the discussion in chapter 7 is Freud's essay *Beyond the pleasure principle*, written in 1920, after he had come to the realization – on the basis of everyday as well as clinical experiences – that the pleasure principle is not universally prevailing in the psychical apparatus. Freud postulated in this essay something that is beyond the pleasure principle, which gradually came to be understood as the death drive. It is in this essay that Freud discussed the death drive for the first time and his last theory of the drive was presented. The essay is complicated and contradictory, but interesting, and it has given rise to various interpretations.

It seems to me that one can sense two conflicting meanings of the death drive in Freud's essay. It is the first meaning that Freud discusses initially, which has to do with the compulsion to repeat, which I give particular importance to in chapter 7. From an economic metapsychological point of view, the compulsion to repeat is about the binding of energy, which thus expresses something completely contrary to the death drive's discharge of energy, which is the other interpretation one can find in the essay. My idea is that what is beyond the pleasure principle – or, better expressed, that which is prior to the pleasure principle – is an affirmation of existence, which I discussed in chapter 4. This is a prerequisite for the activity of the pleasure principle. The discharge of energy is better qualified for the term 'death drive' and is, as mentioned above, the other meaning that can be found in Freud's essay. The essay is distinguished by the fact that Freud attempts to ground the death drive in biology, in a highly speculative manner. In my interpretation of the compulsion to repeat and death drives, I will instead make use of phenomenological insights regarding time.

Scientific activity seeks to obtain knowledge and find truths. I have made the assumption throughout this book that the concrete psychoanalytic process, consisting of the analyst and the analysand, is a scientific project and not solely a psychological treatment. Concrete psychoanalysis is about gaining self-knowledge and finding truths about oneself. We are thereby confronted with the question of what kind of truth concept is applicable to the concrete psycho- analytic project. As I pointed out initially, there are different ideas regarding the scientific status of psychoanalysis. Given that one con- ceives of it as a science, there are many opinions about what kind of science it is. Bearing this in mind, it is hardly surprising that con- sensus is lacking as to what truth concept could be applicable to the psychoanalytic project.

In chapter 8 I deal with the topic of the truth concept in psycho- analysis. The discussion evolves around the two conceptual pairs: con- struction – reconstruction and historical truth – narrative truth. In the first part of the chapter, these concepts are discussed from a his- torical context, focusing on Freud's point of view, the narrative tradi- tion in psychoanalysis and a few of Wilfred Bion's (1897–1979) ideas. It is obvious that these three specific traditions encompass different views on the truth concept in psychoanalysis. The view of the narra- tive tradition differs significantly from Freud's idea that the task of psychoanalysis is to reconstruct historical truths. Within the narra- tive tradition, one rejects the possibility of saying something that is historically valid concerning the life of the analysand. The task of psychoanalysis, instead, is to construct convincing truth narratives. Bion's idea of invariant transformations can be interpreted as a third alternative regarding the relation between construction and recon- struction. Construction and reconstruction are not seen as incom- patible concepts; rather, the reconstruction of psychoanalysis – or, in Bion's terminology, 'invariant transformation' – cannot be achieved without a psychoanalytically constructing perspective.

Bion's position is a challenging starting point for the second part of the chapter, in which I attempt to integrate the concepts of reconstruction and construction, as well as historical truth and truth narratives. I argue that the unconscious, captured through the use of a psychoanalytic construction, must be integrated with the analysand's reconstruction of his/her life story. The psychoanalytic project enables the analysand to create a new story that claims historical validity. It is important in this context, however, not to perceive the term 'historical' in an objectivistic manner, as if it were a question of disclosing objective historical facts. It is instead suggested that the connection between 'the-past-as-it-was-experienced-in-the-past' and 'the-past-as-understood-from-the-present' can be understood in terms of 'fusion of horizons', an expression borrowed from the philosopher and hermeneutist Hans-Georg Gadamer (1900–2002).

# Acknowledgements

During the course of work on this book I have been helped by many people's knowledge in psychoanalysis and/or phenomenology. By their critical reading they have forced me to develop my thoughts and ideas. First of all I would like to express my gratitude to Jennifer Bullington, who has contributed with very valuable comments during the whole process of writing this book. I have had reoccurring and rewarding discussions with Nicolas Smith. I have had the opportunity to discuss parts of the manuscript with psychoanalytic colleagues in a couple of study groups that I have participated in. I want to thank Kajsa Brundin, Birgitta Höglund, Gunnel Jacobsson, Iréne Matthis, Jurgen Reeder, Tommy Tallberg, Synnöve Wallin and Andrzej Werbart. I extend my thanks to a number of other people – friends and colleagues – who in varying degrees have read and helped to improve the manuscript: Catharina Engström, Rolf Künstlicher, Daniela Montelatici Prawitz, Dag Prawitz, Björn Sahlberg, Björn Salomonsson, Gloria Zeligman and Ulf Åkerström.

Parts of this book have been published in other contexts. Chapter 4 is a highly modified version of an article published in the *International journal of psychoanalysis* (2004, vol. 85, pp. 381–400). Chapter 6 is a modified version of an earlier publication in *New research on consciousness* by Jason T. Locks (ed.), (2007, Nova Science Publishers, Inc.). Chapter 7 is a modified version of an article published in *Scandinavian psychoanalytic review* (1998, vol. 21, pp. 37–52), and chapter 8 is a slightly modified version of an earlier article published in *Scandinavian psychoanalytic review* (2000, vol. 23, pp. 3–24). I am grateful to these journals and the publishing company for permitting me to reproduce this material.

# Figures

# 1 Phenomenology and psychoanalysis

At first sight it may appear as if phenomenology and psychoanalysis are opposites. The phenomenological project is concerned with studying consciousness, whereas the field of investigation for psychoanalysis is the unconscious. Freud (1900: 613) describes the unconscious as 'the true psychical reality', and in a well-known metaphor the role of consciousness is limited to the top of an iceberg. One can, in fact, ask: what do these sciences have to do with one another? This question can be answered in different ways. The aim of this book is to discuss the field of psychoanalysis and its basis as science, and for that purpose I believe that phenomenology has the greatest relevance. The impression that phenomenology and psychoanalysis are antithetical changes when one considers the dependence on consciousness for psychoanalytic practice. Psychoanalysis cannot liberate itself from consciousness, owing, among other things, to the fact that the psychoanalytic process both begins with the self-understanding of the analysand and is driven by means of conscious validations and verifications of interpretations of the unconscious. And clinical experience is an important basis when one attempts to characterize the field of psychoanalysis and its scientific ground.

In this chapter I will discuss briefly how I conceive of the relationship between phenomenology and psychoanalysis, and say something about how phenomenology will be used in this work. For the reader who is not familiar with phenomenology, this chapter can serve as an introduction to phenomenological philosophy.[1]

---

[1] The literature about phenomenology is vast. The classical introductory work about the phenomenological movement is Spiegelberg's (1982) *The phenomenological movement. A historical introduction.* Other examples of works of an introductory kind are Sokolowski's (2000) *Introduction to phenomenology* and Zahavi's (2003) *Husserl's phenomenology.*

From a historical perspective there are some interesting similarities between those two movements. Their undisputed founders were contemporaries, born in the same region of Europe, in Moravia, which at that time belonged to the Habsburg empire. Sigmund Freud was born in 1856 and died in 1939. Edmund Husserl lived between 1859 and 1938. Both were Jews, even though Husserl converted to Protestantism. The first full-fledged psychoanalytic work and the first phenomenological work were published at about the same time; Freud's *The interpretation of dreams* was published in 1900 and Husserl's *Logical investigations* was published in two volumes in 1900–1 (Husserl 1970/1900–1). Both Freud and Husserl attended lectures given by the philosopher Franz Brentano (1838–1917), whose influence on Husserl is apparent and significant, while his influence on Freud is unclear but possibly subtle (cf. Cohen 2002). Both psychoanalysis and phenomenology have developed into movements with different branches, a fact that will be reflected in this work. Different representatives for these two scientific movements inspire my analyses, albeit Freud and Husserl hold central positions.

In spite of these historical similarities and their comprehensive production, Freud and Husserl had not much to say about each other. Freud never mentioned Husserl or his phenomenological philosophy in his works. Freud referred to Franz Brentano, who was an important influence for Husserl, in a note in his *Jokes and their relation to the unconscious* (1905a: 31–2, n. 6), and then as someone who had composed some kind of riddles from syllables. Husserl made a brief mention of Freud. On the whole, the interest in psychoanalysis for the first generation of phenomenologists was quite insignificant, which stands in sharp contrast to the later generation of French phenomenologists.

As already mentioned, there is little comment on Freudian ideas in Husserl's work. Among other things, there are a couple of references in Husserl's (1970/1936a) last and unfinished work. The meaning of these references is that the problem with 'the unconscious' also belonged to the problem of transcendental constitution

(p. 188), that is to say, that philosophical project which absorbed his interest at the time. Further on in this work there is a discussion (p. 237) about 'unconscious' intentionalities that had been revealed by 'depth psychology'. Here, repressed emotions of love, of humiliation and of resentment are also mentioned as fields for phenomenological psychology. Besides, there is a somewhat developed and, in my eyes, more interesting point of view in the discussion about 'the problem of the unconscious', written by Husserl's disciple Eugen Fink (1905–75), and placed as an appendix (Husserl 1970/1936b). In particular, Fink argues for the importance of a thorough analysis of consciousness before being able to determine adequately the character of the unconscious. Spiegelberg (1972: 136) points out that the German philosophical phenomenology only had a superficial and casual contact with psychoanalysis – not due to a hostile attitude but rather a difference of interest. With Martin Heidegger (1889–1976), however, in the posthumously published *Zollikon seminars* (2001), one can trace a hostile attitude to psychoanalysis, specifically in his critique of Freud's metapsychology. Heidegger paid attention to the difference – which for him appears to be a contradiction – between Freud's mechanistic and deterministic metapsychology and psychoanalytic treatment's emphasis on liberating the analysand.

The French phenomenological philosophers, however, have shown much more interest in psychoanalysis than the older generation of German phenomenologists. Paul Ricoeur's (1913–2005) comprehensive Freud essay is in a class by itself (Ricoeur 1970). Ricoeur, who conceives of psychoanalysis as a hermeneutic science, takes his vantage point from language philosophy containing several levels of meaning. The psychoanalytic level concerns the 'semantics of desire', whose manifest linguistic expressions are distorted. The relationship of psychoanalysis to language contrasts with a 'phenomenology of religion', which is naïve in relation to the unconscious and where the language is not considered to be distorted, but to manifest something holy that is in need of revelation. When it comes to the psychoanalytic project of interpretation, Ricoeur stresses that psychoanalysis consists of a mixed discourse. Together with a hermeneutic language (meaning, interpretation, representation, and so on), there is quasi-physical energy language (cathexis, discharge, quantity, and so on). It is the distinctive feature of psychoanalysis to comprise this mixed discourse. Even if psychoanalysis incorporates a quasi-physical energy language in the interpretation of meaning, it does not make psychoanalysis into a natural science. It remains, according to Ricoeur, a hermeneutical science, where the quasi-physical language is subordinated to the dimension of meaning. In a later work, Ricoeur (1977) discusses the conditions for validation in psychoanalysis. In line with Ricoeur's *Freud and philosophy: an essay on interpretation* (1970), he argues that psychoanalysis is an interpretive science which, when it comes to the validating procedure, must differentiate itself from the validation in terms of observations that are used in the natural scientifically oriented social sciences. The truth claim of psychoanalysis and the possibility of verification/falsification are based on the narrative character of the psychoanalytic process.

A couple of other French philosophers and phenomenologists need to be mentioned. Maurice Merleau-Ponty (1908–61) was basically sympathetic towards psychoanalysis (for example, 1962/1945, 1963/1942), but was critical of it in two respects (Bullington 1998). In the first place, he objected to Freud's economic point of view concerning the drive energy, which to him entailed an objectification of the human being. In the second place, he considered the psychoanalytic idea about an unconscious as 'idealistic', in the sense that it postulated the unconscious as something transcendent, as something outside the world. For him there was nothing but the incarnated subject who is in the world. Merleau-Ponty took upon himself the task of reinterpreting several important psychoanalytic concepts (for example, libido, repression, discharge), in terms that are in line with his idea about incarnated subjectivity.

Finally, some words about Jean-Paul Sartre's (1905–80) logical critique of Freud's idea about the unconscious and its censorship are appropriate here. Sartre (1956/1942) claimed that it is logically impossible to postulate a censorship whose character is such that it knows what to keep away from consciousness. He launched an 'existential psychoanalysis' whose task was to disclose a person's fundamental choice. In this version of the investigating mind there was no room for anything unconscious; instead he proposed something called 'bad faith' (*mauvaise foi*), which is a chosen, inauthentic strategy of action, which can be described roughly as a choice not to conceive of oneself as a free choosing subject. Whether this concept avoids the logic critique that Sartre directed at Freud's concept about a censorship of the unconscious, however, is debatable.

## ON PHENOMENOLOGICAL PHILOSOPHY

Here I will mention, very briefly, some essential characteristics of phenomenology, whose influence on twentieth-century philosophy is significant and has also been of importance for the social sciences. Phenomenology thus originates from the works of the philosopher and mathematician Edmund Husserl. The task of phenomenology was to study the meaning/significance/essence of a phenomenon. But its relevance was not to be limited to the study of specific philosophical questions in the strict sense, but to work as an epistemological ground for other sciences. The concept 'phenomenology' contains two terms: 'phenomenon' (from the Greek *phainomenon*), which means that which appears/that which shows itself, and 'logy' from *logos*, which in this context can be translated as law/structure/essence. The field of study for phenomenology is thus 'that which appears'/'that which shows itself', and that which appears or shows itself can be anything – for example, perceptual experiences, cognitive processes, emotional experiences, aesthetic experiences or religious experiences. The task of phenomenology is to study the *logos* of phenomenon – in other words, those conditions that are presupposed in order for it to be the phenomenon that it is or is experienced to be. The aim of phenomenology to describe the essence of a phenomenon has to do with identifying and clarifying the necessary conditions for it to be what it is. When we say the necessary conditions, we mean the conditions that are required for the subjective experience.

Phenomenology is a philosophy of subjectivity and consciousness. To give a simple example:[2] What is the essence of 'the perception of a table'? Phenomenologically, this question is answered by studying this perceptual experience and those characteristics or constituents that must be there in this specific experience, in order for it to be a perceptual experience of a table. Each specific experience includes both a contingency – that is, a particularity – and a principal structure, its *eidos* or essence. The perception of the table at which I sit and work consists of things that are contingent – for example, the brown colour of the table – which do not affect the principal structure (the essence) of the table. The table would remain a table even if it were to be painted red. Colour does not belong to a table's essence. However, in the specific experience there is also a 'grasping' of a necessary, principal structure, that which makes me experience it as a table ('the tableness'). It must have a certain consistency, a certain height; I must be able to put things on it, and so on. The necessary or principal structure is, in other words, the structure that is needed in order for it to be what it is.

*The natural attitude and the phenomenological reductions*
Within the framework for his project, Husserl developed different methodological options that are called 'the phenomenological reductions'. The term reduction is not to be confused with reductionism – that is, the project to reduce a phenomenon by explaining it by means of a less complex structure, as is the case when psychology is reduced to biology, biology to chemistry, and so on. The credo of phenomenology is precisely the opposite, namely to be faithful

---

[2] The examples are chosen for pedagogical reasons, with the purpose of illustrating certain ideas. The phenomena that have been studied by phenomenologists are not experiences of banal objects, but important epistemological questions, which will be evident in the next chapter.

to the experience as it shows itself for the subject (human being). Husserl's three most salient reductions (and I do not make any more subtle distinction between reduction and the so-called "epoché") are *phenomenological psychological reduction, phenomenological transcendental reduction* and *eidetic reduction through imaginative variation*. These reductions must be understood against the background of our common, everyday experience of the world.

Husserl has called the attitude which characterizes this everyday experience the 'natural attitude' (Husserl 1962/1913). The natural attitude is the naïve, uncritical attitude to the world. The aspect which Husserl stresses most of all in the natural attitude is the *belief* in (taken for grantedness of) the existence of the world. The object that I see in front of me shows/presents itself as existing *independently* of my perception of it. In this attitude, the world presents itself as a world filled with objects totally independent of the perceiving human being. The natural attitude is a description of our spontaneous, unreflective way of being in the world; when transformed uncritically into a philosophical position it becomes a naïve realistic epistemology, in which the world is exactly the way one sees it, independently of one's perception.[3]

The first two reductions (phenomenological psychological reduction and phenomenological transcendental reduction) are reminiscent of each other in the sense that they try to bracket our everyday attitude (the so-called natural attitude), where we always implicitly

[3] In the psychoanalytic literature there are plenty of expressions of a realistic epistemology. The realistic epistemology exists in different variants. Apart from naïve realism, we have an epistemological realism with respect to the descriptions of science – for example, in postulating that the theoretical concepts of physics (quarks, molecules, etc.) possess an existence independent of the (researcher) subject. The realism in its different variants is objectivistic, in the sense that the characteristics of the object allegedly belong to the object, independent of the subject. In chapter 2 I will critically discuss this kind of realism from the vantage point of Husserl's phenomenology, and in chapter 3 I will discuss an orientation within psychoanalysis, which embraces an epistemological realism. It is obvious that the concept of reality is too briefly and poorly treated in psychoanalytic literature (see Wallerstein 1983, 1985). The concept is rarely problematized and when statements are made they are often of a realistic character.

take the world as existing independently of consciousness. In the natural attitude the achievement or work that consciousness brings about in order for a world to be present is hidden. The world appears as if ready-made and determined, and our experience as if caused by external, independent stimuli. In order to discover the work of consciousness at all, a radical break with this natural attitude is necessary. We must break with our unreflected belief in the existence of the world, in order to reflect on how the phenomenon is given in and through consciousness. For phenomenology the world is nothing that exists independently of us, but the appearance of the world presupposes consciousness and the subject. In the natural attitude we neglect the conditions of consciousness and the subject for the possibility of a world. But in the phenomenological attitude, under the phenomenological reduction, we discover and clarify the link or correspondence between the subject and the world.

Apart from the suspension or bracketing of the belief in the world, the phenomenological reduction implies a bracketing of different systems that attempt to explain the phenomenon. In other words, we set aside theories, sciences, and so on, which try to explain the phenomenon. We are not supposed to explain the phenomenon with something external to the phenomenon in question. The point with the phenomenological reduction is to make us open and unprejudiced towards that which is given in experience. Here we can refrain from the difference between the phenomenological psychological reduction and the more far-reaching transcendental reduction, which brackets not only the world, but also that-in-the-world, including empirical ego.

The phenomenological reduction attempts to answer the following question: how is it *possible* that I experience, for example, the table in front of me as existing, independently of my perception of it? Such a question cannot be answered merely by stating: because the table exists. Suppose I ask the following: how is it *possible* that I experience the table in front of me as existing independently of my perception of it, whereas I do not experience the after-image from a camera flash as existing independently of my looking at it? To answer such a question by stating that the table exists, whereas the after-image does not exist in reality, would not be to answer the question. That would be begging the question. The question about how something is *possible* forces us to reflect on how it is experienced for consciousness. The existence of the world cannot then be presupposed, but we must try to describe the conditions or the possibilities for that which actually exists. This question 'raises' us to an ontological level, which tries to clarify the necessary conditions for the (experience of) existence.

Here, I have attempted to point out the connection between the phenomenological reduction and the question of how something is possible – the ontological question. The phenomenological reduction tries to bracket our belief (judgement, or what is taken for granted) in the existence of the world, with the purpose of making possible an investigation of *how* the object is given in and through consciousness. The bracketing of the existential judgement – the reduction – is not to be understood as a kind of Cartesian doubt. It is not that I doubt the existence of the table; rather, the point is that the belief in its existence has to be clarified. As was shown above, as well as the suspension of the existential judgement, the phenomenological question entails a bracketing of all other theories, systems and sciences that try to explain the experience of the phenomenon. The phenomenological researcher strives to describe the phenomenon as free from preconceived ideas as possible.[4]

Let us now move on to 'the eidetic reduction through imaginative variation'. This can be described as the methodological option that aims to go from the particular to the essential (*eidos* = essence). This is achieved by freely varying parameters (characteristics) of a real or fantasized example of the phenomenon. Thus, one searches for the essential traits that make a phenomenon what it

---

[4] The emphasis on openness that is so important for phenomenology has great similarities with the open attitude of psychoanalysis as it is expressed in Freud's 'evenly suspended attention' and in Bion's 'without memory and desire'.

is. Let us take as an example the phenomenon of 'kindness'. As a point of departure, I take a situation when I am shopping in a store, I am short of time, and a man perceives my pressed predicament and offers to let me stand in front of him in the queue to pay. This experience of being treated in a kind way entails both accidental factors and the essential constituents that make it into an experience of kindness. In the phenomenological reflection, the accidental factors are not reckoned with – for example, that it was a man who showed the kindness or that it was in a grocery store that the kindness was manifested. The phenomenological reflection, on the other hand, aims at making explicit or thematic the (essential) constituents that make it into the experience that it is – in my example, an experience of kindness and nothing else. Without being able to carry out a real phenomenological analysis of this phenomenon here (that presumably is much more complex than one may think at first), we can have a feeling that the essential constituents involve, for example, that the person who exercises the kind act is a subject who carries out an intentional act (a robot cannot be kind) and that there are no ulterior motives behind this act (for example, that it is carried out in order to make me feel pressed to do a favour in return). Thus, the purpose of the eidetic reduction is to articulate those constituents that are essential for the experience of kindness, without which they would not be an act of kindness, and leave aside such accidental traits that happen to be part of this particular case of kindness.

The phenomenological attitude thus aims at making us open to that which is given in and through consciousness, which is achieved by means of the phenomenological reduction's (transcendental or phenomenological-psychological) break with our natural attitude. The eidetic reduction can thereafter be carried out with the purpose of articulating the essence of the phenomenon being studied.

Earlier, I said that the natural attitude conceals the work, the achievement that consciousness brings about in order for a world to be present to us. The phenomenological reductions that are to liberate us from the naïveté of the natural attitude in relationship to the world (the naïve realism) thus open up a new field where the achievement of consciousness and 'part' in the creation (meaning bestowing) of the world is uncovered. The epistemological position of phenomenology can be described neither as traditional idealism (that the subject in its own majesty is the source of knowledge) nor as traditional realism (that the character of the object of knowledge is completely independent of the subject). Expressed in terms of the concept of intentionality, phenomenology maintains the indissoluble relationship between subject and object. And it is within the phenomenological reduction that we can discover intentionality – that is, the meaning bestowing of consciousness. Intentionality is the cornerstone of phenomenology and the analysis of it is complex and sophisticated. Here I will say a few words about it.

*The intentionality of consciousness*

For phenomenology, consciousness is, in its essence, intentional. Husserl inherited the concept of intentionality from his teacher Franz Brentano. Intentionality was the most characteristic trait of the mental in Brentano's characterization of mental and physical phenomena. Psychology was a science of mental life, while natural science studied physical phenomena. The 'directness' of the intentional acts of consciousness was the specific distinguishing mark for psychical phenomena, which means, for example, that in 'presentation something is presented, in judgement something is affirmed or denied, in love loved, in hate hated, in desire desired and so on' (Brentano 1973/1874: 88). Husserl took over and modified, deepened and developed Brentano's concept of intentionality.

Roughly speaking, the concept of intentionality is about the meaning bestowing of consciousness. Intentionality has to do with meaning. The meaning of something – the meant – is dependent on a subjective attitude, a subjective way of being. The experience always stands in a relationship to an experiencing. Consciousness (the psyche) is always consciousness of something. The acts of consciousness 'go beyond' themselves and constitute (meaning bestow) the object or the world. The world for the human being is first and foremost meaningful. Merleau-Ponty expresses the fundamental significance of meaning when he claims that 'we are *condemned to meaning*' (1962/1945: xix; italics in the original). The concept of intentionality implies a rejection of the idea that there would be objective facts, *independent* of a subject/subjective understanding/consciousness. The objectively given fact is always presented in relationship to a subject/something subjective, to a specific subjective attitude, which is the condition to be able to speak about 'something' as an objective fact. Such a non-dualistic point of view implies that subject and object are not two entities independent of each other, but that they are interwoven through intentionality.

It should be acknowledged that the concept of intentionality or meaning is not a simple concept. Perhaps one difficulty is due to the fact that meaning, so to speak, is too close to us. We are too impregnated by it, like the air we breathe. Meaning bestowing, like understanding, is a concept that essentially characterizes human beings. Its ubiquitous presence contributes to the difficulty in making its significance explicit. The phenomenological exposition of the concept of intentionality is thus very complex and implies in the deepest sense an analysis of the subject's temporality.

## IMPORTANT POINTS OF CONNECTION BETWEEN PHENOMENOLOGY AND PSYCHOANALYSIS

It is important to respect the essential differences that exist between psychoanalysis and phenomenology. Psychoanalysis is an empirical science that studies psychic reality, including the unconscious.[5]

[5] It is unfortunately not uncommon that the terms 'empiric(al)' and 'empiricism/empiricistic' are confused when psychoanalysis as a science is discussed. Empirical science means that its field of study concerns real entities. In the case of psychoanalysis, it concerns actual existing people (analysands). Empiricism/empiricistic are terms that refer to an epistemological point of view in which it is claimed that all knowledge is based on experience, and 'experience' is often understood in a very limited way, tantamount to observable and measurable. My point of view is that psychoanalysis is an empirical science (and not only a psychological treatment), but that an empiricistic epistemological ideal is not

Phenomenology can be seen as a philosophical, epistemological-ontological project, which tries to describe conditions and presuppositions for different forms of existence. Later on in this chapter I will specify how phenomenology will be of help when discussing the foundation of psychoanalysis.

Even if phenomenology and psychoanalysis are two different types of scientific projects, they nevertheless have points of connection that are important as a point of departure for my work. Let me present seven points of connection between phenomenology and psychoanalysis and then include common traits as well as differences that can be found.

## Interest in the subjective

Both psychoanalysis and phenomenology have the subjective as their field of study. Phenomenology attempts to describe the subject's experience of different phenomena – in other words, how the world shows itself in and through consciousness. In psychoanalysis also the interest is focused on the subjective experiencing of the analysand. Freud stressed many times that the field of psychoanalysis concerns psychical reality as opposed to material reality. But even if the subjective is a common interest, there are different levels of the subjective that are in focus for the respective science. The field of phenomenology is limited to the subject's conscious intending – that is, to be described as open and as presuppositionless as possible. When I say 'the subject's conscious intending', it should be understood in a broad sense and not be constrained to the explicit, thematic consciousness. Below (under the heading 'Interest in the latent'), I will pay attention to the fact that the concept of consciousness for phenomenology includes that which is given implicitly. Later on in the book it will become apparent that bodily awareness belongs to the concept of consciousness for phenomenology. The 'instance' in

germane to psychoanalysis. The phenomenological view is an alternative to an empiricistic (positivistic) epistemology.

the subject concept, which is the target for the unique interest of psychoanalysis, is the unconscious. Phenomenology in its reflection cannot, I maintain, reach this, but psychoanalysis does, by means of its method of free association.

## The concepts of intentionality and meaning

Both phenomenology and psychoanalysis deal with meaning and intentionality. The concept of intentionality entails a subject's meaning bestowing of an object. The idea about the subject's intentionality is the cornerstone of phenomenology, even if it is conceptualized somewhat differently by phenomenologists. The concept of meaning is also central for psychoanalysis. Psychoanalysis is concerned with the distorted, illogical and pathological, that which appears meaningless, from the assumption that it has meaning, or rather, as I would like to express it, that it is possible to incorporate it into meaning. In the phenomenological project, the concept of meaning does not run into resistance. It is more complicated with psychoanalysis. In line with Ricoeur (1970), one can claim that psychoanalysis consists of a 'mixed discourse', where meaning may have to be transformed by explanation on the basis of a quasi-physical language. Here I will only conceptualize the tension that exists when one presupposes intentionality (interpreting meaning) at the same time as one assumes an unconscious whose character transcends or – to put it even more strongly – breaks with the subject's conscious intending (meaning bestowing). To try to clarify the unconscious is a mammoth task. Nevertheless, I will try to discuss its character and its relationship to consciousness, partly against the background of the concept of meaning (see chapter 4).

## Interest in the latent

I mentioned above that phenomenology is focused on consciousness in a broad sense, including that which is given implicitly, even if it is not unconscious in the psychoanalytic sense of Freud's systematic unconscious. Thus, in a sense, both phenomenology and psychoanalysis are interested in the latent. They are not content with that which is explicit, thematically conscious, but strive to uncover something 'beneath' the manifest. But the latency that phenomenology tries to uncover is carried out, roughly speaking, by means of reflections on the basis of the subject's intending. In order to approach the latency of psychoanalysis – the unconscious – a (theoretical or constructed) metapsychology is required. Ricoeur has discussed phenomenology from the vantage point of the terminology of psychoanalysis – a delicate task, but, nevertheless, one which may fulfil a certain function. He means that phenomenology studies consciousness and the preconscious, but not the unconscious.

### The significance of reflection

The methodological procedure entails reflection on both psychoanalysis and phenomenology. The search for the essence of a phenomenon in phenomenology is carried out by means of a systematic reflection of something that is experienced. Also, in the psychoanalytic process, the reflection on the analysand's material by the analyst and the analysand constitutes a crucial moment in the psychoanalytic investigation/treatment. The Kleinian psychoanalyst R. Horacio Etchegoyen (b.1919) (1991: 549) has paid attention to certain similarities between the analysand's verbalization in the psychoanalytic process and Husserl's so-called eidetic reduction (even though I think it would be more appropriate to refer to Husserl's phenomenological reduction than to the eidetic reduction). Roughly speaking, one can describe the psychoanalytic process of acquiring knowledge as an oscillation between ordinary storytelling, free association and a higher degree of self-conscious reflection of one's experiences.

### The value of openness

Both the phenomenological and the psychoanalytic processes of acquiring knowledge are based on openness. In phenomenology this value has been formulated in terms of 'back to the things themselves' (Zu den Sachen selbst) – that is, to try to be faithful to the phenomenon that we meet in as presuppositionless a way as possible.

Husserl developed the phenomenological reduction for the purpose of assuring oneself about this open attitude. In its investigation of the unconscious, psychoanalysis is dependent on theoretical constructions, but it does not hinder one from trying to be as open and unpresupposing as possible in the psychoanalytic investigation. The importance of openness in psychoanalysis is emphasized more and more. That the psychoanalyst would have a kind of psychoanalytic screen through which the analysand's storytelling is filtered must certainly be considered as an outdated and scurrilous portrait of psychoanalysis. As I pointed out before, Bion's (1988) recommendation to the psychoanalyst to work 'without memory and desire' has gained great popularity (see n. 4 on p. 9).

### The break with the 'common-sense attitude'

Both phenomenology and psychoanalysis represent, in a sense, a break with the everyday, instrumental, common-sense attitude. By 'common-sense attitude' is meant an everyday, uncritical, non-reflective way of being in the world. This attitude is captured in phenomenology by Husserl's expression 'the natural attitude' (see p. 7). It is the natural attitude that phenomenological reduction breaks with. The phenomenological attitude, under the reduction, opens up a field that was previously concealed. The basic rule of free association in psychoanalysis and the psychoanalytic frame also signifies a break with social everydayness, which makes it possible to get a grasp of the unconscious and to make it into a subject for investigation in a way that is not possible under ordinary daily circumstances. Thus, for both phenomenology and psychoanalysis, it is due to a break with the ingrained way of being in the world that it is possible to uncover previously hidden dimensions in our existence, even if these dimensions are not exactly the same for psychoanalysis and phenomenology.

### Responsibility as an ethical principle

As a last and very important point of connection between phenomenology and psychoanalysis, one can mention that they both put much faith in knowledge and self-knowledge as possessing a practical ethical value, and not only a theoretical value. Husserl talks about a striving for a responsible life that presupposes an insight into the subject's meaning-bestowing function. Knowledge acquires ethical implications, an idea that goes back to Socrates' view on the significance of philosophy as a way of living a rational and justified life. It may be surprising that Husserl (1956/1923–24, 1959/1923–24, 1970/1936a) put such an emphasis on this ethical dimension for phenomenology. Zahavi (2003: 67–8; italics in the original) writes that Husserl's motive for philosophizing:

> is not primarily a theoretical motivation, but a practical, or more precisely an *ethical* one – the ethical striving for a life in absolute self-responsibility ... Husserl speaks of an evidence-based self-responsible life that the phenomenological search for a transcendental foundation makes possible. To live in the phenomenological attitude is not a neutral impersonal occupation, but a praxis of decisive personal and existential significance.

And further on (p. 68; italics in the original):

> what is decisive for Husserl is not the *possession* of absolute truth, but the very *attempt* to live a life in absolute self-responsibility, that is, the very attempt to base one's thoughts and deeds on as much insight as possible. And, as Husserl states in one of his still unpublished manuscripts, the self-responsibility of the individual also entails a responsibility for the community. Self-responsibility is fully realizable only in relation to other subjects.

Husserl's philosophical motive for philosophizing would easily qualify as a motive for undergoing psychoanalysis. The ethos of psychoanalysis is also the idea that the analysand's gaining of self-knowledge will make her/him freer to choose and recognize a real responsibility for her/his acts and her/his experiences.

THE FUNCTION OF PHENOMENOLOGY IN THIS WORK

I would now like to say something about how I will use phenomenology in my aim to discuss the scientific foundation of psychoanalysis and its conceptualization of its field of study, the psychical. Phenomenology is a philosophy that presents an epistemological attitude and epistemological ideas, which I will take advantage of. Husserl had the idea that philosophy was to be a science and not, for example, a system of subjective life views. His idea was that phenomenology was to assume this scientific task in philosophy. And he also expressed the idea that phenomenology was even a rigorous science, in the sense that it was not to proceed on the basis of non-analysed conditions, which is the fate of all other sciences, empirical and ideal (Husserl 1965/1910–11). Psychoanalysis is an empirical science, whose field of study is the subject's psychical – not least unconscious – life. A psychoanalysis in search of an epistemological-ontological basis can in this sense take advantage of phenomenological philosophy.

In general, I would like to stress that the project is not about 'phenomenologizing', to make phenomenology out of psychoanalysis, in the form, for example, of 'Dasein-analysis' (Binswanger 1975; Boss 1979) or Sartre's (1956/1942) 'existential psychoanalysis'. I am sceptical of these forms of synthesizing between psychoanalysis and phenomenology, since they risk neglecting the unconscious of psychoanalysis. I am anxious to keep the boundary between phenomenology and psychoanalysis clear. Phenomenology can in no way replace psychoanalysis. Neither is my intention to carry out a dialogue between the two sciences, in which they would give and take from each other. The searchlight will be directed at psychoanalysis, and phenomenology will mainly have an assisting function in my discussion of psychoanalysis.

Even if I think that phenomenology is of great help in order to understand what psychoanalysis is, my analysis of the conditions of the unconscious will rather stress the principal difference that exists between psychoanalysis and phenomenology. Phenomenology does not study the unconscious of psychoanalysis – such an aim is reserved for psychoanalysis. However, phenomenology can help in illuminating the conditions for the possibility of something like the unconscious (see chapter 4).

The overall function of phenomenology in this work is thus of an epistemological-ontological kind. There is an idea in Husserl's thinking that is more clearly spelt out in the next chapter, namely that all sciences are preceded by and, in a certain sense, conditioned by prescientific experiences – in other words, the sciences are grounded in prescientific experiences of the world which Husserl (in particular at the end of his life) came to talk about as the life-world (*Lebenswelt*). Scientific achievements must always be understood against the background of the prescientifically given life-world and by means of phenomenological investigations of life-world experiences. Phenomenology has a general epistemological function to serve for the sciences. The abstract, theoretical constructions in sciences should, in a true scientific spirit, be justified by pointing out their basis in the subjective life-world experience, which can thereby be subject to a critical and systematic investigation. Husserl (1980/1912: 69) could express this idea in the following way: 'Phenomenology in our sense is the science of "origins", of the "mothers" of all cognition; and it is the maternal-ground of all philosophical method: to this ground and to the work in it, everything leads back.'

Apart from this general phenomenological, epistemological point of departure, certain more specific themes in psychoanalytic theory will be elucidated by means of phenomenological thoughts and reflections. These concern themes that are of great clinical relevance, but which have not been satisfactorily investigated in psychoanalysis, nor acquired an adequate place within psychoanalytic theorization. Examples of such themes are the experiences of existence and self-consciousness. These concepts that have been subject to thorough investigations in phenomenology are neglected in the psychoanalytic theory. My hope is that phenomenology will make a contribution to building a firmer bridge between psychoanalytic theory (including the metapsychology) and clinical practice, and thereby make psychoanalytic theory and practice more solid and scientifically cogent.

SUMMARY

This chapter concerns the relationship between phenomenology and psychoanalysis. Psychoanalysis has, among phenomenologists, been received with various levels of interest; some have been enthusiastic, while others have been sceptical and perceived that psychoanalysis, for example, conceives of the human being in too mechanistic a way. Interest in phenomenology among psychoanalysts has usually been limited. My point of view is that there is sufficient common ground of values between them in order for psychoanalysis to benefit from taking part in phenomenological reflections. In this chapter, seven points of connection between phenomenology and psychoanalysis have been identified; these are common traits that nevertheless can entail differences. The points of connection are the following: interest in the subjective, the concepts of intentionality and meaning, interest in the latent, the significance of reflection, the value of openness, the break with the common-sense attitude, and responsibility as an ethical principle.

In this work it is the psychoanalytic conceptualization of the psychical and its scientific ground that are in focus. The task of phenomenology is to help psychoanalysis in its striving to be a cogent science – that is, to help psychoanalysis to be grounded in one adequate (for its purposes and conditions) epistemology. This can be said to be the overall function of phenomenology in this work. In addition, in the discussion concerning more specific themes in psychoanalytic theorization, phenomenological ideas and reflection will be of help.

# 2 The life-world as the ground for sciences

Husserl thought that it was the task of phenomenology to lay the epistemological foundation for other sciences. The expression 'epistemological foundation' in this context means the delineation of the conditions for the possibility of the science in question. Psychoanalysis never became the object for such a specific epistemological grounding. However, Husserl carried out epistemological works for other human sciences, in particular for psychology, as well as for natural science and logic.

Whether psychoanalysis can claim to be a science – and, in that case, what kind of science it is – has been a recurrent subject of contention. The fact that psychoanalysis has had difficulty obtaining scientific recognition within an empiricistic or positivistic frame of reference is hardly surprising. From the vantage point of such a scientific ideal, it seems uncontroversial to declare psychoanalysis either as non-scientific (Popper 1959, 1972) or proven to be scientifically invalid (Grünbaum 1984). However, positivism has lost ground during recent decades, and today one can no longer talk about a unified positivistic orientation. But remnants of positivistic, empiricistic thinking with physics as the scientific model still exist, even within, for example, psychoanalysis.

In the first decade of the twenty-first century, one has been able to discern ideas within psychoanalytic circles that the scientific status of psychoanalysis should be tested by means of other empirical research, as, for instance, when one evaluates the outcome of psychoanalysis on the basis of certain objective criteria. Pragmatic efficiency becomes synonymous with being scientific. The psychoanalytic project in itself is then not considered to be a scientific activity. Such a view of psychoanalysis could be compared to an evaluation of the scientific status of physics by means of the strength of existing bridges. Within natural science and technique, however, one usually differentiates clearly between the specific science in question and the different technical applications that are based on that specific science. Within psychoanalysis, for different reasons, it has been more difficult to maintain this difference in the same clear way, which I believe has been detrimental for a deeper understanding of the conditions for the psychoanalytic project.[1]

In discussing the scientific status of psychoanalysis today, it seems more and more urgent to be acquainted with Husserl's and phenomenological epistemological-ontological thinking. In the previous chapter I mentioned that the overall function in this work is to make up an epistemological basis for psychoanalysis. A science does not develop out of nothing; rather, sciences emanate out of life-world experiences. The basic traits of sciences are already shaped, albeit in a vague way, in the prescientific life-world experiences. Each science has its own specific character, whose outline can thus be discerned in prescientific life-world experiences. But given the monistic scientific ideal of positivism – that there basically exists only one type of science, that is, natural science, such as physics – there is no place for human sciences. In the light of the positivistic scientific ideal, we can see two clearly different trends when it comes to the status of the social sciences. One trend has to do with a methodological aspect, in the sense that subjectivity or the subjective experience cannot be studied under its own conditions but must be operationalized into something measurable – something that can be observed in order to make it into an object for scientific investigations. It is often this kind of thinking that lies behind the idea to make psychoanalysis scientifically legitimate by examining whether it has measurable treatment results. Another trend concerns the treatment of subjectivity or the psychical, as an objective fact in nature, that which goes

---

[1] That psychoanalysis can, and according to my point of view should, be conceived of both as a science and as a psychological treatment might have contributed to the difficulty in maintaining this difference between science and technique.

under the name of 'naturalism'. It is this second trend that we will pay attention to in this chapter and that will be discussed in connection with the so-called 'neuropsychoanalysis' in the next chapter. A brief and concise characterization of naturalism could be the following (Biemel 1971: 668):

> In the scientific approach [naturalism] one has the habit of eliminating the 'subjective' part, or else one looks for something objective to replace the subjective. Thus, when a psychical element is found, it is referred to psychology, to a 'psycho-physical' psychology, which tries to reduce the specific subjective character by replacing it with physical elements.

In other words, naturalism and the ideal that all sciences are basically natural sciences has had the consequence that both the temporal and the logical priority of the subjective life-world experience in relationship to the (natural) sciences has been neglected. Before we can explicate how the sciences are grounded in prescientific experiences, we must reaffirm their priority. Subjectivity, the subjective life-world experience, has been obscured or forgotten, at the expense of the idea that reality, first and foremost, or exclusively, is nature as it is interpreted by natural science. This idea is expressed when, for example, one maintains that consciousness is the brain. Spiegelberg calls this first step a 'mundane phenomenology', before the phenomenological analysis proper of our experiences can begin.[2]

## A CRITIQUE OF NATURALISM

In embracing a naturalistic position, one thinks that one has rendered the *experience* – for example, of a red car – intelligible by characterizing it as the final instance in a chain of events consisting of a physical description of the world. An example of this kind of

---

[2] Spiegelberg (1982: 145) writes: 'As Husserl sees it, a peculiar kind of first reduction, a suspension of science, is indispensable in order to get sight of the life-world and its structures. Thus even the study of the life-world is already a type of phenomenology, though this may still be a "mundane phenomenology".'

scientific, 'physical' description is the number of wavelengths that define the colour red. The *experience* or *perception* of red (we do not experience or perceive wavelengths) is placed secondary to the physical description of red. The idea is that the red car emits wavelengths that impinge on our visual sense organs and through neurological processes are transmitted as 'information' to the brain, where subsequently the *experience* of red arises.

At the extreme, the life-world experience is neglected by *denying* its existence. An example of this is when one asserts that the life-world experience is *nothing but* ... followed by a physical or physiological account of the experience, as in the theory of 'eliminative materialism' (cf. P. M. Churchland 1984), or reducing psychology to a science of neurology (P. S. Churchland 1986). Even if such a reductionistic view is not prevalent today, the spirit of physicalism is still very present. This presence is obvious, for example, in the theoretical frame of reference that is called S-O-R (stimulus-organism-response) psychology. In S-O-R psychology, the starting point in the reconstruction of an experience or action is made up of a stimulus (S), which thereafter is treated by an organism (O) in order to emit a response (R). Stimulus is a natural scientific description (for example, a specific number of a wavelength) in the sense that the stimulus impinges on the sensory organs of a human being, and through efferent neurological processes certain parts of the brain are stimulated, so that the subjective experience emerges in some unspecific way. Stimulus (S) is supposed to be the starting point for a process that leads to an experience. That which is important to note in this context is that the stimulus is made up of a natural scientific description of the world.

The naturalistic attitude breaks radically with a human scientific view of man as an intentional acting person. Husserl (2000/1918: 199; italics in the original) writes:

> But if we place ourselves on the terrain of the intentional
> relation between subject and Object, the relation between person

and surrounding world, then the concept of stimulus acquires a fundamentally new sense. Instead of the causal relation between things and men as natural realities, there is substituted the *relation of motivation* between persons and things, and these things are not the things of nature, existing in themselves ... but are the experienced, thought, or in some other way intended and posited things as such, intentional objects of personal consciousness.

It is important to note that the way the human being is described in natural science corresponds to a specific attitude. Husserl goes on (p. 219) to point out that 'This naturalistically considered world is of course not *the* world' (italics in the original). The different objectivities correspond to different subjective attitudes of understanding, and the naturalistic attitude, for Husserl, is subordinated to that which he calls the personalistic attitude, in which the human being is conceived of as an intentional acting being. It is precisely this relationship of the objectivity to the subjective attitude that is so easily forgotten. In the naturalistic attitude we make the mistake of considering the object as something-in-itself, and we do not see that it is something-for-a-subject. The naturalistic attitude cannot be made into something absolute, but it is always an attitude in relation to a subject. Thus, Husserl (p. 193) gives priority to that which he calls a personalistic attitude:

> the naturalistic attitude is in fact subordinated to the personalistic, and that the former only acquires by means of an abstraction or, rather, by means of a kind of self-forgetfulness of the personal Ego, a certain autonomy – whereby it proceeds illegitimately to absolutize its world, i.e., nature.

In the personalistic attitude the person is conceived of as an intentional subject, and the life and actions of the subject are understood from the vantage point of relations of motivation, and not from the vantage point of causal connections into which the events of nature are ordered.[3] Naturalism, on the other hand, is closely connected to the procedure of natural science, as we have been able to witness, but with one addendum: in the naturalistic attitude, natural science is conceived of as an ontological project – that is, as if the description of the world in natural science were a description of the world's real nature (essence), independent of the subject. By taking part of Husserl's analysis of the grounding of natural science, we can see that it is inadequate or inappropriate to interpret the achievements of natural science ontologically.

## THE GROUNDING OF NATURAL SCIENCE

The question of what is physical stimulus is intimately linked with the question of how natural science is to be understood, since physical stimulus is a natural scientific description of the world. Natural science, in the modern sense of the term, began during the sixteenth and seventeenth centuries. For Husserl (1970/1936a), Galileo Galilei (1564–1642) represented the culmination of the establishment of modern natural science. Galileo's work stripped nature of cultural, religious and subjective significance. Nature was treated as 'pure nature', and Galileo applied the existing mathematical-geometrical system to nature. Nature such as it is studied in physics, for example, is therefore *mathematized*. Physics uses mathematics to explain processes in nature. The mathematical system, for the physicist, is an absolutely necessary 'instrument', without which there would be no physics in the modern sense of the term. A clarification of the meaning of natural science entails the meaning of the mathematical system on which the natural science is built. Let us begin a stepwise analysis of the meaning of natural science with the assistance of Husserl's (1970/1936a) last and incomplete work.

The title of Husserl's last work, *Die Krisis der europäischen Wissenschaften und die tranzendentale Phänomenologie (The crisis*

---

[3] Husserl (2000/1918: 231 ff.) discusses different forms of motivation, one of which is about deeply buried motives, which, according to Husserl, can be brought to light by psychoanalysis (p. 234).

*of European sciences and transcendental phenomenology*), clearly reveals its subject matter. Husserl felt that there was a crisis in the sciences. This crisis concerned not only the young human sciences, such as psychology, but also the successful natural sciences. Indeed, the bulk of his work is about the crisis in natural science. Certainly, this did not pertain to the natural scientific activity concerning the scientist in his/her function as a (natural) scientist. Husserl had no complaints about the concrete methodological procedures in natural science. The claim that there was a crisis in the natural sciences had nothing to do with methodological procedures, but concerned a more fundamental philosophical question. The crisis concerned the epistemological foundation of natural science. How are we to understand the results and descriptions of natural science? We may ask the following questions: are natural scientific results answers to ontological/metaphysical questions? Do they describe an objective world independent of human consciousness? Do they describe the world as it *really* is? An affirmative answer has often been given to these questions.[4]

Let us begin our analysis of the meaning-foundation of natural science by examining Galileo's mathematization of nature, to find out whether natural science yields *true* descriptions of the world, the world as if it were independent of human subjectivity. Galileo himself used traditional Euclidean geometry, without investigating its origins. Geometry was considered to be an autochthonous science – that is, having no foundation outside itself. The mathematical system that Galileo used was taken for granted, and considered as not needing any further grounding and justification. Husserl

---

[4] In the next chapter we will examine a psychoanalytic point of view that represents an epistemological realistic view of natural scientific descriptions. But for now I would like to supply a quote from Freud (1938a: 196) whose meaning implies this realistic character: 'In our science [psychoanalysis] as in the others [any other natural science] the problem is the same: behind the attributes (qualities) of the object under examination which are presented directly to our perception, we have to discover something else which is more independent of the particular receptive capacity of our sense organs and which approximates more closely to what may be supposed to be the real state of affairs'.

did not embrace such a viewpoint. He thought that if we wanted to understand the epistemological foundation of natural science, we needed to go back to the origin of mathematics, or, more precisely, geometry, which was the original achievement in the progress of creating an ideal mathematical system. We are interested in the meaning-foundation of geometry – that is, how it is grounded in a pre-theoretical life-world.

### The origin of geometry

How are geometrical configurations possible when they are not simply perceived or found in the world? Cultural objects surround us in the world, as do nature (which we use for certain purposes), other human beings, and so on. In the life-world there are no geometrical objects to be perceived. The objects that we experience in the life-world are filled with content (meaning) and their shapes are inexact. We see houses, tables, plates, and so on, all of which have meaning and display spatiality: houses are used for living in, plates are used to serve meals on, and so on. The spatiality of the plate, for example, may be round, but when we examine it more closely we discover that it is far from being perfectly round. So the objects of the life-world are neither pure configuration, because they are filled with content (meaning), nor exact, because their shapes are not perfect. A round object is never completely round. Given good measuring instruments, we can always discover imperfection. In this sense, objects of the life-world differ radically from geometrical objects, which are pure forms and exact. We can therefore never (sensuously) perceive geometrical figures in the world. We may *perceive* a circle-like plate, but my perception is never of an exact circular object. Geometrical figures, such as circles, are not given in real space, but they have an *ideal* status. Nevertheless, the first geometrical figures must have originated from geometricians living in a pre-theoretical, subjective life-world, surrounded by cultural objects and other human beings, and it is from this life-world that ideal and exact geometrical figures have somehow been obtained.

So far, the priority of the life-world over the ideal geometrical system has only been hinted at. It still remains to be shown how the life-world provides the foundation of geometry, and how exact shapes can be produced from the subjective life-world. In the beginning of geometry, mankind was able to achieve ideal geometrical shapes from the concrete, inexact life-world. This objectification of the life-world was made possible by the *idealization* of the concretely experienced life-world.[5] Husserl says that it is with the aid of a 'spiritual act' of pure thinking that the acquisition of the ideal objects (configurations) can take place. These ideal objects are objectified entities that remain identical despite the passing of time between the different acquisitions (productions). The meaning of each 'materialized' – that is, as thought, verbalized or written – production of the ideal object remains the same. Although the thinking act, as well as the uttering or writing of the ideal object, is bound in time and space, the sense or meaning of the ideal object 'transcends' its worldly character and thereby the limits of its materialized production, in the form of those specific persons that later on could repeat in different ways the production of the geometrical objects.

The manifestations of ideal geometrical configurations in the world (for example, when I think of the shape of a circle) are concrete psychical acts of thinking that take place at a specific time and in a specific place, whereas the sense or meaning of any such concrete thinking act is not bound to nor constrained by time and place. The sense of the thought of a geometrical object, such as a straight line, has validity beyond all its concrete manifestations. This sense is the same for all the different concrete manifestations, which is why we say it is objective. In other words, the sense of a specific geometrical configuration attains a supratemporal identity, agreed on intersubjectively, despite the multitude of concrete worldly manifestations.

---

[5] Idealization in this context has nothing to do with the psychoanalytic meaning of ascribing more valuable traits to the object than it has. Here, idealization means an abstraction of certain characteristics in the concrete object and retains an ideal geometrical object.

The first ideal geometrical shapes were configurations such as straight lines, circles, and so on, created by idealizing acts out of a perception of sensible bodies in the life-world. Not only is it possible to reawaken or repeat these configurations in psychical acts, but it is also possible to construct new configurations on the basis of these simple shapes. This is what happened in the historical development of the mathematical system. These simple shapes were the ground for *constructions* of new ideal objects. Hence, ideal geometrical shapes are human accomplishments obtained by *idealization* and *construction*. The original meaning of geometry is the idealization and construction by which we overcome the imperfection of objects perceived in the life-world.

The construction of more and more sophisticated ideal shapes can be accomplished without going back to the original meaning of geometry. In the course of time, previous accomplishments were taken as self-evident and became the ground on which the ensuing progress of geometry/mathematics rested. One may be successful in the practice of geometry and mathematics, despite being ignorant of their foundations. Indeed, this is exactly what happened, according to Husserl (1970/1936c: 367):

> The inheritance of propositions and the method of logically
> constructing new propositions and idealities can continue
> without interruption from one period to the next, while the
> capacity for reactivating the primal beginnings, i.e. the sources
> of meaning for everything that comes later, has not been handed
> down with it.

In other words, although the life-world, which was the ground upon which the geometrical configurations were obtained, was neglected, this did not prevent a successful construction of the ideal geometrical/mathematical system. Galileo could consequently inherit and use a system, whose meaning foundation in the life-world was obscured.

### From mathematical system to natural science

We have seen how the mathematical system, developed over thousands of years, provided Galileo with the objectivizing means for studying the world scientifically. The mathematical system guaranteed objective and secure knowledge. Knowledge of geometry had been so sedimented during this historical development that its origin was forgotten. Instead, the application of the mathematical system to nature became the accepted method for discovering the true reality of nature. Nature in its true being becomes something exact and objective which avoids the relativity and subjectivity of the life-world. In applying mathematics to nature, Galileo can be said to be the first to have begun the natural scientific tradition of obtaining exact knowledge about nature.[6] Besides using an idealized and constructed mathematical system, natural science progresses thanks to the improvement of measuring instruments. The more exact and accurate measuring instruments that can be made, the more exact and accurate are the approximations of natural scientific descriptions to the ideal system.

The mathematization of nature obtained by Galileo and later scientists can be described in two steps. The first step is called *abstraction*. In the life-world we experience things in their subjective, cultural meaning – for example, a religious temple as a cultural object, or a stone in its use function to protect a fire from being extinguished. One cannot apply mathematics directly to this primordial, subjective and cultural world. Therefore, the first step in mathematizing nature is to remove/abstract the subjective, cultural meaning from the objects in the life-world and to consider their pure materiality. Through this first abstracting step, the table in front of me ceases

---

[6] When we talk about the exact world of natural science, we describe its progressively increasing capacity to make accurate and exact descriptions, rather than describing complete exactness in the way that the ideal mathematical sciences do. Natural science is still an empirical science, whose goal is to approximate ever more exact descriptions of nature.

to be a table with its subjective, cultural significance, and becomes (only) a materially extended thing – that is, pure nature. The objects of natural science are *abstract objects*. The 'world' of natural science is a de-concretized, decontextualized and de-historicized world, a world where cultural significance has been removed. (It is quite another question that mathematical and natural scientific activities are, in a certain sense, themselves cultural manifestations.)

The second step is the *application of the ideal mathematical system* to nature. The mathematization of nature is not limited to static phenomena, but, as a consequence of the development in mathematics, has also been able to include changes in nature. In the life-world we are accustomed to a certain typical appearance of things. Changes occur in a way that is not usually completely unexpected or arbitrary. Husserl (1970/1936a: 31) writes: 'In other words, through a *universal causal regulation, all that is together in the world* has a universal immediate or mediate way of *belonging together*; through this the world is not merely a totality (Allheit) but an encompassing unity (Allenheit), a whole (even though it is infinite)' (italics in the original).[7] However, this knowledge of the regularities of the world is rather vague and meagre, and gives only knowledge of typical 'behaviour' – for example, if I throw a big stone at the window, the window will break. What is left to create is a method which formalizes the causal connections between the events or occurrences. Thanks to the development of the mathematical system, it becomes possible to formulate causal connections between events. However,

---

[7] The term 'world' in phenomenology does not mean the sum of all things to be found in the world, but rather designates the interconnection and horizon of what makes up everything that there is (exists). 'Husserl demonstrates that the world is not ... the idea of the totality of all existents which could be conceived only after running through the multiplicity of existents: it is not a concept of an object to which nothing corresponds in experience. Rather it is always co-given in experience *as horizon* along with individual objects' (Landgrebe 1981: 189; italics in the original). Neither does the term designate the physical construction of the world (see Landgrebe 1966). There are differences within the phenomenological movement concerning the relationship between man and the world (cf. Dreyfus 1975; Landgrebe 1966).

these functional connections are quite different from the causal typicality in the life-world. Natural scientific laws are based on spatiotemporal occurrences, which are stripped of their subjective meaningfulness. But these natural scientific constructions of causal connections presuppose the regularity which characterizes belongingness between objects in the life-world.

To sum up, abstraction of the life-world from subjective meaningfulness is the first step in the mathematization of nature, and yields abstract forms. The second step is mathematical application, which is a sort of interpretation of the abstract forms. Carr (1977: 205) points out that what has been forgotten in this mathematization of nature is that it rests on 'an abstraction *from* something and ... an interpretation *of* something' (italics in the original). There is nothing in the life-world which compels us to make this abstract, idealized construction of the world. It should be considered as a hypothesis, which, despite possible verification, will always remain a hypothesis. 'It is the peculiar essence of natural science, its a priori way of being, to be unendingly hypothetical and unendingly verified' (Husserl 1970/1936a: 42).

We have come to a point where, given the analysis presented, we can reject the assumption that natural science reveals the real (true) world as it *is*, independent of human subjectivity. Instead, we have seen that it has taken a very elaborate and sophisticated human endeavour for natural science to succeed in constructing an 'objective' world. I will now go on to examine the psychophysical paradigm in light of the analysis of the meaning-foundation of natural science.

## THE PSYCHOPHYSICAL PARADIGM

It is worth repeating that Galileo Galilei's mistake was not the way he treated nature in his role as a natural scientist. On the contrary, it was through the mathematization of nature that natural science could develop with such success. Instead, as stated earlier, the mistake was philosophical-epistemological. Let us look at the ontological claim that followed from neglecting the clarification of the meaning-foundation of natural science, namely that *everything that there is is measurable*. Such a claim can be questioned. The material sphere, which is capable of being measured, is only a part of the concrete life-world. The life-world also contains subjective and cultural layers of meaning, which, more problematically, allow themselves to be measured and described by mathematics.

Galileo not only mathematized pure nature. It was also under his influence that the psychophysical paradigm was systematically developed, even though the Pythagoreans had already observed functional correlations between, for example, the pitch of a tone and the length of a vibrating string. This inclusion of the subjective in the objective scientific sphere could not be made through a direct application of the mathematical system. The mathematical system, as we have seen above, is appropriate for abstract pure forms. Sensory qualities such as smell, sound, colour, and so on, are not amenable to mathematical expression. If there is no way to mathematize sensory qualities directly, how can one render the subjective 'scientific', given Galileo's philosophical-ontological viewpoint? The answer is by mathematizing the subjective indirectly. This is carried out by correlating changes in pure shapes (described in a constructed mathematical system) with changes that take place in the sensible qualities. Galileo advised: 'Measure everything. What you cannot measure directly, measure indirectly' (from McCall 1983: 13).

Now I should like to emphasize the role of the life-world more explicitly. According to the psychophysical paradigm, life-world experience – for example, the perception of a red car – is explained by the language of physical construction – that is, by certain non-experiential wavelengths. The order of primordiality between life-world experience and natural scientific descriptions has thus been reversed: what is derived and constructed by abstraction and application of an idealized mathematical system from the *originally* subjective perception – for example, of a red car – has been placed ahead of the subjective experience, in order to explain it. In other words, *the construction has taken on the task of explaining its own presup-positions.* What this illustrates, of course, is the forgotten ground of the life-world. The life-world has been, if not eliminated, at least considered secondary with respect to natural science.

I will now go on to say a word about how the life-world and life-world experience can make up the foundation on which sciences achieve their legitimacy. It has already been emphasized how Husserl's epistemological critique of natural science was not directed at natural science as natural science. On the contrary, natural science in its mathematization of nature had obtained an appropriate ground. The critique concerned exclusively an inappropriate interpretation of how natural science is to be understood epistemologically. However, the social sciences, such as psychology, had not been grounded in an appropriate way, according to Husserl. Therefore, it may be fruitful to examine Husserl's principal ideas about how sciences should be grounded and how they relate to one another. There is no possibil-ity in this context to discuss in any detail the grounding of social sciences such as psychology, which was the discipline that Husserl discussed first and foremost among the social and cultural sciences (cf. Karlsson 1992, 1993).

THE HIERARCHICAL ORGANIZATION OF THE SCIENCES
Perhaps figure 2.1 below can help us to understand the relationship between the sciences and their ground in the life-world. It ought to be stressed that the figure and the ensuing discussion is a somewhat simplified interpretation of Husserl's hierarchical organization of the sciences.

Let us begin with the rectangle at the bottom of the figure: the life-world. The life-world does not signify a science, but I have never-theless wanted to include it in the figure in order to emphasize the basis of sciences in the prescientific experience of the world, that which Husserl, in particular towards the end of his life, came to talk about as the life-world (*Lebenswelt*). By life-world is meant the expe-rience of our ordinary, cultural world, into which we are born and

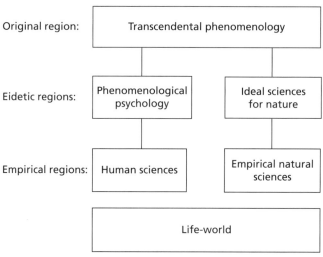

FIGURE 2.1 Husserl's view of the hierarchical organization of the sciences

in which we grow up. Here we have chairs, tables, water to quench our thirst, severe and stingy people, and so on, while there are no atoms, quarks, chemical formulae, superegos or anal erotic people, which are concepts and expressions used in various sciences. The life-world is something that precedes the scientific description of the world, both in the sense that it comes before in time, and as being a logical (necessary) presupposition for scientific descriptions of the world. Without the life-world there is no 'scientific world'. Thus, the scientific world presupposes a life-world, but the life-world can exist in itself, independently of the scientific world.[8] Strictly speaking, one should use the plural form of the concept life-world – that is, life-worlds. A European living in the twenty-first century does not share

---

[8] It is true that even the world of science can, to a greater or lesser degree, be taken up in the cultural life-world, as, for example, when a psychoanalyst directly and spontaneously experiences superego behaviour. But here we are not concerned with such nuances. The scientific theoretical description never becomes completely synonymous with the life-world. In particular, when it comes to natural scientific descriptions, the difference to the life-world is apparent. The natural scientific researcher will never be able to spontaneously perceive her/his kitchen table in terms of atoms and molecules.

the same life-world as a Stone-Age man or an Australian aborigine. One can say that the content of the various life-worlds may differ from one another, but they all share, according to Husserl, a common invariant structure – an issue that we cannot deal with here.

Instead, what I want to emphasize is that the different epistemological domains are already given in the life-world experience, in the ordinary spontaneous experience in and of the world. The different epistemological domains are those that are illustrated in the left- and right-hand sides of the figure. The left-hand side has to do with the subjective, cultural, in terms of human sciences and Husserl's phenomenological psychology. The right-hand side concerns nature in the form of empirical natural sciences and ideal sciences for nature. Let me give an example of when I perceive the wooden computer table in front of me; this experience entails both the dimension that has to do with the subjective and cultural – the computer table in its cultural significance as a table for computers – and something that 'points to' nature – the table's materiality in the form of wood. In the perceptual experience these dimensions are fused together. But in the theoretical, scientific attitude, Husserl claims that those respective dimensions are purified and systematized. This was accomplished by natural science some centuries ago, and the prominent figure in this context, according to Husserl, was thus Galileo Galilei, who conceived of nature stripped from its religious, cultural, subjective significance and mathematized it. Empirical natural science had thereby been grounded in an adequate and consistent way, according to Husserl. However, he argued strongly against the idea (as we saw above) that natural scientific descriptions of the world describe (or are approximations of descriptions of) the world as it really is, independently of consciousness.

The left-hand side of the figure, the one that concerns the subjective and cultural, lacked an adequate philosophical-epistemological ground; psychology at the time of Husserl was, in this sense, pre-Galilean. Husserl's thinking was that his phenomenological psychology was to be the foundation for empirical human sciences – for example, a human scientific psychology. Husserl also discussed the possibility of an empirical psychophysical science, which, apart from being grounded by phenomenological psychology, would also be grounded by empirical and a priori natural sciences, which, however, had never been worked out (cf. Husserl 1968/1928, 1981/1927). Figure 2.1 illustrates the idea of two radically different scientific domains – an idea that runs contrary to the scientific monism of positivism: that there is basically only one kind of science – that is, natural science. Furthermore, the idea is that the empirical sciences are grounded in a different ideal – that is, non-empirical sciences. The ideal sciences depicted in the figure are Husserl's phenomenological psychology and ideal sciences for nature, such as mathematics. These ideal sciences (phenomenological psychology and ideal sciences for nature) also demand their epistemological ground in the original region, which, according to Husserl, was transcendental phenomenology. We do not need to follow him there, but let us remain on the eidetic level.

By working out a phenomenological psychology, Husserl wished to lay the necessary ground for human sciences, which especially occupied him in the middle of the 1920s (Husserl 1977/1925). His phenomenological psychology can be seen as a phenomenological contribution to the philosophy of mind. It is a necessary but hardly sufficient grounding for empirical psychology, for example (Spiegelberg 1967). Thus, the grounding of empirical human sciences comprehends more than that which is achieved by Husserl's phenomenological psychology. However, Husserl's phenomenological psychology makes a crucial contribution in bringing to light intentionality as the essential feature for experience, the subjective and consciousness.

I have obviously refrained from giving a place to psychoanalysis in the figure. Psychoanalysis is, in my view, a human science and not a natural science. But it is a human science that includes a dimension that goes beyond the subject's conscious intending or intention. This particular predicament for psychoanalysis – that in one sense it is an interpretive human science, but at the same time includes something that goes beyond the subject's conscious intending – makes it into a special science. This double character has been formulated in somewhat different ways – for example, that psychoanalysis is a critical hermeneutical science, that it includes a quasi-naturalistic phase in which the hermeneutical understanding is broken by an element that has certain similarities with explanations used in natural science, or that it has a mixed discourse of both meaning and a physicalistic language (cf. Habermas 1972; Lesche 1981; Ricoeur 1970). In chapter 4 I will argue that the unconscious presents itself as something that breaks with the intentionality of consciousness, but which is transformed, with the assistance of psychoanalytic theories, into something meaningful in the psychoanalytic process.

## SUMMARY

In this chapter I have argued that an epistemological grounding of sciences must be located within prescientific life-world experiences. This is a general principle pertaining to psychoanalysis as well as other empirical sciences. The chapter focused on the relationship between natural science and life-world experiences, which is of great importance, due to the way natural science is usually considered today. Natural scientific descriptions are usually understood as descriptions of a factual objective world independent of the subject. Such an understanding of the achievements of natural science is not correct, given the presentation here of Husserl's analysis. Natural science is a kind of construction and not a reflection of the world-in-itself. Besides being an illustration of the overall phenomenological view that the sciences have their ground in life-world experiences, this chapter also forms an important background to the following chapter.

# 3  A critical examination of neuropsychoanalysis

A common opinion among psychoanalysts today is that psychoanalysis has to be integrated with neuroscience if it is to be accepted as a science. Such an opinion would have been met with much scepticism just a few years ago, and could have been conceived of as a consequence of lacking faith in psychoanalysis, and as a threat to the psychoanalytic project. Neurology, which in the last few years has made such impressive progress, has indeed awakened enormous interest among psychoanalysts. In a guest editorial in the *International journal of psychoanalysis* Olds and Cooper (1997: 219) write as follows:

> Freud himself was an early pioneer in biological interdisciplinary study, and we are reminded that he gave up this line of inquiry in part, at least, because neuroscience had not reached the point where such a project could be fruitful.
>
> Now, however, an enormous amount of new information is becoming available through techniques of molecular biology, brain imaging, genetics, computer modelling and other studies and this may be the time to begin thinking anew of the linkages of psychology and the brain. More particularly, we may begin to ask what these new studies can contribute to psychoanalysis, as well as how psychoanalytic understanding of mental functions may help to guide empirical studies of cognition and neural structures.

Mark Solms, perhaps the leading representative for an integration of neurology and psychoanalysis, together with Oliver Turnbull has published the book *The brain and the inner world* (2002), which can be seen as a kind of manifesto for an integrated neuropsychoanalytic science, and which has been given the name 'neuropsychoanalysis'.

There may be reasons to scrutinize this neuropsychoanalysis critically, which raise philosophical and conceptual problems that have to be solved in order for there to be a trustworthy integration between neurology and psychoanalysis. Let us begin by presenting some of the claims that Solms and Turnbull make for this neuropsychoanalysis (2002: 314–15; italics in the original):

> The high road for psychoanalysis is to engage with the neuroscientific issues that should now directly interest it. This will not be an easy task. Most psychoanalysts are unfamiliar with the complexities of neuroscience, and (one must admit) they are often poorly equipped to design and implement systematic scientific investigations. Some psychoanalysts today are, however, keen to rise to the challenge, and this book is designed to aid those who wish to do so. If a critical mass of psychoanalysts should choose this path, there is much to be gained in return for the effort that it will involve. A radically different psychoanalysis will emerge. It will be a psychoanalysis that retains its pride of place as the science of human *subjectivity* – the discipline through which we investigate the stuff of individual experience: the living of a life. But its claims will be far more securely grounded. We will better understand how mental disorders arise. We will be able to target our therapies at those who can benefit most, and in the ways that work best. We may extend our clinical reaches in previously undreamt-of directions. And in the end, we believe, we shall be able to say with confidence at last: this is how the mind *really* works.

This new discipline, neuropsychoanalysis, will not only solve the dead end that psychoanalysis is supposed to have entered,[1] but also brings about a scientific solution to the body–mind problem (more of which comes later).

---

[1] Solms and Turnbull (2002: 298): 'A century on, psychoanalysis has had an adequate opportunity to see how far it can get on its own... the clinical method of psychoanalysis has taken us about as far as it is going to, on its own.'

My intention is to discuss the following themes: conceptualization of the body–mind problem, the attempt to solve the body–mind problem in terms of dual-aspect monism, the alleged epistemological function of neuroscience for psychoanalysis, and the description of subjective consciousness. In a concluding remark, I will point to the fundamental mistake from which I believe this kind of neuropsychoanalysis suffers.

### CONCEPTUALIZATION OF THE BODY–MIND PROBLEM

Solms and Turnbull (2002) think that the solution to the philosophical question of the relationship between body and soul is to transform the question into an empirical (natural) scientific problem (p. xiv). This kind of scientistic expression – that is, that natural science is able to solve ontological/philosophical/conceptual problems – implies a very controversial view of scientific activities.[2] Certainly, there are also occasions when they express a non-scientistic view, which comes out when they make clear that they are 'of the opinion that the nature of the relationship between brain and mind (body and soul) is *not* amenable to scientific proof' (p. 55; italics in the original).

The authors' world-view (*Weltanschauung*) – which most often coincides with a naturalistic opinion – has clearly affected the way in which they formulate the body–mind problem. The question of how body and mind relate to one another is reformulated in their words into a question of 'how matter becomes mind' and, more specifically, 'how does consciousness emerge from the brain' (p. 45). This question should have been formulated in a more neutral and objective way, which would better reflect the discussions that have taken place throughout the entire history of philosophy.[3] The way

---

[2] Solms and Turnbull's (2002: 95, n. 4) scientism is also apparent when they reduce ethical problems to biological facts: 'It even holds out the possibility that answers to the philosophical problem of how to live a worthwhile and fulfilling life might someday be grounded in objective, biological facts.'

[3] In Kaplan-Solms and Solms (2000: 4) one reads, astonishingly, that 'The essence of the mystery [the body–mind problem] was (and always has been) this: how is subjective awareness – consciousness – produced by the anatomical structures and physiological functions of the brain?'

in which Solms and Turnbull have formulated the question is not only biased, but also surprising, since their own idea does not allow one to view the relation between body and mind in terms of causality or as an emergent relation. Let us pause at this issue concerning the relationship between body and mind, and discuss it, from both a methodological and an ontological point of view.

### A methodological comment concerning the correlation between body and mind

Solms and Turnbull seem aware that the neuropsychological investigations and the possible correlations that are found between bodily processes and subjective states of minds in these investigations do' not allow one to say more than that there are correlations between them (2002: 65; italics in the original):

> When we said a moment ago that we know 'what the different chemical processes are that characterize each different emotion', we did not mean that chemicals literally *generate* the emotions. It is more correct (but perhaps too cumbersome) to say that neuroscientists have discovered the specific neurochemical processes that *correlate with* the subjective experiences of specific emotional states.[4]

Despite this awareness, the authors break systematically with an adequate use of language, in favour of a causal or quasi-causal language. It may be more cumbersome to describe the relationship in an adequate way, but owing to the seriousness of this matter, a cumbersome but correct language is preferable. Quasi-causal formulations are innumerable in their descriptions, in which biological processes 'produce', 'generate', 'govern', and so on, subjective experiences. This highly inadequate use of language is in line with the way that they formulate the body–mind problem in terms of 'how matter becomes

---

[4] In a note on p. 80, the same principal standpoint is basically repeated, and this time the use of this misleading quasi-causal language is said to be 'for convenience's sake'.

mind'. As we will see, such a language is also incompatible with their principal solution to the body–mind problem.[5]

## An ontological comment concerning the correlation between body and mind

Solms and Turnbull's ontological thesis (2002), the so-called 'dual-aspect monism', implies a philosophical ontological position on the interpretation of the correlation between bodily states and subjective states of experiences. In brief, the dual-aspect monism can be described as if the mental, subjective and bodily states are two sides of the same thing. Such a formulation excludes seeing the relationship in causal terms, since the dual-aspect monism presupposes that each bodily state is indissolubly correlated with a specific subjective state. The empirically collected correlations do not give us reason to interpret them in causal terms; neither do they give us the right – and this is important – to interpret them as two sides of the same thing. And when it is a question of statistical correlations, which is most often the case, we are, in principle, only justified in saying that under 'X' circumstance, 'Y' will occur with a probability of 'Z' per cent.

### THE THEORY OF DUAL-ASPECT MONISM

This monistic theory concerning the relationship between body and mind implies that we only consist of one stuff: 'we are made of only one type of stuff' (Solms and Turnbull 2002: 56), but appear in two different ways. The authors make clear that these forms of appearance (body and mind) are artefacts of perception – in reality there

---

[5] On the basis of Aristotle's distinction between four kinds of causality (material, formal, efficient and final) Ricoeur (Changeux and Ricoeur 2000: 46) argues that the relationship between neurology and mental states should not be understood in terms of efficient causality, but must be understood in terms of material causality; the neurological state is the substrate of the mental state. My criticism of Solms et al. (Solms and Turnbull 2002; Solms 1997; Kaplan-Solms and Solms 2000) concerns their causal reasoning in terms of efficient causality.

is only one substance:[6] 'The important point to grasp ... is that ... *in our essence* we are *neither* mental nor physical beings – at least not in the sense that we normally employ these terms' (p. 56; italics in the original). And further (p. 56; italics in the original):

> Dual-aspect monism ... implies that the brain is made of stuff that *appears* 'physical' when viewed from the outside (as an object) and 'mental' when viewed from the inside (as a subject). When I perceive myself externally (in the mirror, for example) and internally (through introspection), I am perceiving the *same thing* in two different ways (as a *body* and a *mind*, respectively). This distinction between body and mind is therefore *an artefact of perception.*

What are we then, if we can be understood neither bodily nor mentally, if these forms of appearance are only artefacts of perception? The authors mean that we must put the question to those sciences that can give an indirect answer. We cannot escape this artificial body–mind dichotomy, since we cannot go beyond the limits of our senses. We can only infer what this underlying entity is like and how it functions. This underlying entity, the monistic principle that we are, is the unconscious, which the authors suggest we call 'the human mental apparatus'. Thus, we will never be able to observe directly the human mental apparatus, but only its different appearances in the form of the physical/bodily and the subjective consciousness.

One could summarize the ideas behind Solms and Turnbull's theory of dual-aspect monism in the following way: the entities that appear to us – that is, body and mind – have no autonomous reality, no reality on their own. They are manifestations of an underlying

---

[6] But this idea, that the forms of appearance are only artefacts (and not realities), is described in a varying and contradictory way, because sometimes it is emphasized that experience, the subjective side, exists: 'The inner world of subjective experience, *as we experience it*, is as real as are apples and tables' (p. 297; italics in the original); 'Feelings are real. They exist. They have effects' (p. 296).

reality: the unconscious or so-called human mental apparatus. This apparatus cannot be observed directly, but one is here referred to the two forms of appearance (the subjective consciousness and the brain). When it comes to these forms of appearance, the observations of the brain are more reliable and secure, according to the authors, and it is therefore important for psychoanalysis, and for the solution to the body–mind problem, to engage in natural scientific brain research. The natural scientific brain research is supposed to address the same manifestations which subjective consciousness represents (or is an appearance of).

This suggested dual-aspect monism suffers from a number of obscurities and contradictions. It is hard not to get the impression that this theory is naturalistic, despite the fact that the authors dismiss the so-called 'materialistic monism', which reduces subjective awareness to material brain tissues. This impression gets support from Solms and Turnbull's positivistic ideal of science, which is apparent in the following quote (2002: 294–5): 'There is no denying the fact that although psychoanalysis and neuroscience are both studying the same thing (from different perspectives), psychoanalytic knowledge is far less secure than that of neuroscience'.

In line with the scientific ideal of the authors, the road to knowledge is via visual observations, which precludes the inner subjective life from scientific investigations. This kind of argument to declare psychoanalysis as unscientific is well known (cf. Popper 1959, 1972). The process and dialogue between the analyst and the analysand is thus not acceptable as scientific research on the unconscious. And neuropsychoanalysis is supposed to represent a more scientific alternative compared to the psychoanalysis that we know today (Solms and Turnbull 2002: 314).

The authors assert that psychoanalytic practice is a worse source of psychoanalytic knowledge than that provided by natural scientific brain research. Their idea is precisely that psychoanalysis and brain research study the same thing – that is, the unconscious. And this study object that they have in common can better and more reliably be studied by the neurosciences than by psychoanalysis. To me, this is an untenable standpoint. If we conduct a thought experiment and try to put out of our minds the clinical experiences (the analyst's and analysand's), as well as our own self-analysis, there will be nothing with which the neurosciences can be correlated. The neurosciences' more exact way to describe their study object compared to that of psychoanalysis does not make neuroscience a better or more reliable science, but the crucial issue is the character of the study object. The study object of psychoanalysis, the unconscious, does not have the exact character that the study object of natural science – that is, nature – has. However, it is not only pointless to wish that it would work to describe the study object of psychoanalysis in a more exact way, but it is also an inadequate methodological criterion if its study object, in essence, has an inexact character.

Let us look at another quote that entails the ideal of empiricism, and which displays even greater complications. Solms and Turnbull (2002: 43; italics in the original) write: *'linking* the invisible inner world of feelings, thoughts, and memories with the visible tissues of the body that generate them renders them far more accessible to scientific scrutiny'. I have already pointed out that the authors have chosen to use a quasi-causal language that they themselves in principle dismiss. Here I want to discuss a point that I have only hinted at earlier, namely, whether or not the authors, with their quasi-causal use of language, also undermine their own dual-aspect monism. Their point is that the brain and the subjective life are two sides of the same thing (the same thing being the underlying reality/ the unconscious/the human mental apparatus). However, the quasi-causal language is not compatible with the idea of the subjective and the physical being two sides of the same thing. In quasi-causal language we do not have two sides of the same thing, but one side that generates the other.

Instead, it would be more reasonable to describe the forms of appearance as two sides that do not relate causally to each other. In order to be able to describe a relationship as causal, the two related entities must be independent of each other. We cannot say that 'unmarried man' is the cause of 'bachelor' or that 'heads' are cause of 'tails'. Solms is occasionally aware of the fact that the relationship between the two forms of appearance cannot be described in causal terms; it is exactly this point that he criticizes Searle for.[7] Solms (1997: 701) is very clear on this issue:

> Brain processes can no more cause conscious experiences than a flash of lightning can cause a clap of thunder ... The two modalities of perception [here, the subjective experience and physical brain processes] are not causally related; rather, they are both caused by something else, something in the essence of the natural process or entity they represent ...

An unequivocal picture is depicted here: the forms of appearance cannot be described in causal terms (they are sides of the same thing), but these sides themselves are caused by the underlying reality (more on that later). In the light of this distinct statement that the different forms of appearance are not causally related to each other, it is incomprehensible that this relationship is often described precisely in causal or quasi-causal terms, the most common being that the physical or material causes subjective or mental states. But there are also examples when the subjective is supposed to cause physical/material states, as, for example, when psychotherapy is supposed to change the functional activity of the brain (Solms and Turnbull 2002: 288).

---

[7] Solms (1997: 698; italics in the original): 'It seems to me that Searle perceives a mystery because he does not recognize that the visual images of the processes occurring in your somatosensory cortex and limbic cortex were perceptions *of the same thing* as, respectively, your somatic sensation of pain and your affective feeling of mild unpleasure; all that distinguishes these different images, sensations, and feelings is the fact that *they simultaneously represented the same underlying thing in the qualitative ranges that were peculiar to three different perceptual modalities.* Searle's failure to realize this leads him to wonder how the one perception *caused* the other. But they did *not* cause each other. They were perceptions of a single underlying process, and that process caused all of them simultaneously, which is why they were *correlated* with one another.'

Let us see how the relationship between the underlying reality (the human mental apparatus/the unconscious) and its two forms of appearance (the subjective awareness and the body/brain) is described. This relationship is described in a contradictory way. One way of describing the relationship (as was apparent above) is that the underlying reality manifests itself in two different ways. Such a description is not compatible with a description that the underlying reality is the cause of these two forms of appearance, or a description of the relationship in terms of interaction, but these ways of describing the relationship exist. As was clear from the above quote from Solms (1997: 701) and the quote in note 7 (see p. 48), Solms brings forth the idea that the forms of appearance are caused by the underlying reality. But the causal direction is also described in the opposite way – that is, the forms of appearance affect the underlying reality (Solms and Turnbull 2002: 308):

> one can determine whether, and in what way, a particular function of the mental apparatus has been affected by a brain lesion – for example, the function of 'secondary process' inhibition. We can then correlate the observed changes with the part of the brain that was damaged. This reveals the contribution that the part of the brain in question made to the organization of that mental function.

What is in fact said in this quote is that the physical form of appearance affects that which it is a manifestation of, which is an untenable idea and contradicts the way that the relationship has been described earlier on. We have also seen that the subjective form of appearance can be supposed to affect the material and the underlying reality (the unconscious), since Solms and Turnbull claim that the functional activity of the brain is altered by psychotherapy (p. 288).

These examples suffice to illustrate how obscure and contradictory the description is of the relationship between these two alleged sides of the same thing, as well as the description of the relationship between the underlying reality and the two sides.

THE ALLEGED EPISTEMOLOGICAL FUNCTION OF
NEUROSCIENCE FOR PSYCHOANALYSIS

In this section I would like to argue against the idea that neuroscience has a legitimizing function for psychoanalytic knowledge.
The question is this: is neuroscience capable of legitimizing psychoanalytic knowledge? We have seen that Solms and Turnbull (2002)
hold the idea that natural scientific research on the brain gives the
most secure access to the underlying reality – the unconscious.
Below are two quotes from Solms and Turnbull (pp. 6, 42–3), where
they maintain the idea that neuroscience has an epistemologically
legitimizing function for psychoanalysis:

> Psychoanalysis today is associated with bitter rivalry between
> opposing camps that apparently have no valid means of deciding
> between their conflicting standpoints on various theoretical
> matters. One solution might be to find links between the
> disputed theoretical concepts of psychoanalysis and those of the
> neurosciences.
>
> neuroscience, by virtue of the objective status of its
> evidence, provides a useful set of anchor points from which to
> re-evaluate psychoanalytic concepts.

The idea that neuroscience can constitute a scientific basis for psychoanalysis is often repeated in the text, but there are also occasions
when the relationship between psychoanalysis and neuroscience
is described in a more equal way – in the form of the possibility of
checking conclusions from one type of observation with observations
of another type (p. 274). However, the main tendency in the text is
obvious: neuroscience has a legitimizing function for psychoanalysis.
Given this standpoint, one would have expected to be offered examples
of cases where psychoanalytic conceptions are disproved or corrected.
Furthermore, it would have been interesting to see the resolution of
one of the conflicts occurring between different psychoanalytic orien-
tations determined on the basis of neuroscientific discoveries. But
none of that is fulfilled – quite the opposite, the tendency is to show

that the neuroscientific findings support psychoanalysis. Against this background, one can say that the authors' rejection of the present status of psychoanalysis is somewhat surprising.

However, there is one example when they discuss a possible refutation of a psychoanalytic idea. The background is the so-called Ribot's law in neuroscience, which seems to contradict certain ideas within psychoanalysis. The meaning of Ribot's law is that recent memories are more vulnerable and less durable than memories from the past. At first, this seems to contradict the psychoanalytic idea of infantile amnesia. Let us look at how Solms and Turnbull (2002: 148–9; italics in the original) handle this situation:

> Any account of infantile amnesia must explain why it violates Ribot's law. In psychoanalysis, the explanation is that early childhood memories *are* very robust; they only *appear* to be forgotten, but in fact are just unavailable to conscious awareness. The question then becomes: Why are they not available to conscious awareness? (The answer, in psychoanalysis, is repression.) It is not clear how the alternative account explains this violation of Ribot's law.

At this critical point, the neuroscientific experience seems to weigh lightly compared to the psychoanalytic experience. My criticism, of course, is not aimed at the fact that the authors defend the psychoanalytic standpoint, but it is a kind of ad hoc reasoning to introduce psychoanalytic concepts and ideas in order to explain away the applicability of the neuroscientific law to psychoanalysis. Nor is it convincing to avoid the problem by means of unconventional semantic definitions – that childhood memories are robust or only appear to have been forgotten. Remembering belongs to the sphere of consciousness. From the perspective of being conscious, I can remember and forget, but to talk about the unconscious as an instance that remembers and forgets is to do violence to the use of language. (What would the difference be between an unconscious that forgets and one that remembers?) I believe that this example shows how difficult it is to comprehend the dual-aspect monism in our understanding of concrete psychoanalytic standpoints. What we risk losing in the theory of dual-aspect monism is its dynamic thinking, which has to do with conflicts between different impulses and with the disturbing effect of the unconscious on conscious life.

The basic problem is that the subjective side and the bodily side (the brain) are two radically different perspectives that cannot be connected or bridged. The two perspectives are, on the one hand, a first-person perspective, by which is meant the person's own and unique subjective experiencing, and, on the other hand, a third-person perspective, by which is meant observations of external objects, such as the brain. This circumstance – that subjective consciousness is a first-person inside perspective, while observation of the brain is a third-person external perspective – is recognized by Solms and Turnbull, but this recognition does not seem to entail any obligation. They do not take this unbridgeable gap between these two perspectives seriously. Instead, they talk about it as two sides of one and the same thing, and by means of the allegory of the blind men and an elephant they attempt to illustrate how the different perspectives are synthesized to one and the same thing. (This allegory is also found in Kaplan-Solms and Solms 2000.)

Let us take a closer look at this allegory and find out what kind of perspective it presupposes. In this allegory of the blind men and the elephant, each one's perspective – that is, the trunk for one person, a rear leg for another, a front leg for the third, and so on – is a different part of one and the same thing. This implies that every perspective or part of the elephant blends in a harmonious way with all the other parts. Or, to formulate this in a somewhat different way, each part in itself points to and opens onto, in its extension, the possibility of embracing all the other parts (the whole). This can be imagined by letting the blind man who touches the trunk go further than the trunk and, by means of further tactile impressions, he will be able to form a synthesized whole of all the different parts. It is this that makes it possible to talk about different sides of one and the same thing in this context. But when it comes to the theory of dual-aspect monism, with its two alleged sides, there is no such harmony. A first-person subjective perspective cannot reach or be synthesized with a third-person perspective, no matter to what extent this first-person perspective is developed. In my subjective experiences, I can follow the threads that are opened up by my experience, but no matter how far I go with my experiencing from the first-person perspective, it will not lead into that which is produced by a third-person external perspective. Here we are dealing not with a concept of perspective in which the different perspectives are harmonious with one another, but one which reveals two essentially different attitudes. We are reminded of Sartre's (1948: 5) apt description of the difference between facts and meaning. It is just as impossible to come to meaning by collecting facts, no matter how many facts we collect (because, basically, it is a question of different attitudes), as it is to reach 1 by adding figures to the right of 0.99.

In the relationship between a first-person perspective and a third-person perspective, one has not yet found any way to bridge from one perspective to the other; nor does there exist any overriding third level of discourse under which these two different perspectives can be subordinated.

This idea of the two sides of one and the same underlying reality is thus problematic. The mental side possesses certain qualities that cannot be caught by observations of nature (the brain), according to Solms and Turnbull, but the implications of this remain unclear. And then we have the brain, which is supposed to yield more reliable knowledge about the underlying reality. But access to consciousness via the brain becomes problematic when we apply this reasoning to everyday (life-world) experiences. This becomes obvious as soon as Solms and Turnbull discuss the problem of perceiving the other as someone with a consciousness. Then it sounds like this (pp. 67–8; italics in the original):

> We cannot enter the consciousness of another being to determine directly if it is like our own, and indeed if it exists at all. Each one

of us knows for certain that we, *ourselves*, possess consciousness. For the rest, we rely on inference since other people *behave* in roughly the same way as we do, and since their brains are *constructed* in roughly the same way as ours, it seems only reasonable to *infer* that they, too, possess a consciousness like ours.

Several objections to this quote could be raised, but I want to restrict myself to a comment on how subjective experience has been depicted. The perception of the other as an alter ego must be understood on the basis of life-world experiences. To make observations of my own brain as a sound basis for the belief that my neighbour also has a consciousness, as the authors do, is far-fetched. And who has observed their own brain?

What this quote reveals, among other things, is that the authors' constructed explanation neglects the originality of subjective life in favour of a constructed and derived natural scientific perspective. The constructed perspective is subsequently used to explain something that has already been carried out; the understanding is already a reality. We recognize this critique from chapter 2, in which the priority of the life-world had been neglected within the psychophysical paradigm. Let us look in more detail at how subjective life is described within neuropsychoanalysis.

THE DESCRIPTION OF SUBJECTIVE AWARENESS

The descriptions of subjective awareness in neuropsychoanalysis are inadequate, which makes it more difficult to reveal the incorrect thinking that forms the basis of dual-aspect monism. One is struck by the lack of sensitivity with respect to subjectivity and its conditions, which, of course, is regrettable from a psychoanalytic perspective. It would appear, according to Solms and Turnbull (2002: 46), that we have better access to atoms, molecules, quarks – that is, the non-perceivable perception of the world – than to our own subjective perceptual experiences.

Lack of sensitivity for subjectivity and subjective experiences is expressed in many different ways within the neuropsychoanalytic

tradition. Subjectivity is treated in an objectifying way, which essentially means that the subject, in terms of a meaning-bestowing, intentional subject, disappears. Pally and Olds (1998: 975) objectify the
subject/person in the psychoanalytic situation into a third-person
neuter:

> A patient lying on a couch has a rather static visual
> environment, especially with the eyes closed. Because the brain
> is always looking for change, on the couch with so little external
> distraction it will look for change and follow the change in the
> stream of thoughts and associations.

Another problematic way to describe the mental within this tradition is in terms of a perceptual observation of something internal.
This perception of the internal is called 'introspection': 'our mental experience arises out of introspection; *we* perceive the mind
(as opposed to matter) by looking inwards' (Solms and Turnbull
2002: 67; my italics). The idea that is expressed here implies several
problems, regardless of how one interprets this sentence. If one takes
the sentence literally, the idea is that the mental life does not arise
until the act of introspection is carried out. But then it is difficult
to understand who and what this 'we' is that carries out the percep-
tion/introspection. If one is not to understand the sentence in this
literal sense, but rather in the sense that introspection illuminates
the mental (pre-introspected) state, then introspection means a kind
of reflecting of one's pre-reflected experiencing.[8] But in such cases

---

[8] Solms and Turnbull use the concept 'introspection' as a kind of perception of
our inner life. The idea that we perceive our inner life can be criticized because
it describes experiences of inner life as analogous with experiences of the outer,
objective world. Outer objects and the world are perceived by our visual looking
at the object, for example,, while the inner life cannot be experienced in accordance with this pattern of perception. (It is not by accident that psychoanalysis
is a listening science and not a science of observation.) A better alternative to
'introspection' can often be the term 'reflection'. Inner life is thematized, is
brought into focus by means of reflecting acts of consciousness that thematize
something that has already been lived through, but has not been explicitly
known. The presupposition for reflection is thus a pre-reflected experiencing. I
am free to use the concept reflection and avoid using introspection, since introspection tends to neglect pre-reflected inner life.

one misses a description and understanding of the pre-reflected lived experience. On the whole, one can notice that the subjective and consciousness are limited to connoting abstract reflected (introspected) states, at the expense of the pre-reflected experiencing of the subject and of consciousness. In other words, the concept of consciousness tends to be apprehended in much too narrow a meaning.

Solms and Turnbull place on an equal footing reflection of one's inner life (in their terminology, introspection) with perception of the external object. However, reflection is not, as has been pointed out, a perceptual act, but it reflects, thematizes something that has been lived through but not thematized, such as a spontaneous visual perception, for example, of the bus that takes me to work in the morning. Husserl (1962/1913: 127) has described metaphorically the reflecting acts as 'swimming after' the acts which the reflection is directed upon.

Neuropsychoanalysis, in line with the naturalistic attitude, places mental life on a par with nature: 'The mind is an aspect of nature' (Solms and Turnbull 2002: 297). The intentional relation between a constant stream of conscious acts and their objects (in the widest possible meaning) remains undiscovered. Mental life and the transcendent character of consciousness always to go beyond itself are reified and treated as any things or facts in the world. One does not make any principal distinction between nature and subjective living – that is, between, on the one hand, a stone, a piece of wood, a planet, and, on the other hand, a *wish* for consolation, a *grieving* for the death of a close friend, a *perception* of a smiling child. Indeed, the idea of a *subject* is completely lacking in neuropsychoanalysis. And in consequence the *world* is also missing, with all that goes with it – other human beings, history, future projects and a relation to oneself. In neuropsychoanalysis the human being is depicted in a one-dimensional image: a human being who is closed in in a sensory now-state, without being open towards the past, the future or other people and without a capacity for self-reflection. Solms (1997: 685) states the following about the conditions of man:

> First, we are aware of the natural processes occurring in the
> external world, which are represented to us in the form of our
> external perceptual modalities of sight, sound, touch, taste,
> smell, etc. Second, we are aware of the natural processes
> occurring within our own selves, which are represented to us
> in the form of our subjective consciousness. We are aware of
> nothing else. These are the only constituents of the envelope
> of conscious awareness, which defies the limit of human
> experience.

This quote reminds us logically about the sceptic's self-contradiction
when (s)he, in his/her utterance that there is no truth, rejects something which is presupposed in the utterance. Solms' description of
man deprives him of his reflecting capacity that goes beyond those
alleged representations of external and internal processes. But one
may wonder if Solms' utterance, in fact, does not presuppose a
reflecting capacity; how else could it otherwise be possible for him
to involve himself in this meta-perspective that the quote implies?

Another problem with how the subject (human being) is
treated consists of the simplified and inadequate way in which the
character of consciousness' self-consciousness is described. In Solms
and Turnbull (2002: 76–7) we read the following: 'The mind itself
is unconscious, but we perceive it consciously by looking inwards.
It is this capacity for "looking inwards" (for introspection or self-
awareness) that is the most essential property of a mind'. A first
complication here is that consciousness is described in a way that
may contradict earlier descriptions. In this latter quote, the idea is
expressed that the introspection is a capacity of consciousness that
goes against the idea that consciousness arises out of introspection,
which was the literal sense of the quote I discussed earlier. However,
this is not the only troublesome aspect in this latter quote. In fact,
consciousness is described in two diametrically different ways in
these two sentences. In the main introductory clause of the first
sentence ('The mind itself is unconscious'), consciousness in itself

is unconscious, which must in all likelihood mean that it is not conscious of itself.[9] In the subsequent sentence, on the other hand, self-consciousness belongs essentially to consciousness ('the most essential property of a mind'). Yet another problem with the quote is that introspection is equated with self-consciousness. Introspection (in the sense of reflection) is an act that is directed towards a pre-reflected act, an act of a higher order, in other words. However, self-consciousness cannot consist in consciousness reflecting oneself by means of another act of consciousness of a higher order. It may be possible, however, that Solms and Turnbull embrace the so-called 'reflection theory', which means precisely that self-consciousness of consciousness is constituted by a conscious act's reflection on itself. In this theory one neglects the fact that self-consciousness *cannot* be ascertained through an act of reflection. Reflection of myself pre-supposes a consciousness that is aware of itself. How could I know otherwise that it is myself that the act of reflection reflects on? In other words, self-consciousness must be based on pre-reflected acts of consciousness (see Zahavi 1999).

Also as regards the ideas of body and 'bodilyness', one sees that the descriptions are objectivistic and one-dimensional. The body is described in terms of the objectified body, deprived of intentionality and subjectivity (Solms and Turnbull 2002: 77): 'The body is not the mind. Bodily processes are not intrinsically mental; they can even be performed by machines'. This description of an objectified body from a third-person perspective neglects to take into account the subjectively lived body – that is, 'my body'. Despite the explicit wish of the authors to avoid Cartesian dualism, the above quote bears witness to a view that resembles Descartes' division of subjective awareness as something immaterial and the body as something material and mechanical. To reduce the body to something mechanical and material seems to be obsolete and refutes the attention paid,

---

[9] The idea of a second unconscious consciousness apart from consciousness is an idea that Freud conceived as absurd (see chapter 4).

in the last few decades, to the body as something subjectively lived (Bullington 1999; Husserl 2000/1918; Merleau-Ponty 1962/1945), the erogenous body (Freud 1905b), the creative/thinking/speaking body (Lerner 1999; Matthis 1997; McDougall 1989), the body in terms of a 'skin-ego' (Anzieu 1989), and pre-symbolic body experience in terms of an 'autistic-contiguous position' (Ogden 1992). These different ways of conceptualizing the body are of great importance for psychoanalytic thinking.

Thus the body is treated in an objectifying and one-dimensional way. Different body parts, whose givenness is fundamentally different, are treated as if they were comparable and on a par with one another. The body, as an object for external perception, can be oneself, as in the example of looking at oneself in the mirror (Solms and Turnbull 2002: 56). This perception of my body that I see in the mirror is compared to the perception of my brain. However, here one must object that my brain is not a perceptual object for me. In fact, I have no experience of my brain, but the function of the brain is something that I have been taught and told about. The objective knowledge that I possess of the brain is something that affects neither my identity nor my experience of myself.

A central problem with the cognitive neuropsychological tradition, as has been pointed out, is that its use of language is badly anchored in lived experience, which leads to consequences that are contra-intuitive and where the relationship between psychical processes becomes reversed. Within this tradition, we are like closed-in monads; we do not reach out to the world, but are closed in in representations of the world. The world is not presented to us, but is given in an indirect way as a representation. The character of perception, to put us in a direct relation with external objects here and now, is transformed into a memory of something we have learnt: 'much of what we take for granted as "the way the world is" – as we *perceive* it – is in fact what we have *learned* about the world – as we *remember* it' (Solms and Turnbull 2002: 154; italics in the original). Such a description is the opposite of our intuitive experience and reverses the relationship between memory and perception. Perception becomes reduced to an execution of memories. In reality, the relationship between perception and memory is rather the opposite. When remembering, we remember earlier perceptions; we reflect earlier perceptions.

Furthermore, perception is described in a too abstract and cognitive manner. Earlier experiences can by all means take part in and form the perceptual experience. But it is not difficult to find examples when knowledge shows itself powerless in relationship to perceptual illusions – as, for example, when one drives a car on a hot, sunny summer's day and one thinks one sees a surface of water on the asphalt road ahead. It is difficult, if not impossible, to liberate oneself from this perceptual illusion, despite one's knowledge that in reality there is no water on the road, which is consequently confirmed perceptually once one has reached the point where one thought the road was covered with water. How would one like to explain such an experience on the basis of memory?

With this unsatisfactory analysis of perception, it follows that man is not supposed to reach out into the world, and our perception can only be indirect and be a re-presentation of the world. Solms (1997: 693) stresses that perception does not have to do with reality itself, even if we experience it in such a way. Perception is instead of consciousness itself: 'Stimuli arising from the external world can be perceived only on the external surface of consciousness' (Solms 1997: 695).[10] This counterintuitive theory demands an explanation why, in such a case, we experience that perception puts us in direct contact with the world.

Perception of the external world is also on a par with that type of observation that is conducted within natural scientific research by means of different instruments (Solms 1997: 690). One neglects the essential differences between the perception of external objects and observations by means of instruments in natural scientific

---

[10] Pally and Olds (1998: 978) also clearly express this counterintuitive standpoint: 'Despite the subjective experience that we sense the outside world, it is the brain's neural activity patterns that "simulate" reality'.

research. Our common spontaneous perception puts us in direct contact with the world, while the instruments in natural scientific research make it possible to postulate something that it is not possible to perceive. The natural scientific observations, by means of specific instruments, are supposed to correspond with entities that cannot be perceived with the naked eye, and sometimes not even by means of instruments.

## CONCLUDING REMARKS

My examination has shown that Solms' and his co-authors' neuropsychoanalytic project suffers from serious conceptual and philosophical problems. The number of contradictions is so high that the project appears to be a failure, concerning the question of understanding both the psychoanalytic conceptualization of the unconscious and the philosophical body–mind problem. There are several reasons for this failure, and some of the contradictions are so obvious that they could probably be cleared up in a more cogent way within the framework of the neuropsychoanalytic project. However, in the end, I believe that this failure must be understood against the background of the epistemological traditions within which this neuropsychoanalytic project has developed. I am thinking, firstly, of the positivistic and realistic epistemological tradition.[11] Within this epistemological tradition, one does not understand the achievement that scientific activity implies in an adequate way. The lifeworld that makes up the prescientific ground for scientific activity is neglected. It is also obvious that the scientific description is left hanging in the air and does not contribute to the understanding of the intuitive life-world experience. Nor is the scientific achievement

---

[11] The epistemological debate of the last few decades has dealt to a large extent with how to understand scientific theories and concepts. Against the realistic standpoint – that is, that the concepts and theories refer to something existing independent of the research/researcher – we have the instrumental position, where it is claimed that scientific theories and concepts are instruments in order to understand the world, but without any claim that they would describe a world independent of the research/researcher.

understandable as long as the life-world is neglected as the pre-scientific ground.

Let us take a closer look at the complications that have to do with embracing a realistic epistemology and the neglect of the life-world as prescientific ground. Solms emphasizes that we cannot get direct, only indirect knowledge about the unconscious: 'The unconscious is the psychical reality; in its innermost nature it is as much unknown to us as the reality of the external world' (Solms 1997: 685). For my part, I believe that the idea that the unconscious is unknown, even something 'unknowable' (p. 687), is incompatible with a realistic epistemological view of scientific descriptions. One can summarize Solms' standpoint in the following way: *the unconscious is in itself unknown, even unknowable. All our knowledge of the unconscious is necessarily indirect, but (and here the realistic view of natural scientific descriptions is introduced) the way in which natural science describes the unconscious is the way in which it exists in itself independent of us, and the procedure with which we obtain knowledge about it.* This summary is, I think, the most reasonable way in which Solms (1997: 688; italics in the original) should be understood:

> the external processes occurring inside our own selves are ultimately unknowable. Freud recognized that just as we can never know external reality *directly*, so too we can never know our inner selves directly.[12]

The obvious conclusion of this position is that the concepts we use in describing the unconscious (and nature) are dependent on the human subject. By saying that the unconscious in itself is unknown/

---

[12] That Solms places the subject on a par with nature is obvious. Not only does he explicitly express the idea that the unconscious of man is of the same kind as processes in nature, but in his rhetoric he also maintains that nature in itself is unconscious: 'the external world is not conscious. The external world is made up of natural elements... which are *in themselves* unconscious' (Solms 1997: 686; italics in the original). This use of language, to apply a discourse belonging to man (consciousness, the unconscious) to nature, reminds us of pan-psychology.

unknowable, we imply that the concepts with which we describe this reality cannot be claimed to reflect this reality in itself, independent of the way humans construct, acquire and organize knowledge. But it is exactly this kind of realistic epistemological claim that Solms makes. The contradiction here may be said to lie between, on the one hand, the ontological position that something exists that is unknowable, and, on the other hand, the realistic epistemological position that our description has a validity independent of us. Let us look at a quote from Solms that illustrates my point (Solms 1997: 686; italics in the original):

> The external world is made up of natural elements (which physicists describe as particles, waves, energies, forces and the like) which are *in themselves* unconscious, although they are consciously *represented* to us in the form given them by our external perceptual modalities – that is, as sights, sounds, feelings, tastes, smells, etc.
>
> If there were no sentient beings equipped with the sensory organs that generate sound, touch, taste, smell, etc., then the natural elements of the universe would presumably still exist in and of themselves, but they would no longer exist in the familiar form in which they are represented to *us* ... In short, what are constant (and therefore truly objective) are the natural elements themselves; what is inconstant (and therefore less reliable) is perceptual awareness ...

This quote contains, as far as I can understand, two incompatible theses. On the one hand, it is claimed that the external world in itself is unconscious, which means that it is unknowable in itself. On the other hand, it is claimed that this world consists of natural elements, such as particles, waves, energies, forces and the like, which are supposed to exist independent of man and his knowledge-acquiring activities. One wonders on what ground the validity of the natural scientific description is postulated.

My idea is that this incompatibility is a result of the neglect of accounting for the subjective life-world. Here we can witness the importance of that which was presented in chapter 2, namely, the importance of understanding the scientific achievement's relation to the prescientific life-world. In grounding and justifying psychoanalysis (as well as other sciences), one has to find the place and access point where the investigation can begin. And this is what I would like to delve into in the next chapter.

## SUMMARY

This chapter contains a critical examination of a project that is claimed to solve the dead end that psychoanalysis is said to be in, and which presents a way of conceptualizing the body–mind problem. The solution for psychoanalysis is said to be neuropsychoanalysis. The work that is primarily examined in this chapter was written by Solms and Turnbull. The examination concerns many aspects of neuropsychoanalysis. The authors' formulation of the body–mind relationship in terms of a dual-aspect monism is unsatisfying and contradictory. The principal manifesto that the subjective consciousness and the physical (body/brain) are two sides of one underlying reality (the unconscious) is never carried out in a trustworthy way. Many of the authors' ideas are instead naturalistic, and the subjective tends to be reduced to physical material. The description of the subjective is not done in a way that does it justice, which is to be regretted, not least owing to the fact that it is the psychoanalytic field that is in focus.

One conclusion from my examination is that this version of neuropsychoanalysis does not succeed in accomplishing what was promised, namely, an integration of neurology and psychoanalysis. I believe that the problems, essentially, are due to the neglect of an adequate recognition of subjective life, as we saw similarly in the previous chapter, when the naturalistic attitude was shown to neglect subjectivity/the life-world experience.

# 4 The conceptualization of the psychical in psychoanalysis

The task of discussing the conceptualization of the psychical in psychoanalysis entails a search to determine the character and preconditions of the unconscious. Psychoanalysis is indeed the science of the unconscious, even though its field of investigation cannot be limited to the unconscious as a system in Freud's sense. How should one go about being able to say something about the unconscious? Hermeneutics stresses the importance of entering the hermeneutical circle in an appropriate way. And how is one to enter that circle appropriately in order to increase our understanding of the unconscious? We must avoid taking our point of departure from a constructed system, from science other than psychoanalysis. We must begin our investigation where the unconscious shows itself for us in the psychoanalytic process. And it is here that the question of consciousness comes in.

The psychoanalytic process begins with the analysand's conscious self-understanding and is driven forward with the assistance of conscious validations of interpretations of the unconscious. Our knowledge about the unconscious always takes place from the vantage point of consciousness, and in this sense we never reach the unconscious directly, but only through the means of metaphors (cf. Enckell 2002). In other words, one can say that the constitution of the unconscious takes place from the vantage point of consciousness, which is the reason why we must first understand what essentially characterizes consciousness in order to understand what the unconscious is. In discussing the features of consciousness, I will be helped by phenomenological reflections and ideas.[1]

[1] As has been pointed out before, it is not a question of trying to conduct a phenomenology of psychoanalysis, a phenomenological (existential) psychoanalysis (cf. Binswanger 1975; Boss 1979; Sartre 1956/1942), nor to carry out a dialogue between these two sciences, where each would give and take from the other.

A discussion about the conceptualization of the psychical in psychoanalysis includes, among other things, the question of the relationship between consciousness and the unconscious. The unconscious can be said to lie between something that I will call 'the ego's conscious intending' and a rudimentary body-ego experiencing. Against the background of the intentional structure of consciousness, I will discuss the essential difference between consciousness/self-consciousness and the unconscious, and present the reason why the unconscious can only be captured by means of a construction (cf. chapters 5, 6 and 8 in this volume; Karlsson 2000). I will argue that the unconscious can only arise given certain presexual processes, consisting of a body-ego's formation of continuity, coherence and wholeness. The body-ego belongs to the sphere of consciousness/self-consciousness, even if self-consciousness here is only given implicitly and not as a full-fledged 'I am conscious that I ...' I am entering neglected areas of psychoanalysis here; the phenomenon of self-consciousness and the concept of existence. It is in self-consciousness that the subject's ability to 'affirm existence' has its source. The chapter ends with my attempt to show the importance of the 'affirmation of existence' for psychoanalysis (cf. chapter 7 in this volume). The subsequent chapters can be seen as a deepening of themes that are introduced in this chapter.

Let us take a look at some of Freud's ideas about consciousness, which will lay the groundwork for further discussion in this chapter, and help us to chisel out a first important distinguishing trait between consciousness and the unconscious.

## ABOUT FREUD'S VIEW ON THE RELATIONSHIP BETWEEN CONSCIOUSNESS AND THE UNCONSCIOUS

Freud's challenge to gain acceptance for the unconscious involved a confrontation with the question of what consciousness is. Let us

Psychoanalysis will be in focus, while phenomenological reflections and ideas will mainly be playing an assisting role in the attempt to conceptualize and structure the psychoanalytic field of investigation.

look at Freud's partly contradictory conceptualizations of consciousness. He expressed the idea that consciousness is immediately given (Freud 1938a: 144) and that its character is indubitable (p. 157). The indubitable character of consciousness seems even to justify the absence of discussing it: 'There is no need to discuss what is to be called conscious: it is removed from all doubt' (Freud 1932: 70; cf. also Freud 1938a: 159).

It might seem reasonable to conclude from the above quote that Freud thought that the character of consciousness was so uncomplicated and easily understood that no further investigation was required. But at the same time there are occasions upon which a completely different attitude towards consciousness comes to light. In a letter to Wilhelm Fliess in 1896, Freud talked about consciousness as 'this most difficult of all things' (1995/1887–1904: 185). And in connection with his writing about the immediacy with which we know consciousness, he admitted that consciousness 'defies all explanation or description' (Freud 1938a: 157).[2] The slightly more than 40 years that divide these quotes do not, apparently, mean that Freud thought that he had gained a better understanding of the character of consciousness.

Regardless of the degree of complexity of consciousness, Freud was aware that the psychoanalytic project could not do without consciousness. As I pointed out at the beginning of this chapter, the psychoanalytic process begins with the analysand's conscious self-understanding and is driven forward with the assistance of conscious validations of interpretations of the unconscious. The unconscious can never be reached directly, but is traced out in conscious and preconscious material: 'Now all our knowledge is invariably bound up with consciousness. We can come to know even the *Ucs.* only by making it conscious' (Freud 1923: 19; cf. also 1915a: 166, 1938b: 286).

[2] Even if one can hardly assume that Freud considered how the immediacy and closeness of consciousness to us could be a source of the difficulty in getting to grips with it, others (for example, Heidegger 1980/1927: 69) have paid attention to the paradoxical unity between that which is closest to us and that which is constantly overlooked.

Thus, Freud occasionally expressed the view that consciousness is epistemologically prior to the unconscious, in the sense that the unconscious can only be understood on the basis of consciousness. This is an idea that we can recognize from Husserl, as Eugen Fink has presented it in Husserl's last, unfinished work (Husserl 1970/1936b: 386):

> One thinks one is already acquainted with what the 'conscious', or consciousness, is and dismisses the task of first making into a prior subject matter the concept against which any science of the unconscious must demarcate its subject matter, i.e., precisely that of consciousness. But because one does not know what consciousness is, one misses in principle the point of departure of a science of the 'unconscious'.

If Freud would have liked to express the epistemological priority of consciousness to the unconscious in such a clear way, however, is doubtful.

For Freud, it was clear that consciousness and the unconscious differed radically. Freud made clear, on many occasions, that the unconscious is *not* a kind of second consciousness, which is united with the consciousness that we know (Freud 1915a: 170). The idea of a second consciousness is absurd, according to Freud: 'And after all, a consciousness of which one knows nothing seems to me a good deal more absurd than something mental that is unconscious' (Freud 1923: 16, n. 1; cf. also Freud 1912: 263, 1925: 32).

The quotes above highlight two important aspects: (1) consciousness and the unconscious differ radically, and accordingly the unconscious cannot be understood as another second (unconscious) consciousness; (2) consciousness possesses self-consciousness, which is not the case for the unconscious.

Freud understood that consciousness entails self-consciousness: 'Now let us call "conscious" the conception [*Vorstellung*] which is presented to our consciousness and of which we are aware, and let this be the only meaning of the term "conscious"' (Freud

1912: 260). And in his essay 'The unconscious' (1915a: 170), he conceived of self-consciousness as the 'most important characteristic' of consciousness.

Even if Freud realized that self-consciousness intrinsically belongs to consciousness, he nevertheless ignored self-consciousness and never discussed it in any substantial way, which is not so surprising owing to his attitude to consciousness as something that we do not need to describe and as something in fact indescribable (Freud 1938b, 283). He focused on the notion of *Selbstbewusstsein* (self-consciousness) only once in his collected works, namely in a footnote in his essay 'On narcissism' (Freud 1914: 98, n. 1). There he discusses the censoring agency's alertness during sleep and wonders if a differentiation of the censoring agency from the rest of the ego may constitute the distinction between consciousness and self-consciousness.[3]

Zahavi (1999: 204) criticizes Freud for his naïveté when it comes to understanding self-awareness, and is of the opinion that Freud embraced a kind of reflection theory – that is, the idea that self-consciousness consists of a reflecting act of consciousness on itself by means of a second act, an act of a higher order. One neglects, in the reflection theory, the fact that reflection presupposes that self-consciousness is anchored in pre-reflective acts of consciousness. One makes the mistake of placing self-consciousness (being conscious of oneself) on a par with perceptions of external objects – for example, the perception of the table in front of me. The opinion that

---

[3] I have stressed that the psychoanalytic theorizing has not been focused to any large extent on understanding the significance of self-consciousness. Nevertheless there are interesting examples of how self-consciousness, at least implicitly, has been taken into account in clinical experience. Freud (1938a: 201–2) writes: 'Even in a state so far removed from the reality of the external world as one of hallucinatory confusion (amentia), one learns from patients after their recovery that at the time in some corner of their mind (as they put it) there was a normal person hidden, who, like a detached spectator, watched the hubbub of illness go past him.' And Bion (1987: 46) writes: 'I do not think... that the ego is ever wholly withdrawn from reality... On this fact, that the ego retains contact with reality, depends the existence of a non-psychotic personality parallel with, but obscured by, the psychotic personality.'

comes forth in the reflection theory excludes that the experience in itself directly and implicitly entails self-consciousness. Thus, Freud conceptualized self-consciousness according to perceptual object intentionality, which is apparent, among other things, in the following quote: '"Being conscious" is in the first place a purely descriptive term, resting on a perception of the most immediate and certain character' (Freud 1923: 13–14).

Let me summarize and look forward. We have seen that despite Freud's ambivalent view concerning the significance of taking consciousness into account, there are occasions when he expressed the view – in line with phenomenological thinking – that consciousness constitutes the point of departure for investigating the unconscious. So far, self-consciousness is the distinguishing trait between consciousness and the unconscious. It is now time to explore the grounds of this alleged radical difference between consciousness and the unconscious, and with it the connected idea that the unconscious can only be captured by means of a construction. I will make use here of phenomenological reflections when discussing consciousness, or, more precisely, that which I call 'the ego's conscious intending'.

The 'I' or ego is to be understood here in a naïve, experiential way, and not as a theoretical term, as, for instance, an 'agent' in Freud's structural theory. I am thinking of the 'I' as a 'part' in the subject, which would comprise – apart from the ego – the unconscious and the body-ego. My use of the ego concept has similarities to Federn's ego concept – that is, ego-feelings. Federn (1952) describes the ego as a bearer of consciousness and, simultaneously, as conscious of its own ego. Anzieu (1989: 91) points out how this ego-feeling normally goes on without being noticed, and does not become noticeable until it goes wrong.

## THE EGO'S CONSCIOUS INTENDING

To begin with, I want to clarify an essential trait belonging to consciousness. Consciousness can be divided analytically into a subject side – with its constant stream of acts of consciousness – and an object side – the object to which the acts of consciousness are directed. According to phenomenology, consciousness is characterized by intentionality. The notion of intentionality entails both an act of consciousness directed towards an object (other than itself) and that it is conscious of itself. In this section the focus will be on consciousness directing itself towards an object, and later on in this chapter self-consciousness will be in focus.

The experience of perception is one of many possible ways in which intentional acts of consciousness can be manifested. 'Higher' forms of intentionality are, for example, voluntary processes (I wish that ... I decide that ...) or cognitive processes (I judge that ... I expect that ...). But here I will choose a visual perceptual example in order to describe certain traits in intentionality. The intentionality of perceptions highlights some points that I want to make, among other things, to connect it with the body-ego intentionality in the latter part of the chapter.

In order to illustrate the intentionality of consciousness, let me take a perceptual example of seeing the table in front of me. In the phenomenological attitude, I cease postulating it as existent in order to reflect on how this table is given to me in and through consciousness (see chapter 1). In the reflection, my interest is thus focused on how this existence is given to me. That which previously was experienced unreflectively appears thematically in the phenomenological attitude – that is, I am thematically aware that the table is given *perspectively*.

The perception of the table is in perspectives, in profiles. Only one side is sensorially given, so to speak.[4] The phenomenological analysis of perception shows that in the perception of an object, one perspective of it can be said to have a privileged position,

---

[4] I have chosen to comply with a non-phenomenological language and use the expression 'sensorially given'. It would have been more adequate to describe it in terms of, for example, 'that perspective which is given in a privileged way', but here I choose a simpler alternative and hope that the reader will not associate it with theories of perception within the physicalistic tradition, within which the term 'sensorial' belongs.

namely, the actual perspective from which the object is perceived (that which is sensorially given). The other perspectives are given as *possible other perspectives* from which it can be perceived. These possible other perspectives make up the 'inner horizon' of the object (see, for example, Gurwitsch 1964; Husserl 1962/1913; Merleau-Ponty 1962/1945). I perceive the table from one side, and sensorially only this perspective is given, whereas the infinitely many other perspectives – for example, from below, from straight above – are 'co-perceived' in the form of an inner horizon – that is, there is a more or less determined 'idea' about what characterizes those perspectives.

Regardless of what perspective I perceive the table from, it is thus only given in profiles – which is the case for all external, transcendent objects. However, I experience it immediately as a *whole object*. I do really perceive the table, not (only) the top side of the table. The outer visual perception of things is immediate. It is not that I make a conclusion based on cognitive processes that it is a table I perceive. I do not add over time the different sides until I reach an experience of a table, but the perceptual experience of the table is, as I said, immediately given in perspectives. In other words, that which is characteristic for visual perception is the immediate givenness of the perceived object as a *whole-object-in-perspectives*. The perception is an original presentation of the world and not a re-presentation. It gives something immediately present.

The purpose with this perceptual example is to illustrate certain traits in the intentionality of consciousness, in order subsequently to contrast consciousness with the unconscious. We can see that the intentionality of consciousness consists of a striving towards wholeness. There is a tension between that which is (sensorially) given (that which is explicitly present – that is, one side of the table) and that which is intended/meant (the table in its wholeness). All sides are not simultaneously given explicitly, but only one side is given explicitly, while the others are implicitly co-constituted. These co-constituted sides can, in their turn, be given explicitly. One can also express it in the following way: there is a tension between the (explicitly) present and that which in one sense is absent (the co-constituted implicit sides), but that nevertheless participates in constituting the object. Thus, there is something absent in the conscious acts' constitution of external objects. I can, however, make these absent sides – that is, the co-constituted sides – present (explicitly conscious), either by reflection (in the phenomenological attitude) or by more concrete perceptual acts (in my everyday/natural attitude).

One finds in the perceptual experience a 'projecting' of what the implicit perspectives must contain in order for the object to be what it is (experienced to be). Let us take the example of the table that I have perceived from above. Perceived from this perspective, I hold as implicitly true that the co-constituted perspectives contain, for example, table legs, a bottom side of the table, and so on. The absent sides must be assigned a character in accordance with the side that is thematically given, and must be able to be confirmed when I move my body, for example. It may be that these co-constituted sides are not confirmed in new views. If such is the case, my perception of the object will 'explode', and that which I previously took the object to be will be shown to be wrong.

If these co-constituted sides appear in accordance with the side that is thematically given, we have coherence in the stream of conscious acts. Then, the one act of consciousness – for example, that the table is perceived from above – is coherent with the next act – for example, when the table is perceived straight in front – and the ensuing act – for example, when the table is seen from the bottom. 'The table' is only a table as long as these infinitely many possible perspectives harmonize with one another in the constitution of the object as a table. The coherence between the acts is a necessary condition for the perception of one and the same object.

Another way of expressing this coherence between the acts is to say that there is continuity between them. The acts are synthesized with one another. The intentionality of consciousness can be summed up here by the concepts *coherence, continuity* and *wholeness*. These concepts can be seen as three sides of one and the same phenomenon. It is this structure that enables us to reconstruct a psychic process. By means of reflecting acts of consciousness and/or memory acts, I can reconstruct experiences and earlier acts of consciousness. The reconstruction is a rendering of something that I have experienced, as, for example, when I remember previous perceptual experiences or other events. That which is rendered/reproduced concerns something that I have previously experienced as directly and immediately present, and which now can be actualized again by new acts of consciousness, but then in such a way that they once have been directly and immediately present. To qualify as a reconstruction, a rendering/reproduction or re-experiencing is needed of something that earlier has been constituted as directly present in my stream of consciousness.

Let me summarize this description of the intentional character of consciousness. Intentionality is a presupposition for grasping an object in perception. There is an intrinsic striving towards wholeness, which is possible due to the acts' synthesizing capacity. The coherence and continuity between the acts are a condition for the constitution of one and the same object. Together with this continuity, coherence and wholeness, we have the streaming of different acts, with the constant possibility that a particular act will not cohere with the previous one, as in the case, for example, of visual illusions. Perhaps one can say that consciousness entails the possibility of 'rupturing' within itself.

The synthesizing of conscious acts corresponds to unification from a plurality. A plurality of acts of consciousness is needed for unification. The object (the world) can only receive its consistency – that it is one and the same object – from the vantage point of a plurality of acts. The plurality of acts means that every single act's projecting character is tied to the preceding and ensuing acts, to something coherently unified. The synthesizing in this constant stream of acts, however, can be disrupted.

But all these ruptures that take place within the stream of consciousness are not necessarily of the same kind that characterizes the break of the unconscious with consciousness. Without being able to discuss this issue here, it should nevertheless be pointed out that the stream of consciousness allows for breaks of different kinds, in a very complicated manner, without being understood from the vantage point of the unconscious. Breaks within the sphere of consciousness can be occasional breaks with the synthesizing. One throws oneself out into something unknown, which breaks with a previous harmony and familiarity. But this new unknown waits to be transformed into something familiar, something that is constituted again in a harmonious flow of acts of consciousness. Or one identifies another culture as something foreign, but still as something that will become familiar in due time and/or as something foreign to oneself, but which, nevertheless, possesses its own constituted harmony. This is a topic for a so-called generative phenomenology (see Steinbock 1995).

Here I want to bring out an essential difference between consciousness and the unconscious, which may be said to be the reason why the subject's conflicting predicament is *not* something temporary or surmountable.[5]

[5] A fundamental difference between phenomenology and psychoanalysis, according to my point of view, is that phenomenology is limited to studying consciousness, while psychoanalysis includes the unconscious. This difference corresponds to the difference between reconstruction and construction. In chapter 1 I pointed out that the French phenomenologist Maurice Merleau-Ponty was basically sympathetic towards psychoanalysis, but that he was, among other things, critical towards Freud's economical aspect and drive theory, which implied, according to him, an objectification of human beings (Bullington 1998). He tried to avoid Freud's drive theory by reformulating several important psychoanalytic notions – for example, libido, repression, discharge – in terms that were in line with his idea of the incarnated subject. I see an apparent difficulty with this 'phenomenologizing' of psychoanalysis, where there is a risk, for example, that the unconscious is not taken into account: 'Phenomenology and psychoanalysis are not parallel; much better, they are aiming toward the same *latency*' (Merleau-Ponty 1982–83: 71; italics in the original). In an article, Pontalis (1982–83) has analysed Merleau-Ponty's and Freud's different projects, and summed up the difference by stating that for Merleau-Ponty the unconscious is the other side (cf. the perceptual example and the co-constituting sides), whereas for Freud the unconscious is the other scene.

THE DISTINGUISHING QUALITY OF THE UNCONSCIOUS

When consulting psychoanalytic literature, one will discover how very diversely the unconscious is presented. Already in Freud we find a division between the unconscious, which has been conscious and subsequently repressed (repression proper), and primal repression, which has never seen the light of consciousness. We find another example of a division of the unconscious in Sandler and Sandler (1983), who – in their so-called 'three box model' – make a division between an unconscious that is constituted before the age of latency and an unconscious that belongs to the present. Many times it is very difficult, not to say impossible, to draw a clear boundary between preconscious and unconscious material. Matte-Blanco (1988) has, by means of a gradation of five stratified structures, differentiated the unconscious from consciousness.[6]

My contention is that the unconscious (as a system in Freud's sense), in its most radical form, breaks with the intentional character that constitutes consciousness. The unconscious, in its most radical form, shows itself in its negativity, in its breaking with the harmoniously synthesizing stream of consciousness. The unconscious appears as something strange, something contradictory to the intending of consciousness. Breuer and Freud's (1893–95: for example, 6, 165, 290) discovery of hysteria takes place in a context where the trauma shows itself as something unpleasant for the analysand, something that the analysand cannot remember, and the psychical causal context cannot be understood. The psychical trauma and the unconscious are also described as a 'foreign body' in consciousness (Breuer and Freud 1893–95: 61, 165, 221, and on p. 290 it is described as 'an infiltrate'). In the essay 'The unconscious', Freud (1915a: 170) describes how the analysis of the unconscious reveals

---

[6] Here I will emphasize the essential difference between consciousness and the unconscious. The important question concerning becoming conscious of unconscious material, which presupposes a certain 'communication' between the unconscious and consciousness, will not be dealt with here (cf. Bernet 1996; Freud 1915a: 190).

'peculiarities which seem alien to us, or even incredible, and which run directly counter to the attributes of consciousness with which we are familiar.'

The wild and untamed character of the unconscious is perhaps best shown when Freud describes the id (Freud 1932: 73):

> [The id] is the dark, inaccessible part of our personality; what little we know of it we have learnt from our study of the dream-work and of the construction of neurotic symptoms, and most of that is of a negative character and can be described only as a contrast to the ego. We approach the id with analogies: we call it a chaos, a cauldron full of seething excitations.

According to Laplanche (1999a: 188) Freud's id can be said to be a deepening of the unconscious, and is attached to the death drive in Laplanche's monistic drive theory. It may be worthwhile to take note of some of Laplanche's thoughts in order to characterize the unconscious.

Laplanche (1989: 83) emphasizes that the unconscious and sexuality are the major discoveries of psychoanalysis. He embraces the idea of a drive psychology, but rejects a dualistic form where Eros and the death drive are two different drives. Nevertheless, he finds his own monistic drive theory to be in accordance with Freud's ideas, since Freud only deals with one type of drive energy, namely, libidinal energy. The death drive becomes the extreme expression of the discharge of the libido. It is the least civilized, least socialized part of sexuality, and functions in accordance with the principle of free energy and the primary processes (Laplanche 1979). I would like to describe the death drive's rush towards the zero point in line with the Nirvana principle, as an increasing degree of liberation of affections from ideal representation/meaning, where bodily sensations come more and more into the foreground, and where sexuality, aggression, insanity and images of death are increasingly difficult to distinguish from each other. However, the discharge of libido never reaches zero, since the zero point is an asymptotic border (cf. Ey 1978: 361). The death drive, in this sense, does not concern a biological, organic death, but has to be understood in a metaphorical, psychic way, as Laplanche stresses (1986: 14; italics in the original):

> the death referred to in the 'death instinct' is not the death of the organism, but the death of this 'organism' which, in human existence, represents the interests of the biological organism, that is to say, the ego.

Thus, Laplanche's non-biological, sexual death instinct functions in an opposite way to the ego's striving towards a harmonious synthesizing. It represents a threat to the ego's conscious intending and is, in its essence, in conflict with the intentional character of consciousness.

Consciousness produces, in its intentionality, a stream of harmonizing acts, and these acts can be reflected and reconstructed with the assistance of reflections, whereas the unconscious presents itself as something that does not allow itself to be reconstructed as earlier harmonic acts of consciousness. The possibility of reconstruction lies in the rendering/reconstruction of earlier experiences, whose character is a sufficiently good, harmonic and synthesized whole. Through the unconscious and its death drive we are facing – within the subject – a way of functioning that is not compatible with reconstructing reflections or acts of memory. The possibility of rendering unconscious material through reconstructing acts of consciousness is ruled out. The unconscious is thus not something that has once been perceived in its presence as something coherent and whole and which now is given in acts of memory/acts of reflection (cf. Fletcher 1999: 37). We fill the unconscious, in its negativity, with theoretical concepts. We fill the 'un' in the unconscious with theoretical constructions, such as in the metapsychological theories, theoretical models and different clinical theories.

The insufficiency of reconstruction in relationship to the unconscious also shows in that the psychoanalytic method does not base itself on reflections of the ego first and foremost, but must use a method – free association – that goes beyond the ego's conscious intending.

This is the most radical description of the unconscious, as it has been characterized in Freud's id and Laplanche's version of the death drive. I would claim that the unconscious in this most radical form signifies a state that is beyond experience, but nevertheless 'inside' the subject. It is something that has never been lived through, something that has never been grasped in conscious experience. The unconscious, in its most radical meaning, is not – and has never been – available within the content given in our conscious experiencing (cf. Freud's primal repression). In other words, the unconscious can only be captured by means of a theoretical construction. I will return to this idea and develop it in the next chapter and, in particular, in chapter 6.

The way that I have characterized the unconscious introduces an interesting tension between the meaning-bestowing consciousness (intentionality) and, in a certain sense, the de-signifying, dissolving movement of the unconscious. Laplanche makes a point of describing the unconscious in terms of 'the other thing' (das Andere) – that is, not 'the other person' (der Andere). 'The other thing' connotes thing-like ideas and has a reified character. The unconscious is by all means a 'phenomenon of meaning', but one which at the same time has been closed off to meaning (Laplanche 1999a: 107). Put in a simplified manner, one can say that meaning is formulated in the psychoanalytic process through analytic translations of the unconscious.

This struggle to try to make the unconscious compatible with meaning is interesting. Psychoanalysis deals with meaning and treats all human expressions as meaningful in principle. There is nothing that basically is meaningless for psychoanalysis. Despite this fact, I want to claim that the unconscious in its most radical form is perhaps better described as something that has an effect or influence, rather than being understood as something that contains a specific, determined meaning. I also believe that this must be the

implication in the commonly expressed point of view among psychoanalysts that the unconscious in itself is unknowable.

The unconscious, as the other thing, has its source in the enigmatic message that the infant takes part of from the adult world.
It is the primary caregiver – for example, the mother and a breast
that is erotic for her – that unconsciously communicates enigmatic,
seductive messages. Sexuality and the unconscious are implanted
in the infant from outside; it is an event in time that comes from
the outside. I find Laplanche's ideas useful for my purposes, as they
help us to understand the essential traits of the unconscious and to
see how the unconscious is constituted in relation to another desiring subject (the mother). But I also maintain that Laplanche's theory
about the mother's inevitable seduction of the infant, the so-called
'general theory of primal seduction', needs to be complemented with
another containing type of mother that makes up the condition for
the development of the ego.

What, then, is the pre-sexual background against which sexuality, the pleasure principle and the unconscious are constituted?

## THE PRE-SEXUAL CONDITIONS OF THE UNCONSCIOUS

Once again, we are dealing with psychical processes that belong to
the sphere of consciousness/self-consciousness, but now in the form
of a body-ego, which is not a full-fledged self-conscious ego (cf. Ey
1978: 329, 369). One could possibly designate this field as the 'unconscious of phenomenology', that at least to a certain extent corresponds
to Freud's descriptive unconscious. The level of meaning can be of such
a deep and obscure character that, in practice, it may not be possible to
carry out reconstructions from a first-person perspective, but it does
have a constructed character. But such a constructed reconstruction
of meaning, that sometimes may be assumed to lie beyond the reflecting ego's capacity, is *not*, however, a construction of the kind that I
depicted in the previous section as the unconscious of psychoanalysis (see also n. 10 on p. 88 and chapter 8). In this type of constructed
reconstruction, it thus belongs to the sphere of consciousness, and is

still a question of a phenomenon whose ground is an intentional syn-thesizing. Before discussing this body-ego, I will briefly present some psychoanalytic ideas, conceptualized somewhat differently, but all embracing the idea that Freud's unconscious, ruled by the pleasure principle, presupposes another kind of psychical process.

Long before psychoanalysis was enriched by thoughts about a body-ego, Freud embraced the idea that the discharge of the psyche presupposes a state of bound energy. In the *Project for a scientific psychology*, Freud (1950/1895: 301) writes that 'the exigencies of life' require a stored quantity of the intercellular order of magnitude, a function that is taken care of by the ego. In *The interpretation of dreams* (Freud 1900), the wish and the dream's hallucinating wish fulfilment – ruled by the pleasure principle – presuppose a previous bodily perceptual experience (in the form of both a previous satisfac-tion and an experienced absence of the object). The child must be capa-ble of storing a certain amount of bound energy, with its continuity and unity over time, before the pleasure principle can be effective. One could also argue that the striving of the pleasure principle to reduce the tension from a logical point of view presupposes a cer-tain amount of bound energy. Discharge of energy cannot be accom-plished from a zero-point level. Another example from the beginning of psychoanalysis can be found in Freud's (1905b) idea that the libido rests on the self-preservative drives. Later on in Freud's work, in his biologically speculative essay *Beyond the pleasure principle* (Freud 1920), we find the idea of a protective shield against stimuli.

In one reading (Karlsson 1998) of *Beyond the pleasure prin-ciple*, I have argued that what Freud postulated as beyond – or rather on this side of – the pleasure principle has to do with a rudimentary affirmation of existence. It is an affirmation of existence in the sense that the subject (infant) experiences/strives for something constant, something that has a quality of a gestalt. This affirmation of exist-ence is presumably something that precedes and constitutes the condition for the functioning of the pleasure principle and for the possibility of wishing (see also chapter 7 in this volume).

Didier Anzieu, with his concept of the 'skin-ego', is probably the psychoanalyst who has best developed a model that gives an original function to a containing, protecting envelope, before something like the pleasure principle begins to function. In his theory of the skin-ego, it is pointed out that a containing skin-ego is required for a discharge of energy to take place (Anzieu 1989: 39), and, furthermore, that it 'remains true that genital or even auto-erotic, sexuality is accessible only to those who acquired a minimum sense of basic security within their own skins' (Anzieu 1989: 39). Another illuminating quote is the following: 'The Skin Ego fulfils the function of providing for *supporting sexual excitation*' (Anzieu 1989: 104; italics in the original).

Another suggestion, within a Kleinian theoretical framework, is Ogden's (1992) conceptualization of the autistic-contiguous position in making up the most primitive psychological organization, the 'underbelly' of the schizoid personality organization. This position concerns a sensory-dominated, pre-symbolic generation of experience. The term 'autistic' is not to be understood in a pathological sense, but as a kind of 'normal autism', designating isolation and disconnectedness. The term 'contiguous', in this context, connotes the sensory connections – for example, the touching between the infant and the mother. It is in this original position that a rudimentary 'I-ness' arises, according to Ogden.

The pre-sexual condition of the unconscious seems to point towards processes that have to do with bodily experiences, which, among others, Anzieu has captured with his concept of the skin-ego, but which Freud already touched on with his body-ego.[7] In other words, one can say that the system, the unconscious, lies on the border between the ego's conscious intending and consciousness in the form of a body experiencing continuity and existence. My point is that this body-ego belongs to the sphere of consciousness, even if we

---

[7] Freud writes in *The ego and the id* (1923: 26): 'The ego is first and foremost a bodily ego; it is not merely a surface entity, but is itself the projection of a surface.'

cannot, on this 'level', talk about a consciousness having the character of a full-fledged 'I am conscious that I ...' Nevertheless, even this consciousness of the body-ego belongs to self-consciousness. In this respect, we stick to an insight that, as we have seen, Freud also expressed, namely, that self-consciousness belongs intrinsically to consciousness. The fact that self-consciousness is necessarily entailed in the concept of consciousness can perhaps be accepted without difficulty when it concerns the thematic consciousness, but is probably met with objections when we have to deal with a body-ego. Therefore, I will try very briefly to trace out a connection between the ego's conscious intending and the body-ego, showing that self-consciousness is not only limited to the ego's conscious intending.

No doubt there are great differences between, on the one hand, a 'full-fledged' self-reflecting ego (*ego cogito*), with its personal biography and history and that can remember and exercise reflections, and, on the other hand, an 'anonymous' body-ego (which by all means could be conceptualized as a *descriptive* unconscious). Nevertheless, these two ego-structures have something in common that makes it possible to talk about them in terms of consciousness. The first experience of existence as a sense of coherence, continuity, wholeness will have to be related to the subsequently developed and conceptualized thematic self-consciousness (*ego cogito*) – that is, 'I am conscious that I ...'[8]

---

[8] Within the language-oriented analytic philosophy, one has faced difficulties trying to avoid a circular reasoning when it comes to the question of self-consciousness. Bermúdez (2000) tries in an interesting way to avoid the 'paradox of self-consciousness'. The essence of this insolvable paradox is that to be able to think first-person thoughts (I think), one must have a command of linguistic self-reference, and in order to be able to refer to oneself linguistically, one must already be able to think first-person thoughts. We are locked in this conflict as long as we define self-consciousness in terms of a linguistic command of the first-person pronoun. The solution of this paradox, according to Bermúdez, is to take into account that the full-fledged conceptual self-consciousness is based on pre-linguistic forms of self-consciousness – that is, states of affairs with non-conceptual first-person content. A non-conceptual content can be assigned to the person, without him/her being able to specify the content conceptually. Bermúdez builds his analysis on, among others, the perceptual psychologist

I would maintain that the ego's thematic self-consciousness is in an embryonic form in the pre-reflective, bodily experience of continuity and coherence (see n. 8 on p. 83). When I exemplified the intentionality with a perceptual example earlier on, I pointed out that the perception of an object always includes the co-constituted sides (the so-called 'inner horizon'). This intentional constitution of objects correlates with a kinaesthetic awareness of bodily movements, which makes up a kind of 'pre-objective' condition for the constitution of external objects. Thus, we have here an intimate and mutual connection between body intentionality and object intentionality. This body intentionality is, in other words, a pre-reflective bodily awareness that accompanies all my experiences of the world and objects in the world.[9] Self-consciousness which belongs to the body-ego is thus not a thematic reflection about oneself, and it is important to differentiate between a body-ego's pre-reflective self-consciousness and a full-fledged ego's self-consciousness: 'it is necessary to differentiate pre-reflective self-awareness, which is an immediate, implicit, irrelational, non-objectifying, non-conceptual and non-propositional self-acquaintance, from reflective self-awareness, which is an explicit, relational, mediated, conceptual, and objectifying thematization of consciousness' (Zahavi 1999: 33). This pre-reflective self-consciousness is not characterized in terms of object intentionality (the conscious acts' relating to/constituting of an object), but constitutes a necessary dimension in the subject's experiencing (in the act itself). The self-awareness of kinaesthetic movements and the bodily capacity indicates that the original self-awareness entails an awareness of 'I can' (if, for example, I turn my head somewhat, I will get a glimpse of another view of the object).

Gibson's theories and infant research, which shows that from the beginning the infant has an experience of itself. See also Norman's (2001) psychoanalysis with infants that illuminates bodily self-reflections and the pre-lexical level of meaning on which this psychoanalytic process rests.

[9] For a phenomenological exposition of the importance of the body for human existence, see, for example, Husserl 2000/1918 and Merleau-Ponty 1962/1945, 1963/1942.

In other words, the phenomenal level of experiencing, the experience of something, presupposes an implicit self-consciousness. Experience, from the beginning, is given as my own experiencing. In the experiencing there is, at the same time, an implicit self-consciousness. On the bodily, rudimentary level, it is not a question of an explicit self-consciousness (*ego cogito*), but of an 'anonymous' I-experiencing. In experiencing pain, it is *my* pain. The experience of pain is not followed by the question, whose pain?, but the pain is immediately and directly connected to an experience of the ego. Different psychical means of externalizing the pain outside myself only confirm that it is my pain after all.

## SELF-CONSCIOUSNESS AND ITS SIGNIFICANCE FOR PSYCHOANALYSIS

Self-consciousness needs to be considered as something ontologically given and which, in a strict sense, lies outside the field of psychoanalytic research. However, the psychical significance of self-consciousness for our existence is of great interest for psychoanalysis. Psychoanalytically, the issue of concern is *the affirmative potentiality of self-consciousness.* It is a question of affirming something, not of creating it. The affirmation becomes a way of consolidating and strengthening experience. The significance of self-consciousness is more visible when we have to deal with certain forms of psychical suffering and pathology. The ontological and the psychological levels become apparent, for example, in states of depersonalization, when a person has the experience of being invaded by others' thoughts. This experience does not refute the ontologically indisputable fact that it is still I who thinks or experiences these strange thoughts. These depersonalized states always need to be qualified in that it feels 'as if' somebody else is thinking in me.

Here we have an interesting fact in the sense that the ontological givenness of self-consciousness, which focuses on the person's own individual relation to him/herself, from the psychoanalytic standpoint, discloses the importance of other significant people.

This self-conscious character of consciousness exists necessarily in a field, which includes other people and physical surroundings. The mother, or the primary caregiver, can prevent or promote the ability of self-consciousness to affirm existence. In this discussion we will be helped by Anzieu and Winnicott, whose thinking elucidates the relation between a 'containing ego' – that is, an ego-development where the self-consciousness of consciousness is able to affirm existence – and the early mother–child relationship. Anzieu (1995: 262) expresses it in a pregnant way:

> It can even be the case that consciousness co-exists with life
> ... it is to simultaneously have consciousness of being oneself
> and of being present to the world; in a complementary way it is
> also to be conscious of [the fact] that the primordial object at the
> same time is conscious of being present to the world, for herself
> and for me, and thus that she can and/or wants to envelop me.

In Winnicott, we can see it expressed thus (1965/1960a: 54; italics in the original):

> With 'the care that it receives from its mother' each infant is
> able to have a personal existence, and so begins to build up
> what might be called *a continuity of being*. On the basis of this
> continuity of being, the inherited potential gradually develops
> into an individual infant.

We can discern the idea of the affirmation of self-consciousness in Winnicott's (1965/1963: 239) idea of an 'I AM feeling', and perhaps even more obviously in Federn's and Anzieu's writings. The 'Ego feeling' that Federn describes entails this consciousness of myself, which Anzieu also takes up: 'The mental (or psychical) Ego feeling has its rational formulation in the *cogito, ergo sum*' (Anzieu 1989: 92; italics in the original). Without this affirmation it is difficult to experience joy of life, to feel alive. This joy of life, whose structure is not to be confused with the discharge of the libido, is manifested in *the affirmation of existence.* In the affirmation there is a confidence or, to use Anzieu's expression, a belief (Anzieu 1989: 131):

> Belief is a vital human need. It is impossible to live without believing one is alive. One cannot perceive the outside world without believing in its reality. One is not a person if one does not believe in the identity and continuity of the self.

We should not interpret this 'belief' in terms of a subject's cognitive belief in a specific characteristic of an object. A traditional epistemological point of view is not relevant here. Anzieu (1989: 131) consequently lets us know that 'these beliefs, which make us cleave to our being and enable us to live our lives, do not have the status of knowledge'.

Self-consciousness plays a crucial role in understanding the possibility of man to affirm truth and existence. Within psychoanalysis, a theoretical development has occurred more in respect to the denial than the affirmation of existence, quite in line with the fact that self-consciousness has met with such little interest, and probably also that the concept of existence in psychoanalysis is often treated in an objectivistic manner. One misses the point that existence is existence *for a subject,* that it is constituted as existence and presupposes a subject. Let me discuss 'the affirmation of existence' in relationship to traumatic experiences that the subject has not been able to contain (cf. Kaplan 2002).

In cases of severe traumatic experiences, one can focus on affirming a reality that has actually taken place, but that has not been able to be perceived in its wholeness (or, more precisely, sufficiently intact), and thereby one cannot think about it or carry out reflections. When consciousness contains large gaps, it may be the task of the psychoanalyst to affirm a real event and to function as a 'first witness' (Künstlicher 1994; see also Halling 1997). Here we are dealing with a pure reconstruction, as opposed to the reconstruction that emanates from unconscious material (ruled by primary processes and the pleasure principle), which should be called rather a constructed reconstruction (cf. Karlsson 2000).[10]

When it comes to traumatic experiences, one can, I believe, describe that which happens in severe traumatic events in terms of a lack of, or incomplete synthesis of, the stream of consciousness. This kind of 'lack' in the intentional synthesizing of consciousness is not in the form that I described as the (dissolving) function of the unconscious. Instead, we are now on a primordial level, where the relationship between consciousness/self-consciousness and the world is threatened and/or does not allow itself to be established in a harmonious (adequate) way. Laub and Auerhahn (1993: 290) point to this when they assert that massive psychic trauma 'defies the individual's ability to formulate experience'. We also learn that the reality character of events cannot be affirmed, but that 'we can only relate to the events as if they had not happened' (Laub and Auerhahn 1993: 288). Without a sufficiently intact intentionality, in terms of continuity, coherence and wholeness, there is no chance for the pleasure principle to emerge and no wishing is possible. The repetition compulsion that Freud discovered clinically, and which made up the basis for *Beyond the pleasure principle*, can be viewed as the first step in 'affirming the existence' of unendurable, incomplete experiences, before one can start to think about meaning and significance.[11]

However, the relevance of 'the affirmation of existence' is not limited to being an important factor in traumatic experiences, but makes up an important aspect of the psychoanalytic process as a

[10] The 'pure' reconstruction of a real event does not preclude that it is in need of a kind of construction, but in such a case this construction is on a 'common–sense' level and does not imply taking a theoretical perspective. This construction is about filling in incomplete external perceptions of something that we can agree upon (constitute) intersubjectively as factual reality. The constructed reconstruction of unconscious elements takes place from the vantage point of a certain psychoanalytic perspective and is not about the factual external reality (see also chapter 8).

[11] Compare Anzieu (1989: 201) who writes: 'In extreme cases, inflicting a real envelope of suffering on oneself can be an attempt to restore the skin's containing function not performed by the mother or those in one's early environment, which we shall also see illustrated below: I suffer therefore I am.'

whole. Schafer (1993) points out that the psychoanalytic attitude is characterized by an 'affirmative' quality. Killingmo (1989) also talks about the importance of affirming the analysand's experience in order to promote a feeling of identity and meaning with the analysand. The affirmation becomes a means of clearing away doubts about the validity of the experience. Affirmation as a therapeutic intervention is used, first of all, when we are dealing with derivatives of insufficient relationships, belonging to the early mother–child interaction. On this level of psychical functioning, the task of psychoanalysis is to affirm, rather than revealing psychical conflicts through interpretation. We are concerned here with deficits rather than conflicts. Another way of expressing deficits in this context is to formulate it as an inability to constitute continuity, coherence and wholeness.

Thus, the psychoanalytic technique needs to be adjusted according to whether the aetiology of the suffering originates from deficits in the intentionality of consciousness/self-consciousness (difficulties in affirming existence) or from repressed unconscious intra-psychic conflicts. When it comes to problems in the sphere of consciousness/self-consciousness, our interventions do not concern interpreting unconscious conflicts 'behind' that which is said or expressed, as with Freud; nor do they concern interpreting 'who makes what with whom', as with Klein. Here we are dealing with something more basic: what it is the analysand experiences or attempts to experience (cf. Alvarez 1992; Monti 2005). The question concerning 'what something is' is the first question and it does not require the same developed psychic capacity as, for example, the question about 'why something is'. The expression that I have coined in order to catch the spirit of this type of intervention is thus 'the affirmation of existence'.

The affirmation of existence is not an 'either/or' phenomenon, but a 'more or less' phenomenon. On one side, we have a state of mind where the affirmation of existence is very poor, and on the other side, we have a state of mind where this affirmation of existence is established and spontaneously affirmed. In the latter case it is a silent experience, reminding us to a certain extent of Winnicott's 'going-on-being'. As a silent experience, the reflecting capacity of the person is not brought to the fore. Perhaps one can say that *most deeply the experience of existence is constituted in a spontaneous, non-reflected living in the present.* But there are occasions when the silently affirmed existence fails, and the person is in need of reflecting acts in order to affirm the existence, for instance, of emotional states of mind.

There is a transforming power in the affirmation itself. We can experience this when we affirm painful feelings and experiences. The affirmation, for example, of one's vulnerability or the feeling of being very small in a situation can make the difference between feeling lost, disintegrated and full of anxiety, and being in touch with oneself, feeling collected and present. My point is that there is a psychic growing in the affirmation itself. The affirmation of difficult and painful feelings is, then, not firstly a means of ridding oneself of something (that would be to reduce the affirmation to an instrumental value), but the 'affirmation-in-itself' entails psychical growth. I think it is this quality in the affirmation that can explain analysands' common paradoxical description in the course of the analytic process that they feel worse than ever and at the same time stronger than they have ever felt before (cf. Karlsson 2004).

I will have reasons to return to 'the affirmation of existence' and its relationship to sexuality and the pleasure principle in chapter 7.

## CONCLUSION

I have suggested that the unconscious can be said to lie on the border between the ego's conscious intending and a rudimentary body-ego experiencing. The unconscious, governed by the pleasure principle, presupposes consciousness/self-consciousness, which, however, has not hindered me from emphasizing their radically different ways of functioning. There is a tendency in psychoanalytic thinking and writing to neglect the importance of consciousness, at the same time as the tendency to treat the unconscious as a second unconscious consciousness – a description of the unconscious that Freud found absurd. A conclusion from my discussion should be that psychoanalytic investigations cannot be limited to the unconscious, but must extend to obscure and dark regions of consciousness. My characterization/definition of consciousness and the unconscious does not rest on the degree of obscurity with which the fields are given, nor the degree of difficulty with which they can be investigated. My aim has been to clarify these fields with respect to their structures and ways of functioning.

The importance of the affirming potentiality of self-consciousness was discussed. The affirmation of existence can concern an affirmation of factual events (external objects) as well as an affirmation of subjective experiences. To affirm the factuality of external events, for instance, can correspond to a greater capacity to contain and reconstruct traumatic events in terms of a sufficiently intact and harmonious stream of consciousness. The affirmation of the subjective experience is consciousness' illumination of itself. The psychoanalytic attitude (Schafer) and the 'affirmative' psychoanalytic interventions (Killingmo) can be said to be in alliance with an affirming self-consciousness. What we – psychoanalysts and analysands – ultimately achieve in affirmation is not to validate or legitimize experience by means of external norms or criteria. What we do is open (unfold) ourselves for experience such as it is experienced.

SUMMARY
This chapter deals with the question of the conceptualization of the psychical in psychoanalysis, which includes the determination of the character and presuppositions of the unconscious. I argue that the unconscious lies on the border between the ego's conscious intending and consciousness in the form of a bodily experiencing of continuity and existence. In my discussion I tie the unconscious

to its most radical characterization, such as has been described by Freud's id, or the death drive in Laplanche. This unconscious does not come first, however, but presupposes the sphere of consciousness/ self-consciousness.

At the end of the chapter I stress the importance of taking into account the affirming potentiality of self-consciousness. The psychoanalytic investigations should not be limited to the unconscious, but must extend to unapproachable parts of consciousness/ self-consciousness. My distinction between consciousness and the unconscious does not rest on the degree of obscurity or accessibility of these respective fields. My aim has been to clarify these fields – consciousness and the unconscious – with respect to their structures and ways of functioning.

# 5   The libido as the core of the unconscious

In the previous chapter I argued that the unconscious lies on the border between the ego's conscious intending and a body-ego experiencing. The character of the unconscious was tied to human sexuality. In this and the following chapter, I would like to elaborate on the significance of sexuality for the concept of the unconscious (as a system). From the very beginning, sexuality has had a central position in the theory making of psychoanalysis, and for Freud played the role of explaining pathological suffering.[1] Thereafter the significance of sexuality in the understanding of psychopathology has diminished. Today there are well-known French psychoanalysts who claim that sexuality has been neglected within the psychoanalytic movement (Green 1996, 2003; Laplanche 1999b). Laplanche points out how infantile sexuality has been lost with Freud's successors (Laplanche 1999b: 236–7; italics in the original):

> If it is difficult to grasp infantile, non-genital sexuality –
> precisely as in our anecdote, where alimentary function and
> pleasure are not distinguished from oral sexuality, with its
> pleasure, its zone, its specific object – then it will be, purely
> and simply, abandoned. Reference will still be made to orality
> (anality) or to oral (anal) object relations, but practically no
> longer at all to oral or anal *sexuality*. Who amongst the Kleinians
> ever speaks now of infantile sexuality? Who is interested in
> pre-genital erogenous pleasure?

For Freud it was sexuality in its struggle against another driving force which ruled human behaviour. Freud was always a drive

---

[1] Even if sexuality was of primary importance for Freud, it was never everything – an accusation that he defended himself against (Freud 1916–17: 351).

dualist – that is, his theorizing involved two different types of drives. In his first theory of drives, we have sexual drives (libido) and self-preservative drives (ego-drives); sexual drives were regarded as the more interesting from the vantage point of psychopathology. This first drive theory – libido versus ego-drives – was henceforth followed by making a division between ego-libido and object-libido. Thereafter, in the 1920s, Freud formulated his last theory of drives, that between Eros (life drives) and Thanatos (death drives). Laplanche (1999a) has stressed that through Freud's interest in narcissism during the first decade of the twentieth century – and in line with this interest, the division between ego-libido and object-libido – the wild and untamed character of sexuality was lost. Indeed Laplanche tries to rehabilitate this distinguishing trait for sexuality by means of an original interpretation of the death drives, which was discussed in chapter 4. Traditional views have tended not to tie Thanatos together with sexuality, but to let the death drives function as the opposite of Eros/life drives. The importance of sexuality has diminished at the expense of the death drive or the drive of destruction in this traditional conceptualization of the life and death drives. This relative depreciation of sexuality in Freud himself has continued since with, among others, Melanie Klein and her successors, where aggression and destruction have taken the dominant position.

## SEXUALITY IN FREUD'S EARLIEST WORKS

With his interest in neuroses and psychoses, Freud focused early on sexuality. We find already in Freud's pre-psychoanalytic writings an idea of the importance of sexuality.[2] It was in the essay 'The neuro-psychoses of defence' (Freud 1894) that sexuality received a primary aetiological role, but Freud had a presentiment of its importance before this (cf. Andersson 1962). Anzieu (1986: 65) points out that Freud referred to the aetiology of sexuality in neuroses in a letter to

---

[2] Breuer and Freud's (1893–95) work, *Studies on hysteria*, commonly counts as the starting point for psychoanalysis. The concept 'psychoanalysis', however, was used for the first time in 1896 (Freud 1896: 151).

Wilhelm Fliess, dated 18 December 1892. In this letter, Freud mentions a lecture that he delivered in 1893, which concerned the psychical mechanism of hysterical phenomena and in which it is made clear that 'erotic ideas' exist in connection with hysteria (Freud 1893a). The earliest discussion that I have found in Freud's collected works on the sexual aetiology of hysteria is an essay published as early as 1888, from which one can read the following (Freud 1888: 51; italics in the original): 'conditions related *functionally* to sexual life play a great part in the aetiology of hysteria (as of all neuroses), and they do so on account of the high psychical significance of this function especially in female sex'. It is also worth noting that by this time Freud already talks about the importance of the aetiology of sexuality for neuroses in general, and that a more general psychological significance for sexuality is hinted at.

Freud's view of the aetiological significance of sexuality should not be limited to being based on experience that he acquired in his clinical practice. May (1999) suggests that the aetiological significance of sexuality for neuroses was something of a 'vision' for Freud that he spent his life trying to verify. Freud's conviction that the significance of sexuality is nourished from sources that are outside and precede the clinical experience does not, of course, diminish the validity of his discoveries. However, it shows that Freud was governed by a certain – to use a hermeneutical expression – pre-understanding in his clinical interpretation of the analysands in his practice. May comments (1999: 777; italics in the original): 'I think it important to note Freud's visionary certainty and not, for example, to imply that his *leading idea* was purely empirical in character, derived from observation and thoroughly validated by observations'.

My idea is that this vision of the aetiological significance of sexuality has its basis in Freud's personal experiences from his everyday life, his life-world experience. These are experiences we can all have; however, Freud had the capability to use these experiences in his scientific research. Thus, we can imagine that it is sexuality as it shows itself in the life-world experience that awakened Freud's thoughts about its significance, and which led further to fitting sexuality into formulated, scientific theories. In the next chapter I will try to ground the concept of libido in sexual life-world experiences.

Freud was far from alone among his contemporaries in the view that sexuality played a role in neuropathology, but he distinguished himself by placing sexuality as a part within a greater structural context (May 1999). The aetiological significance of sexuality for neuroses and psychoses cannot be understood unless one takes into account the defence of the ego against sexual impulses. Sexuality and the defence against it together constitute the pathological suffering. The concept 'sexuality' for psychoanalysis entails the ego's relation to sexuality.

What Freud accentuated in a unique way was that the amnesia that hysterics suffer from is to be understood in the sense that the ego defends itself (later on, the term 'repression' was to be used) against sexual impulses. It was Freud, in contrast to Breuer, who took the step of conceiving the splitting of consciousness as a result of psychic resistance and defence. From Freud's position, we can discern several interesting implications, a couple of which I would like to illuminate. Firstly, we have the idea that neuroses and psychoses have a psychological, in contrast to a physiological, aetiology. Even if the picture is contradictory and complex, one must admit that Freud mainly entertained a psychological view of the aetiology of neuroses and psychoses, which distinguished him from his literary colleague Josef Breuer.[3] It seems that there was always a tendency in Freud to think that psychoanalysis would be possible to ground biologically. We see this clearly in Freud's *Project for a scientific psychology* from

---

[3] May (1999: 774) points out that there were many specialists in medicine and neuropathology who worked independently of one another and before Freud embraced the idea that neurotic symptoms had a psychic cause. Geerardyn (1997: 132) summarizes the difference between Freud and Breuer in the following way: 'While Breuer's theory remains essentially physiological, Freud adopts a clinical-psychological position. By putting the psychical mechanism of defence in a central position, Freud presupposes the patient's speech as a point of departure.'

1895, but published posthumously in 1950 (Freud 1950/1895), and in his *Beyond the pleasure principle* from 1920, as well as in his later works. This biological materialistic view can be conceived of as his utopian *Weltanschauung* (Lesche 1981: 62), but that did not influence his concrete psychoanalytic method of treatment and investigation.[4]

Secondly, we have an idea about an 'ego' that defends itself against sexual impulses. Let us dwell on the ego concept that Freud used in the beginning of psychoanalysis, long before he developed his ego-psychology in the 1920s, in which the ego is conceived of as an agent that has to orient itself in relation to the superego and the id. In contrast to the ego as an agent in the structural model, the ego concept in the beginning of psychoanalysis connotes a non-theoretical, rather phenomenological ego-experience. Andersson (1962: 150) points out that the ego is synonymous with 'the person', 'the individual' or 'the consciousness' of an individual. Here the ego refers to an everyday, non-theoretical ego.[5] Sexuality presents itself as something that I-consciousness, or merely the ego, defends itself against. It is in this conflict between sexuality and the ego's self-esteem that sexuality is not allowed free discharge, but comes to expression in a distorted way. Andersson (1962: 149) writes: 'the sexual ideas that were assigned etiological significance in hysteria and obsessional neurosis had only one feature in common: that they were in painful opposition to the person's "ego" or "consciousness".'

Let us consider a couple more sources of Freud's scientific discoveries of sexuality – sources that can be found within a scientific

---

[4] Anzieu (1986: 41–2) is one of those who has expressed surprise about the fact that despite Freud's psychoanalysis being a form of psychological treatment, one can always find in Freud the idea that it was to be confirmed by biology: 'one is constantly startled, when reading Freud, at the insistence with which the inventor of psychoanalysis, a purely psychological therapy, hoped throughout his life... that advances would enable neurosis to be treated more quickly and more radically.'

[5] The life-world as a source for Freud's discovery of the aetiological significance of sexuality can thus have been expressed in the form of (1) a sexual life-world experience, which I attempted to point out with respect to his alleged pre-scientific vision of the aetiological significance of sexuality, which was to be confirmed scientifically, and (2) an everyday, prescientific ego concept.

context. Firstly, we have other contemporary researchers (neuro-scientists) who belonged to Freud's environment (for example, Krafft-Ebing, Preyer). And if we extend the circle of influence to thinkers outside natural science, we can add a couple of philosophers who were used in Freud's exposition of the significance of sexuality for the human being. First of all we have Schopenhauer (for example, Freud 1905b: 134), but also on occasions Plato's talk about how the original human beings were split up into two halves – man and woman – that are reunited in love (for example, Freud 1905b: 136). Freud's discovery and launching of the significance of sexuality take place in a scientific surrounding where the view of the aetiological role of sexuality is more and more discernible. But May (1999: 772) lets us know that: 'Psychiatry and neuropathology in the decades before the turn of the twentieth century lacked an aetiological theory and hence also a soundly based classification of the nervous and mental diseases.' Freud came with an innovative contribution to the aetiological theory making of sexuality. His view deviated in several respects from the ideas of his contemporary colleagues. Above, I made a point of the fact that Freud put sexuality in a context in which ego-defences were also involved – perhaps the most important distinguishing character of Freud's contribution, but not the only one.

He classified certain neuroses as being psychically caused and others on the basis of a biological and physiological aetiology. Hysteria, paranoia and hallucinatory psychosis or confusion were classified as psychically conditioned. He believed that phobias and compulsion symptoms could be of both psychical and physiological origin. Neurasthenia and anxiety neuroses were exclusively somatically conditioned, according to Freud. Only pathologies with a psychical aetiology could be treated with psychotherapy. In other words, he introduced a psychological view on neuroses, which has had a great impact on the treatment of psychopathology.

Sexuality was, for Freud, the only cause of neurotic and psychotic disturbances. Sexuality never obtained such a dominant position among his contemporary colleagues as it did for Freud, even though others attached great importance to it. Besides, sexuality was a general factor for different kinds of pathological states, according to Freud. However, instead of getting deeper into these problems, I want to illuminate yet another very important source of his scientifically formulated theories about the aetiology of sexuality, namely, his clinical practice and the transference situation in clinical experience.

It is in the relationship to the analysand that Freud in his early professional activity experienced the immense force and plasticity of sexuality. The handling of the sexual transference became a watershed between Breuer and Freud. Both of them were interested in the patient's life history, which distinguished them from the great theoreticians of hysteria Charcot and Bernheim, who did not show any interest in understanding the meaning of the symptom. Breuer and Freud, as I have said, had another attitude to patients: they wanted them to recount their life histories. However, their agreement broke down when it came to sexuality and the sexual transference. Geerardyn writes (1997: 117; italics in the original): 'The generalisation that all neuroses result from a sexual factor, which Breuer disapproved of, involves much more than a simple transposition from another field of research ... Freud ... is also alluding to the phenomenon of *transference*'. In Anzieu (1986: 63) there is an event recounted from 1892 when Freud related to Breuer how 'a patient (a nurse) threw herself into Freud's arms during a hypnosis session. It was this event that finally brought home to him the sexual aetiology of neuroses – a discovery which Jones says "greatly excited" Freud'.

Freud's greatness was his capability of refusing to avoid the tender and erotic feelings of the patient in relationship to the therapist, and of dealing with these feelings as something to be understood. He could thereby gain insight into how these feelings originated from earlier relationships that the patient had had with significant objects, first and foremost with their parents. The insight that there existed something like transference, displacement of feelings from one person to the other, had significance for the development of the clinical practice. Geerardyn (1997: 131) points out that 'there is no Psyché without Amor, i.e., no psychotherapy without a theory on psychosexuality and transference'.

In a way, we have here the seed of how Freud progressed from the cathartic method that consisted of giving full expression of the unconscious affects, to a method whose aim was to make the psychical conflict conscious. By becoming conscious of the conflict, the patient could be cured of her/his neurotic suffering; thereby, psychoanalysis becomes both a research/knowledge project and a therapeutic (treatment) project.

## THE DEVELOPMENT OF THE DRIVE THEORY

Drives and their validity as an explanatory concept in Freudian psychoanalysis are of crucial importance. The libido or the sexual drive is something different from sexuality and the sexual experience. By means of, among other things, the concept of drives, Freud sought to construct a model of the psyche and a theory of the unconscious. It is impossible to imagine the unconscious being the raison d'être for Freudian psychoanalysis without drives. Not all psychoanalysts embrace Freud's ideas of the necessity of the drive concept, which is one of the reasons that we do not talk about one, but several psychoanalyses today (Wallerstein 1992). Despite the central and crucial importance that the drive theory has for many psychoanalysts, the concept suffers from obvious obscurities. Freud was well aware of this and expressed on several occasions discontent about the obscurity of the concept. In a metapsychological essay from 1914 – that is, the year before his 'Instincts and their vicissitudes' (Freud 1915c) – he complained about 'the total absence of any theory of the instincts which would help us to find our bearings' (Freud 1914: 78). In *Beyond the pleasure principle*, he declared both the importance and the obscurity of the drive concept in very obvious terms: 'at once the most important and the most obscure element of psychological research' (Freud 1920: 34). The similarity of this sentence to what he wrote in 1924, in a footnote added to his *Three essays on the theory of sexuality* (1905b: 168, n. 2) is striking: 'The theory of the instincts is the most important but at the same time the least complete portion of psychoanalytic theory'. And in his 'New introductory lectures on psycho-analysis', published in 1932, we find the following sentence: 'The theory of the instincts is so to say our mythology. Instincts are mythical entities, magnificent in their indefiniteness' (Freud 1932: 95). Igra (1998: 9) summarized in a succinct way Freud's relationship to the theory of the drives: 'For Freud the theory of drives remained both indispensable and inscrutable'.[6]

Let us follow Freud in his development of the drive theory. Edgcumbe (1990) presents four phases in the development of the drive theory. The first phase, which is divided into two sub-phases, is between 1894 and 1911, and concerns the conflict between sexual drives and ego-drives (self-preservative drives). The concept of

---

[6] There is a complicated ambiguity in Freud's presentation of the drive and its relationship to soma and psyche. On the one hand, there are statements where the drive is placed between the mental and the somatic and is a psychical representative for endosomatic stimulation (see for example, Freud 1905b: 168, 1911: 74). On the other hand, there are occasions when Freud distinguishes the drive from the psychical representative and where the idea is the representative of the drive (see for example, Freud 1915a: 117, 1915b: 152). According to Strachey (1957: 113), the latter view predominates, but he also wants to diminish the conflicts between these two views: 'It may be, however, that the contradiction is more apparent than real, and that its solution lies precisely in the ambiguity of the concept itself – a frontier-concept between the physical and the mental.' The purpose is not to go deeper into these different views, but the idea that the drive is a frontier concept between the mental and the physical may need to be qualified. One can easily understand this idea in a dualistic, substantial way, where the body is equated with the scientific, biological conceptualization of the body and the mental/psychical is understood as a non-bodily phenomenon. This traditional dualistic idea is unfortunately very common when body and psyche are dealt with in psychoanalytic discussions. From the vantage point of Merleau-Ponty's (1962/1945) phenomenological analysis of human subjectivity, the human being is an embodied subject. That is to say, there are no thoughts, feelings, and so on, that are not connected in some way to a bodily dimension, and there is not in our original bodily experience – the lived body – a bodily course of events that is not related to subjective intentionality. We must liberate ourselves from the traditionally derived and scientifically constructed concept of the body and take possession of the originally lived body. And I believe that an application of Freud's sentence that the drive is a frontier concept between the mental and the physical opens up new, fruitful conceptualizations, in line with the idea that was presented in the previous chapter, namely, that the unconscious lies between the ego's conscious intending and a rudimentary body-ego experiencing.

ego-drives is not used until 1910 (Freud 1910: 214) – although in the English translation it is unfortunately translated as 'ego-instincts'. The second phase runs from 1911 to 1914, when narcissism becomes part of the libido development, and a distinction is made between ego-libido and object-libido. In the third phase, from 1915 to 1920, Freud's essay 'Instincts and their vicissitudes' (1915c) plays a central role. In this essay, the conflict between the libido and the ego-drives returns, where love is tied to the libido and feelings of hatred to the ego-drives. The aggressive tendency is also given attention, even though aggression is still not considered to be a drive on its own. The fourth and final phase, Edgcumbe places from 1920 to the death of Freud in 1939. This consists of the two drives of Eros (life drive) and Thanatos (death drive). The libido is joined to the life drive and the death drive is conceived as having a conservative character – that is, it strives to return to a previous state, ultimately, through death, to the inorganic state. The death drive is described as destructive and aggressive.

After this rough background, I would like to present and discuss certain themes in Freud's drive theory. To begin, let us return to Edgcumbe's first phase, 1894–1911, which consisted of yet another division, in which the first period was between 1894 and 1897. During this period, psychoanalysis was born and several important works were generated, among them 'The neuro-psychoses of defence' (Freud 1894), *Studies on hysteria* with Breuer (1893–95), and *Project for a scientific psychology* (Freud 1950/1895). Edgcumbe (1990: 26) describes this phase in the following way:

> During these years Freud's assumption of opposing biological drives, self-preservative and sexual, was implicit, but not discussed. At this period, what he put forward was essentially an affect theory, and his discussion of mental conflict was in terms of opposing 'ideas' or 'wishes'. Though he already emphasized the importance of sexuality, his emphasis was still heavily on external traumata and physical events, in the form of seduction, as the origin of mental conflicts.

Here the conflict is described in terms of ideas and wishes, which can be seen as phenomenal and experiential processes. Later on, ideas and wishes are to be seen as drive derivates, but at this point the concept of drives has not seen the light of day in Freud's published works.[7] Edgcumbe (1990: 28), however, maintains that Freud 'implicitly assumed the existence of sexual and self-preservative drives, which he viewed as sources of constant somatic stimulation operating within the organism'. Despite the fact that here Freud deals with an endogenous stimulation, his main focus is nevertheless on traumas caused by external events. The thread that I want to pick up from this early phase of the history – or even the prehistory – of psychoanalysis, is Freud's idea of a quota of affect (*Affektbetrag*). The idea that there is a quota or sum of excitation that ties itself to the affect (a qualitative entity) has a lasting and very important significance in his theorizing. His idea about a quota of affect can be seen as the beginning of a construction of a theory of drives. The quota of affect is mentioned in an article from 1893 (Freud 1893b), and in 'The neuro-psychoses of defence' we can read the following (Freud 1894: 60):

> I refer to the concept that in mental functions something is to be distinguished – a quota of affect or sum of excitation – which possesses all the characteristics of a quantity (though we have no means of measuring it), which is capable of increase, diminution, displacement and discharge ...

It is striking how Freud in his early theorizing formulated traits that he later took up and that became essential to the drive. As I said, the quota of affect, a quantitative factor belonging to the idea, remained a

---

[7] This statement is a qualified truth, since it was used a few times in his early works – for example, in *Project for a scientific psychology* (Freud 1950/1895: 317), published posthumously in 1950, in which the term 'drive' (although in the English translation rendered as 'instincts') was used on one occasion and the idea of an energy (drive) in the psyche is also to be found. Below we will see that it was in Freud's *Three essays on the theory of sexuality* (Freud 1905b) that the concept of drives reached a clear and substantial meaning.

leading idea in Freud's metapsychology (the economic point of view) and in his drive psychology. The above quote contains a couple of important things to take into account. We learn that the quota of affect cannot be measured, in spite of being a quantitative entity. Here we are dealing with a psychical concept that, at best, can be specified by means of qualitative quantities, such as increase, diminution, more or less. The psyche is a place with different driving forces, and the quota of affect is of crucial importance for the outcome of this dynamic. It is also a precondition to understanding essential characteristics (displacement, condensation) in the plasticity of the unconscious. Freud (1894: 53) was aware that such mechanisms were not observable, although they could be obtained by inference:

> The separation of the sexual idea from its affect and the
> attachment of the latter to another, suitable but not incompatible
> idea – these are processes, which occur without consciousness.
> Their existence can only be presumed, but cannot be proved by
> any clinico-psychological analysis.

The continuation of this extract is of particular interest in this context and reads as follows (Freud 1894: 53):

> Perhaps it would be more correct to say that these processes are
> not of a psychical nature at all, that they are physical processes
> whose psychical consequences present themselves as if what is
> expressed by the terms 'separation of the sexual idea from its
> affect' and 'false connection' of the latter had really taken place.

According to my interpretation of these extracts, it seems as if Freud's horizon of understanding was limited in the sense that if there were no psychical, phenomenal processes, then they must be physical processes. There is a tendency in Freud to think in accordance with the conditions of epistemological realism.[8] In Freud's

---

[8] By 'epistemological realism' is meant (as was pointed out earlier) the epistemological idea that conceives of scientific theories and descriptions as real objective processes independent of a constituting or constructing researcher/subject.

later works, however, we find examples where he presented more explicitly the idea that the drive concept was a kind of construction, but throughout his life there was a tendency to think realistically on epistemological issues.

Let us follow the fate of the quota of affect in his developed drive theory, such as it was presented in 1905 in *Three essays on the theory of sexuality* (Freud 1905b). As was shown above, Freud's first drive dualism consisted of libido (sexual drive) versus ego-drives (self-preservative drives). For my purpose, the libido is of the greatest interest. The Latin term *libido* means wish or desire. Freud asserted incorrectly that he borrowed the term from Moll 1898, as is mentioned much earlier in the letters to Fliess. The first time the term is mentioned is in a letter, which – with great uncertainty – has been dated to June 1894 (Freud 1995/1887–1904: 80). The first time 'libido' appears in a published essay is 1895, where there is a discussion about 'sexual libido or sexual desire' (Freud 1895: 107). In the 'Editor's note' to this essay in *The standard edition of the complete psychological works of Sigmund Freud* (Strachey 1962: 88), it is stressed that in his earliest works Freud conceived of the libido as psychical, and that there is no clear distinction yet made between psychical and conscious. But in 1897 the libido is already accepted as something potentially unconscious. Laplanche and Pontalis (1985: 239) admit that it is difficult to give a satisfactory definition of Freud's libido concept: the concept itself has not been clearly defined and, besides, the libido theory has been developed in parallel with the development of the drive theory.

From my point of view, I would like to claim that the view of the libido goes from being a descriptive and phenomenal concept to one that describes something unconscious and where the libido eventually acquires a more constructed character. In the first edition of the *Three essays* from 1905 (Freud 1905b), the libido is still roughly synonymous with sexual desire (cf. Laplanche and Pontalis 1985: 240). But in a section added in 1915, the libido becomes an energy concept which describes the pressure of the sexual drive: 'We have defined the concept of libido as a quantitatively variable force which could serve as a measure of processes and transformations occurring in the field of sexual excitation' (Freud 1905b: 217).

Three essays on the theory of sexuality – one of Freud's most important works – is a very rich text, from which I will only deal with some important traits. I want to (1) show that Freud's characterization of sexuality breaks with a conventional idea about what sexuality is, and (2) present the drive structure which has sexuality as its model.

### Freud's characterization of sexuality

At the beginning of this chapter, I referred to Green's and Laplanche's critiques of how sexuality has been neglected in contemporary psychoanalysis. One easily neglects Freud's wide definition of sexuality and misses its infantile character. Nor is it uncommon that one gets the impression that sexuality in today's allegedly open and unprejudiced society is not that source of psychical pathology and difficulty that it was during Freud's puritanical time. I believe that psychopathology has changed, to a certain extent, since Freud treated his analysands. Culture and history leave their mark on the psychical curse of time. But I think one is wrong to hold the view that today's openness about sexuality (a conventional idea that really needs to be discussed) has any significant effect on the kind of sexuality that is interesting for psychoanalysis. Only if one defines sexuality in a rather limited way can one get the idea that the changes in lifestyles and attitudes with respect to sexuality that have occurred since Freud's time would have any effect on the sexuality that psychoanalysis deals with and that many think is the core of the unconscious. The psychoanalytic definition of sexuality perhaps has more to do with an existential rather than with any cultural aspect. Due to the non-conventional nature of Freud's definition of sexuality, I find it necessary to shed more light on this definition here.

In Freud's opening paragraphs of Three essays, he makes clear how radically he diverges from traditional ideas, which – as indeed is common even today – see human beings' sexuality as something innate, something naturally given and limited to heterosexual genital relations. Freud (1905b: 135) writes:

> Popular opinion has quite definite ideas about the nature and characteristics of this sexual instinct [that which science calls libido]. It is generally understood to be absent in childhood, to set in at the time of puberty in connection with the process of coming to maturity and to be revealed in the manifestations of an irresistible attraction exercised by one sex upon the other; while its aim is presumed to be sexual union, or at all events actions leading in that direction. We have every reason to believe, however, that these views give a very false picture of the true situation. If we look into them more closely we shall find that they contain a number of errors, inaccuracies and hasty conclusions.

He goes on to complicate the issue even further (Freud 1905b: 146; note added in 1915):

> from the point of view of psycho-analysis the exclusive sexual interest felt by men for women is also a problem that needs elucidating and is not a self-evident fact based upon an attraction that is ultimately of a chemical nature.

For Freud, the infant is also a sexual being. The unifying genital sexuality is preceded and built up by partial drives, which can be derived from inner bodily processes that generate sexual excitement at a sufficient level of excitation. Mechanical bodily movements, for example, can have a sexually exciting effect. We can easily imagine other motives than health motives when, as adults, we exercise physically. Freud (1905b: 203) also speculates on whether the sexual excitement conditioned by muscular activity could be one of the roots of the sadistic drive.

Apart from these indirect sources of sexual excitement, the partial drives also originate from the bodily parts that Freud signifies as *erogenous zones*. The first erogenous zone is the mouth, lips that are charged sexually when the infant sucks the mother's breast. Other erogenous zones are the anus, clitoris and genitals. In principle, any part of the body skin can become an erogenous zone. The connection of the partial drives to one's own body turns them into autoerotic to begin with, even though the starting point in the development of the drives is constituted by an external object, namely, the mother's breast. But there are also partial drives that are not primarily based on one's own skin, but which involve other people, such as the drive to expose oneself (exhibitionism) and the drive to watch (scoptophilia).

In so-called 'normal development', the drive goes from being autoerotic to becoming satisfied by sexual intercourse with a person of the opposite sex. But even in heterosexual intercourse, the partial drives are manifest in terms of foreplay: kissing, caressing, and so on. In other words, there is a sense in which Freud thinks about a 'normal development' and which he discusses in relation to deviations from such normality. The deviation, in this case, is about sexual perversion.[9] What was mentioned above concerning sexual partial drives is closely connected to Freud's view on perversion. The sexuality of the child that Freud describes as 'polymorphously perverse' consists – as we saw – of a number of partial drives, and, as pointed out, also becomes manifest in the adult's 'normal' relationship to sexuality – for example, in the form of foreplay. For Freud, perversions are characterized by a residue of the partial drives which achieves the main role. They are, thus, not just a means to a fulfilment of heterosexual genital intercourse. Another trait of perversion entails that the expressed partial drive also succeeds in generating an

---

[9] Laplanche and Pontalis (1985: 308) discuss Freud's normative concept, and they point out that this does not put a social aspect on what is to be considered normal or deviant at different times in history. They ask and answer: 'Is it then the establishment of the genital organisation that institutes the norm in that it unifies sexuality and subordinates partial sexual activities to the genital act, so that the former are relegated to a preparatory role *vis-à-vis* the latter? This is the explicit thesis of the *Three Essays*'.

orgasm; however, for the non-perverse, the orgasm is the end result. To express oneself in clinical-technical terms, Freud maintains that perversion is a regression to an earlier libido fixation.

What I consider to be of importance in this discussion is Freud's view that perversion is not something essentially detached from the so-called normal sexuality, and Freud's inventive way of defining neurosis as 'the negative of perversions' (Freud 1905b: 165, 231, 238), all of which captures how these early partial drives still live within us, even though, consciously, we do not want to have anything to do with them. The difference between the neurotic and the perverse is thus repression. The neurotic has repressed these infantile, sexual, pleasurable experiences and they appear as ego-dystonic, whereas for the perverse, these infantile, sexual, pleasurable experiences do not give rise to any deep unpleasantness for the ego.[10]

This discussion about Freud's definition of sexuality has shown the breadth of the concept, but it has not dealt with the constructed character of libido. When we now move on to the second point, to present the drive structure that has sexuality as its model, the question of the constructed character of libido will be brought to the fore.

### The structure of drives

Freud developed the structure of drives in *Three essays* 1905, in terms of *source, aim* and *object*. In addition, in 1915, *pressure (Drang)* also came into being; this has a special interest since the pressure of the drive belongs to the metapsychological economic point of view and signifies a quantitative energy aspect. But first to the terms that were being used by 1905. In brief, the *source* of the drive is defined as the somatic place where excitation appears (in other words, an

---

[10] It may be of value to make a clinical comment in this context. Laplanche and Pontalis (1985: 309) warn against the misleading description of conceiving of perversion as 'the brute, non-repressed manifestation of infantile sexuality'. The fact is that perversions have very different characters, and that other defence mechanisms than repression are present in perversions – for example, denial and splitting of the ego.

erogenous zone), and where the aim of the drive is to abolish this excitation and thereby generate the experience of pleasure. As was mentioned above, the somatic organs that make up the source of the drive are called erogenous zones, some of which are predestined because of their anatomical location. These erogenous zones are the mouth, the anus and the genitals. But possible erogenous zones do not end there, as the whole body can function as an erogenous zone. Freud (1905b: 183) therefore declares that:

> the quality of the stimulus has more to do with producing the pleasurable feeling than has the nature of the part of the body concerned. A child who is indulging in sensual sucking searches about his body and chooses some part of it to suck – a part which is afterwards preferred by him from force of habit; if he happens to hit upon one of the predestined regions (such as the nipples or genitals) no doubt it retains the preference.

The *aim* of the drive is the way in which excitation is resolved and satisfaction obtained. The drive itself is, in principle, always active, whereas the aim can be both active (the wish to watch, sadistic pleasure) and passive (the wish to be watched, masochistic pleasure). If we stick with the example of sucking the mother's breast, the sucking is then that way – that aim – in which a satisfaction of pleasure is achieved.

The *object* of the drive is that object or bodily part by which the drive can obtain its aim. The first object for sexual satisfaction is the mother's breast; thereafter follow autoerotic objects. Thus, Freud's theory of drives is not characterized by the lack of objects, which is sometimes the way it is presented in contrast to the theory of object relations. What is characteristic for the object of the drive is its plasticity. The object for the satisfaction of the drive can change. The breast as the first object can be replaced, for example, by one's own thumb. But Freud lets us know that the sucking of the mother's breast remains as a prototype in each love relationship: 'The finding of an object is in fact a refinding of it' (Freud 1905b: 222).

Apart from these characteristics of the drive – source, aim and object – we have to add (as mentioned before) yet another characteristic, namely, the *pressure* of the drive. The pressure of the drive is not included in Freud's theory of drives from 1905, but was added 10 years later, in 1915. The pressure is the force that the drive exercises, or – as it is expressed in another interesting way in one of his metapsychological essays – 'the measure of the demand for work which it represents' (Freud 1915c: 122). As has been said, the drive is active, which Freud points out on several occasions, even though its aim may be passive. The activity of the drive is exactly this pressure – the force that it exercises in order to be satisfied. In order for this drive pressure to be expressed in a wish, a mind is demanded that has a capacity for metaphor. In themselves, the drive and unconscious are unknown. (Concerning the significance of metaphor within psychoanalysis, see Enckell 2002.)

One can detect a view in Freud that the drive's pressure represents the drive's distinctive feature, when he asserts that: 'The characteristic of exercising pressure is common to all instincts; it is in fact their very essence' (Freud 1915c: 122). It is the drive's pressure that shows the constructed character of the drive, which is why it has a special interest for us. The idea of a quantitative factor, however, is not new, as we saw above. What is new is the designation 'pressure'. My idea is that the constructing character of the libido concept becomes clarified by the fact that the concept 'pressure' came to be used in 1915, although the idea of a quantitative factor is older on account of the expression 'quota of affect'. But the theoretical and metapsychological status of the pressure of the drive probably became ever more clear for Freud, which explains that the drive's pressure as the concept was not introduced in *Three essays* until the 1915 edition, at the same time as he wrote his metapsychological essays.

Let us move on and try to understand the character of the drive in Freud's thinking after the important year 1915, when the drive concept was given a more elaborated and metapsychological presentation in 'Instincts and their vicissitudes' (Freud 1915c), and when the concept of the pressure of the drive appeared in print, both in that essay and in the 1915 edition of *Three essays*.

## LIFE DRIVES VERSUS DEATH DRIVES

The last phase in Freud's developing of the concept of drives is the dualism that he depicts between life drives and death drives, between Eros and Thanatos. This drive dualism is introduced in his much discussed and controversial essay *Beyond the pleasure principle* (Freud 1920). Freud's essay is a remarkable text in the sense that two very different figures of thought are presented with the aim of representing the death drives. The background of the essay is that Freud discovered the existence of both everyday and clinical phenomena that were manifested in repetition compulsion (see chapter 7). Freud was forced to realize that this compulsion to repeat could not be explained from the vantage point of the pleasure principle and its striving to discharge energy; this is the reason for the name of the essay, *Beyond the pleasure principle*, although it might have been more appropriate to designate it 'prior to' the pleasure principle (Pösténeyi 1996). In chapter 7, I will return to the meaning of repetition compulsion and how one can interpret it. Here it is sufficient to establish that in Freud's essay *Beyond the pleasure principle*, this repetition compulsion later becomes conceptualized as the death drive, the very opposite of a life drive.

Freud struggled to try to get some order into his new dualistic drive theory of the life drive (Eros) and the death drive (Thanatos), and how it could be understood in relation to the old distinction between ego-drives and sexual drives (libido). Eros, or life drives, can be described as a hybrid between the old pair of drives, ego-drives (self-preservative drives) and sexual drives: 'the libido of our sexual instincts would coincide with the Eros of the poets and philosophers which holds all living things together' (Freud 1920: 50). To Eros is attributed the function of binding and preserving. What had earlier been the characteristic of libido – to be ruled by the principle of free

energy and the striving of the pleasure principle to discharge as fast
as possible – instead became a defining property of Thanatos (death
drive) in Freud's last drive theory.

The most common way to interpret the death drive is as an
aggression or destruction drive, an interpretation that has certain
support in *Beyond the pleasure principle*, but which became more
evident with Freud in his later works, perhaps, in particular, in
'Civilization and its discontents' (Freud 1930).[11] In Kleinian psychoanalysis, the death/aggression drive has been stressed and even considered to be original. I will not repeat Laplanche's idea of the death
drive as the most extreme expression for the discharge of libido,
which was presented in chapter 4. However, here it may be of interest to mention Laplanche's idea about the emergence of the death
drive in Freud in the 1920s, as a result of the loss of these drives'
untamed and wild character in Freud's theorizing about narcissism,
where drive dualism was represented by ego-libido and object-libido.
In 1920, this wild and untamed side of libido reappeared, but in the
guise of the death drive, according to Laplanche (1999a: 191):

> Sexuality ran the risk of being entirely monopolised; one risked
> seeing no more in sexuality than this bound, invested, calm and
> quiescent aspect.
>
> Consequently, in 1919 came the need to reaffirm
> something that had been lost, that is to say, non-connected
> sexuality, sexuality that could be described as 'unbound' in the
> sense of the drive – sexuality that changed its object, having
> only one aim, which is to move as fast as possible towards

[11] With the launching of the death drive, aggression thus received the status of
being a drive for Freud. Before that, sexual drives entailed aggression as an
aggressive component (for example, Freud 1905b), which was changed in 1915 in
'Instincts and their vicissitudes' (Freud 1915c), where aggression belongs to ego-/
self-preservative drive. Freud's disciple Alfred Adler, who broke with Freud in
1911, suggested in 1908 an aggression drive, an idea that Freud commented on in
his *Analysis of a phobia in a five-year-old boy* and explicitly rejected: 'I cannot
bring myself to assume the existence of a special aggressive instinct alongside
the familiar instincts of self-preservation and of sex, and on equal footing with
them' (Freud 1909: 140).

satisfaction and the complete appeasement of its desire. In other words, this is the complete realisation of desire via the shortest possible route; thus, at this moment it became necessary to reaffirm something essential in sexuality, which had been lost – its demonic aspect, subjugated to the primary process and the repetition compulsion. From this point on, you can see that the content of which sexuality was comprised from the beginning was now split into two aspects, eventually to be regrouped by Freud under the terms 'life drives', or 'Eros', and 'death drives'. Eros does not represent the totality of sexuality, but those of its aspects, which were attached to preserving the object, and also to preserving the ego as primary object.

Thus, Laplanche tried to make a stance for the wild dimension in sexuality in his reinterpretation of Freud's death drive. The concept that best matches this wild and untamed side in human life is probably the id (*Das Es*), which we will now address.

### THE ID AND THE UNCONSCIOUS

Some years after the introduction of the death drive, in 1923, Freud develops the structural model, consisting of the id, ego and superego. All these three instances can be comprised of the unconscious, even though it is the id, primarily, that belongs to the unconscious. The concept of the id is especially interesting, since it illuminates that which is chaotic in the human being and in the unconscious. Freud's description of the id also contains ideas and traits that I do not touch upon here – for example, biological interpretations.

Freud inherited the concept from Georg Groddeck (1866–1934), but changed its meaning in important aspects. Freud thought it was adequate to call this instance the id – an impersonal pronoun – since its most apparent trait is its ego-alien character. The specific characteristic of the ego to synthesize and harmonize is totally lacking with the id. The id presents itself as the opposite to that which characterizes the ego and is best described in negative terms (Freud 1932: 73):

It is the dark, inaccessible part of our personality; what little we know of it we have learnt from our study of the dream-work and of the construction of neurotic symptoms, and most of that is of a negative character and can be described only as a contrast to the ego. We approach the id with analogies: we call it a chaos, a cauldron full of seething excitations.

The id represents the untamed drives; there is no logic that excludes the existence of conflictual impulses, no idea of time, no historical awareness; rather the impulses of the id remain always the same, with no recognition of the passage of time. Freud furthermore stresses that the id is free from values, without any moral dimension from which good and evil can be judged. The closest we come to a positive definition of the id is to describe it in terms of energy, drive: 'The economic or, if you prefer, the quantitative factor, which is intimately linked to the pleasure principle, dominates all its processes. Instinctual cathexes seeking discharge – that, in our view, is all there is in the id' (Freud 1932: 74).

Laplanche (1999a: 188) maintains that the id constitutes an intensification of the unconscious and he links it to the death drive in his theory of drives, in which we have seen that death drives are the most radical, untamed and wild aspect of sexuality. The unorganized and the unstructured in the unconscious are given prominence by the id. The id is the principle of free energy and is ruled in accordance with primary processes. And in order to sustain a discourse about drives, it is the drive's economic point of view that the id latches on to, which is pointed out by Laplanche (1999a: 168): 'Perhaps what is interesting about this second theory [that is, the structural model], that of the id, is that it puts more emphasis on this energy point of view, under the name of the drives'.

Perhaps one can say that in Freud's thinking, from the very birth of psychoanalysis, sexuality has always been regarded from an energy point of view, concerned rather with a quota of affect than with ideal representations, and that exerts a pressure towards its realization. This idea has been captured by means of different expressions: a quota of affect, the pressure of the drive, and, latterly, it is the id that is to satisfy this indispensable but elusive phenomenon in Freudian theorizing. Sexuality constitutes the unconscious, and the energy aspect of sexuality is not a descriptive, phenomenal term, but has a constructed character, which is, however, in need of development and further clarification.

## SUMMARY

Sexuality, which has been of central importance in Freud's theorizing from the very beginning, must be understood against the back-cloth of being in conflict with other forces within the person, such as the ego or ego-drives/self-preservative drives. In this chapter I have attempted to present the development of Freud's theory of drives, with the focus on libido/sexual drives.

Furthermore, the libido concept must be understood in a broad sense, including not least infantile sexuality with its partial drives. The point of view presented in this chapter is that libido/sexual drive is not synonymous with experienced sexuality, but that it has to be understood as a theoretical construction. In particular, I put emphasis on the pressure of the drive, which is the fourth element in the structure of the drive that Freud designated in 1915. The previous three are the source, aim and object of the drive.

Principally, one may argue that the pressure of the drive has been included from the very beginning in terms of the notion 'quota of affect'. The quota of affect, or pressure, sets the searchlight on the quantitative, energy aspect of sexuality. It is, nevertheless, a quantity, albeit a quantity that does not allow itself to be measured.

My main point in this chapter has been to show the theoretical, constructing traits in Freud's concept of the libido. The basis of this theoretical construction will be discussed in the next chapter.

# 6    The grounding of libido in the life-world experience

In the previous chapter – The libido as the core of the unconscious – I discussed the development of Freud's drive concept, in particular with respect to the libido/the sexual drive. We saw that in Freud's concept of the drive, a quantitative factor was included, although it was not measurable. Freud's idea that a quantity belongs to the drive was essentially there from the start, but it did not become explicated as the pressure of the drive until 1915. The constructed character of the drive concept thereby became more obvious. This pressure of the drive – that is, its energy and quantitative factor – is perhaps the most important part of Freud's metapsychology. Freud himself described it as the essence of the drives (Freud 1915c: 122).

The functioning of the psychical apparatus in accordance with the so-called 'pleasure principle' implies a striving towards immediate discharge of energy. This striving can be described in line with the Nirvana principle – that is, a discharge of drive energy towards the zero point, an extinguishing of psychical life. This way of functioning for the psyche/the unconscious in accordance with Freud's thinking can also be captured by means of a number of other important concepts. In Laplanche's interpretation of the death drive, it is argued that the death drive is the most extreme expression of the discharge of the libido. The death drive is sexuality when it is the least civilized and socialized. It functions then in accordance with the principle of free energy and the primary process (Laplanche 1979). This type of description of the death drive reminds us of Freud's id, whose elusive character makes him talk about it as 'a chaos, a cauldron full of seething excitations' (Freud 1932: 73). But Freud also makes an attempt to define the id against the background of the metapsychology's economic standpoint: 'The economic or, if you prefer, the

quantitative factor, which is intimately linked to the pleasure principle, dominates all its processes. Instinctual cathexes seeking discharge – that, in our view, is all there is in the id' (Freud 1932: 74).

My idea is that all these different concepts and expressions –
the pleasure principle, the Nirvana principle, the principle of free
energy, primary process and the id – are to be understood as frontier
concepts, which do *not* refer to phenomenal, experiential entities.
They are to be conceived as idealized, theoretical constructions.[1]

The aim of this chapter is to ground the meaning of the theoretical construction of the libido concept in life-world experiences. As
I pointed out in the previous chapter, the source of Freud's discovery
of the aetiological significance for pathological suffering cannot be
limited to observations in his clinical practice. In accordance with
May (1999), we should understand that the aetiological significance
for neuroses was nourished by a prescientific 'vision' that Freud spent
the rest of his life trying to confirm. It is in this context that the life-
world concept, used within phenomenology, becomes of interest. My
hypothesis is that it is sexuality as it shows itself in our life-world
experience that awakens Freud's thoughts about its importance and
that in turn leads him further to adapt sexuality into formulated,
scientific theories. To ground the meaning of the constructed libido
concept in sexual life-world experiences means that one identifies
the conditions for the construction on the basis of life-world experiences. Such an ambition can be said to fulfil an epistemological,
legitimizing function. We will thus be able to understand the constructed libido concept of psychoanalysis against the background of
prescientific life-world experiences.[2]

---

[1] Idealized/idealizing in this context has nothing to do with the psychoanalytic meaning of ascribing more valuable traits to the object than it has. In this
chapter, as in chapter 2, where idealized/idealizing was used in the creation of
geometrical configurations (see chapter 2, n. 5), the designation of it is that one
abstracts certain characteristics in the concrete being or experience – for example, a specific sexual experience – with the purpose of achieving a pure structure.

[2] The analysis of this chapter is, in its structure, influenced by Husserl's
(1970/1936a, 1970/1936c) analysis of modern natural science and how its

To begin with, I will briefly outline certain characteristics in the life-world experience, the way that it most often manifests itself. Thereafter I will say something about the life-world experience on occasions of injury and sickness, whose structure deviates from the 'normal' life-world experience. My hope is that these descriptions can serve as a background against which the character of sexual life-world experiences can be explicated. In other words, the first step consists of showing the specific character of sexual life-world experiences. In the second step, the construction of the libido on the basis of the character of sexuality is discussed. The idea is, thus, that it is the specific and unique character of sexuality that serves as the ground for the transformation of the sexual experience into libido. The libido is to be understood as a non-experiential, constructed, scientific, metapsychological concept that provides us with a psychoanalytic perspective, from the point of which subjective life can be understood and explained.

## SOME CHARACTERISTICS OF LIFE-WORLD EXPERIENCES

The life-world – a concept that is used (although not exclusively) in phenomenological thinking – can be said to be an 'operative' concept – that is, the concept has still not reached a thematic clarity, but nevertheless fulfils an important function within phenomenological thinking. In chapter 2, I emphasized the priority of the life-world in relationship to scientific descriptions and constructions of the world. The life-world is the historical, cultural and social conditioned world we are born into and in which we grow up. The concept of life-world is attached first of all to the later thinking of Husserl's unfinished philosophy from the 1930s. Other descriptions resembling the life-world concept are to be found much earlier. Other phenomenologists have also thought and theorized about the life-world, although under other designations. The meaning of the

meaning ground is to be understood from the vantage point of subjective life-world experiences.

concept is not restricted to representatives within the phenomeno-logical philosophy. Alfred Schütz (1962) points out the great similar-ity to William James' concept of 'sub-universes', developed in James' *The principles of psychology* (1890).

Inspired by various phenomenologists' discussion and charac-terization of the life-world, I would like to outline certain charac-teristics pertinent to my specific aim. Thereafter, I want to show the deviant structure of sexuality, in crucial respects, in relation to everyday life-world experiences – in other words, the dominant way in which we are living in the life-world.

Schütz (1962) discusses different realities in our existence. For our purpose, it is the 'reality of the world of daily life' that is the most interesting. The world of daily life is an intersubjective world, with an inherited significance and meaning into which we are born. This world is characterized by the so-called 'natural attitude', with its pragmatic and practical interests.[3]

We can describe, with the help of Heidegger (1980/1927), the primordial way in which we are in the world in terms of a prac-tical, non-reflective and non-theoretical engagement. Instead of talking about how we are in the world, we can talk about how we understand the world. How we are in, or how we understand, or how we relate to the world connotes one and the same thing in this context. Heidegger calls this primordial way of being in the world 'hermeneutical-existential'.[4] In this hermeneutical-existential way of understanding the world, the objects that we encounter in the world are understood in their function, in their use value – that is, as equipment. By calling objects 'equipment' (*Zeug*), Heidegger wants to emphasize our concernful dealings with them and their usability

---

[3] The concept 'natural attitude' – which stems from Husserl (1962/1913) and is described on p. 7 of this volume – signifies our everyday common-sense attitude. In the natural attitude we take the existence of the world for granted; we do not doubt it or question it. On the whole, the question of existence is not an issue. On occasions when we suffer from perceptual illusions, for example, our belief in the existence of the world in its totality is not yet affected.

[4] The term 'existential' for Heidegger signifies an essential way of being for man. Man is by necessity understanding, according to Heidegger.

value, and where each piece of equipment belongs to a 'totality of equipment'. For instance, the pencil that I use when writing this chapter about the life-world relates to a whole meaningful totality of equipment. It is equipment in terms of its belonging to a context of other equipment: the eraser, the paper on which I write, the table at which I sit, and so on. Heidegger (1980/1927: 97) writes: 'A totality of equipment is constituted by various ways of the "in-order-to", such as serviceability, conduciveness, usability, manipulability'.

Thus, the equipment with which we deal appears as something to be used in order to accomplish something. Equipment manifests what Heidegger calls 'readiness-to-hand' (*Zuhandenheit*). The equipment points further to an activity. The pencil as a piece of equipment points to an activity – in this case, writing a chapter about the ground of the libido in life-world experiences. Furthermore, in my concernful dealing with the equipment, it is given in an implicit way and not thematically – that is, I'm not thinking of the pencil, but simply use it in my activity. In other words, we have a comprehension of what pieces of equipment can be used for, despite the fact that our comprehension is neither theoretical nor thematic. Rather, our understanding of the equipment shows itself through how we use it; our understanding and knowledge of it is of a 'know-how' character. This is the case at least as long as it fulfils its function. However, there are occasions when the equipment stands out, when our attention is focused on the usefulness of the equipment. This is the case when its readiness-to-hand and its usefulness are disrupted. The day when I come to write with the pencil and discover that it is broken, then its meaning – the meaning of the equipment – will be in focus. But as long as it fulfils its function, when I carry out the task (the writing) unreflectively, I do not pay any attention to it. What is given attention, rather, is the activity – to continue with my example, the writing of this text. We see here that the piece of equipment (the pencil) points to or refers to an activity (the writing). However, the chain of references does not end with my work or activity. The activity – in this case, the writing of this chapter – does not take place in a vacuum. It points to another reference, namely, to a human being, or, to use Heidegger's term, *Dasein*. The activity serves a purpose, which is carried out to satisfy human desires, wishes and needs. We thus have a chain where a piece of equipment, included in a totality of equipment, points towards an activity, and now we can see also that the activity, in turn, points to that 'for-the-sake-of-which' (to use Heidegger's expression). In this case, the writing of this text is done for the sake of publishing a book on psychoanalysis. The chain of references ends with the primary 'for-the-sake-of-which' of a human being.

What is important is not only that the chain of references ends with the purpose or the sake for which the activity is done, but also that our primordial understanding of the objects (equipment) in the world already entails the whole structure of references that has been sketched here – that is, our primordial understanding of the pencil entails the whole system of references: the pencil pointing to the activity of writing, which in turn points to the purpose of the writing, that is, my wish to publish this book. So, at the moment of seeing or dealing with my pencil, I grasp its use character and understand its potential (for writing my book). Again, this understanding is not thematic and theoretical. Heidegger calls this type of concernful dealing in the world for 'hermeneutical-existential understanding'. The world and the objects (equipment) in the world present themselves first of all as possibilities to fulfil intentions and satisfy wishes. This is our original and practical way of being in the world.

Heidegger's critique of the philosophical tradition was that the tradition had prioritized an abstract, decontextualized description of the human being's understanding of the world, and where the objects in the world are conceived of as separate, objective things. Such a decontextualized, abstract way of describing the world and objects in the world is expressed when I describe the pencil as 10 centimetres long, yellow in colour, made of wood, and so on. In this derived way of describing the object (the pencil as a thing), the primordial hermeneutical existential way of understanding the world is concealed.

My purpose is not to discuss, in detail, what characterizes our primordial way of being in the world. Here, I simply want to highlight in the above description our *practical, future-oriented* and *instrumental* way of being in the world. These are the three characteristic traits in life-world experiences that I want to preserve in this context, in order to discuss these characteristics further in relation to sexual experience. What is especially striking, when reading Heidegger's explication of how we are/understand the world, is, I believe, the absence of one's body or one's body experience. This fact may say something about how our body and our bodilyness is the zero point from which we live in space and the world, and which is always with us, but not as an object of our consciousness. In order to get a grasp of our body in life-world experiences, we need to consult Merleau-Ponty, who has developed a 'phenomenology of the body'. Merleau-Ponty has captured the status of the body in the following way (Merleau-Ponty 1962/1945: 90; italics in the original):

> It is particularly true that an object is an object, only in so far as it can be moved away from me, and ultimately disappears from my field of vision. Its presence is such that it entails a possible absence. Now the permanence of my own body is entirely different in kind: it is not at the extremity of some indefinite exploration; it defies exploration and is always presented to me from the same angle. Its permanence is not a permanence in the world, but a permanence on my part. To say that it is always near me, always there for me, is to say that it is never really in front of me, that I cannot array it before my eyes, that it remains marginal to all my perceptions that it is *with* me. It is true that external objects too never turn one of their sides to me without hiding the rest, but I can at least freely choose the side which they are to present to me.

Merleau-Ponty's conceptualization of 'the lived body' implies that my body is not separate or split from my consciousness, but my 'I' is an embodied subject. It is a pre-reflective body experience before

I possibly reflect on my body. Human beings are, for Merleau-Ponty, body–mind entities existing in and towards the world (être-au-monde). Bullington (2004: 110) summarizes Merleau-Ponty's idea about the relationship between body, mind and world in the following way:

> The lived body can thus be described as a lived relationship to the world. Through this relationship human experiences arise. There is no understanding that is not rooted in bodily existence, and no bodily experiences that do not at least have a rudimentary meaning, and no world without a body–mind presence. These three poles are, according to Merleau-Ponty, the fundamental basis for all further investigation and reflection.

Bullington and Karlsson (1997) have discussed different body experiences, one of which is called 'the functional body'. This form of functional body should be understood, in Merleau-Ponty's terms, as an 'embodied subject'. The body is given in an immediate meaningful way. The condition for talking about a functional body is that there is a specific relationship between 'I' (the self) and the body. The relationship between 'I' and the body is about a subject's embodying. The body is not an object, split from the 'I', even though the body can assume different 'values' in relation to a person's intentions and wishes. The body can, for example, be felt as pliable, when it is only on the fringe of the experience, or it can feel obtrusive and obstinate, when it is in focus for attention.

This way of describing the body experience may be in need of comment. The division between the 'I' and the body is an analytic division and not an ontological division between two different substances. There is no dualism hidden behind the distinction that has been made here between the 'I' and the body. Instead, we must situate this description within the framework of Merleau-Ponty's way of approaching the body–mind question (Merleau-Ponty 1962/1945: 88):

> Man taken as a concrete being is not a psyche joined to an organism, but the movement to and fro of existence which

at one time allows itself to take corporeal form and at others moves towards personal acts. Psychological motives and bodily occasions may overlap because there is not a single impulse in a living body, which is entirely fortuitous in relation to psychic intentions, not a single mental act which has not found at least its germ or its general outline in physiological tendencies.

When the body in a pliable way exists on the fringe of the experience, we have a body experience where the 'I' and the body are fused. This original position can be broken and the body can then be experienced as dysfunctional – it becomes obtrusive and obstinate. But in the ordinary, practical and unproblematic way of being in the world, the appearance of the body can be captured with the following terms: *automatic* (one does not need to think what to do), *smooth and easy* (it flows from intention to action without disturbance) and a feeling of *competence* (faith in one's capacity). This is a holistic background feeling, in the sense that when one moves around – for instance, when going for a walk – there is a harmonious cooperation between the different parts of the body, and the spontaneous experience of the body demands no separate awareness about the different parts of the body. Usually, one's awareness is not of a thematic kind, but rather an awareness on a bodily level about how one carries out activities. Thoughts about what one is doing become more likely disturbing, perhaps to the extent that the activity cannot be carried out. For example, when I am writing on the keyboard of the computer, my fingers find the right keys to press automatically and smoothly. If I try to think where to put my fingers to press the keys, at worst it may make the typing impossible. It can also be difficult to remember cognitively where the letters are on the keyboard, whereas my fingers find the right keys without problem. The lived body is not regulated by a 'superior' thinking about how I should carry things out. However, thinking about how I should act bodily may have special importance when I learn different tasks and activities.

In one's normal flow of the body, when one carries out activities with an automatic and pliable capacity, there is also room for a simultaneous capacity. I can carry out several things at the same time, without lacking in concentration or focus. For example, I can walk down the street on the way to the shop and simultaneously be engaged in a conversation with a person, while touching my pocket to make sure that I brought my wallet with me, and besides this I am able to observe a car that is approaching us at high speed. My body is compliant with my activity and resembles the implicit and anonymous character that the equipment possesses, which I describe above. My body is there, on the fringe, without making any 'noise'.

This bodily 'anonymity' gives me a freedom in the conscious flowing life. The body does not demand attention, does not occupy me in my way of throwing myself out into the world. Indeed, it could happen, in line with the fact that the equipment can occupy my attention when it does not function, as I have described above. The broken pencil makes me thematize the usability of the pencil. In the same manner, the body can be obtrusive and obstinate, and can be experienced as an obstacle to my activity. The experience moves from being 'I am my body' to 'I have a body', which then may present itself as something problematic and obstinate.

## The lived body in ill health

Inspired by Heidegger's description of being-in-the-world, Svenaeus (2001) has analysed our way of being in the world when in ill health. In ill health, our familiar way of being in the world ruptures, and we are thrown into a homeless being-in-the-world. And this changed way of being in the world also entails a changed relationship to ourselves/our own body, in that the body shows itself as something incomprehensible and something that becomes an obstacle to our familiar way of being ourselves.

We have seen that the lived body shows itself as a silent, marginal and anonymous presence in normal functioning, and that it becomes thematized, paid attention to on those occasions when it does not exist smoothly in the fulfilling of intentions and wishes. The body then shows itself as obstinate and obtrusive. In this section, very briefly, I will pay attention to an example of the obtrusive body, such as it shows itself in ill health. When I suffer from a high fever, for example, I am no longer capable of going to work, or a stomach flu might obstruct me from continuing to read the book I started before I became sick. The competence of my lived body breaks down and my body's anonymous presence on the fringe of my experience transforms into a body that is paid attention to. Toombs describes such a change in the following way (Toombs 1992: 70–1; italics in the original):

> illness engenders a shift of attention. The disruption of lived body causes the patient explicitly to attend to his or her body *as* body, rather than simply living it unreflectively. The body is thus transformed from lived body to object-body. This objectification results in the apprehension of the corporeal nature of the body as a physical encumbrance, as an oppositional force, as a machine-like entity and as a physiological organism.

Not only does an objectification of my lived body take place, but it also appears as a non-functional physical object. My broken arm is noted exactly in its incapacity to saw a piece of wood. Murphy describes the big change in the experience of oneself and of the world after a spinal tumour (from Kielhofner et al. 2002; italics in the original):

> I no longer know where my feet are, and without the low-level pain I still feel, I would hardly know I had legs … I have become rather emotionally detached from my body, often referring to one of my limbs as *the* leg or *the* arm … As my condition has deteriorated, I have come increasingly to look upon my body as a faulty life-support system, the only function of which is to sustain my head.

The objects too, which used to be lived through smoothly, without giving them a thought, are now problematic for my body. The steps that took me to the floor upstairs appear now as an obstacle for my broken leg to overcome. This whole harmonious field of body–mind–world is changed in ill health. Toombs (1992: 64) writes:

> in response to the demands of illness, the contextual organization of the body and the complexity of body/mind/world must shift in varying ways. Such adjustments in the contexture are experienced as 'foreign', alien, unnatural. 'I'm just not myself today' or 'Things just don't feel right', express in part this perceived change in bodily experience.

Toombs (1992) also points out how spatiality and temporality change in ill health. My spatial experience is first and foremost a spatiality that concerns the situation, and not a geometrical, physical room. I relate to a situation, where objects (equipment) are placed at an appropriate distance, or, for example, too far from me in relation to my lived body and its capacity. Under normal conditions, the world and the surroundings open up when I move, but in ill health and weakness the world tends to be restricted to a *here*. And not only to a *here*, but also to a *now*, in that the capacity to delve into future projects is lacking.

## THE SEXUAL EXPERIENCE IN THE LIFE-WORLD AND ITS RELATION TO THE CONCEPT OF LIBIDO IN PSYCHOANALYSIS

By sexual experience in the life-world is meant experienced sexuality, including orgasm, as well as the sexual excitement preceding it. Abraham (2002) noted that the specific experience of orgasm has received little interest from psychoanalysts. One has neglected to study the subjective experience, and to the extent that the orgasm has been in focus, it has been dealt with from the vantage point of the organ – for example, the clitoris or the vagina. The manifestation of the sexual experience in the life-world is contrasted with, and to a certain extent even breaks with, the way that the life-world experience shows itself in its everydayness for us.[5] Let me now

[5] I want to refer to Stein's illumination of sexuality as an extraordinary phenomenon, inspired by, among others, Bataille's and Laplanche's ideas (Stein 1998a, 1998b, 2008).

discuss the characteristic traits of sexuality against the background of the above description of the everyday life-world experience. The body experience that represented the everyday body experience was the functional body, which could show itself both as ego-syntonic and ego-dystonic in relation to the intention and wishes of the person. We are now going to treat the body and body experience from another life-world aspect, namely, as the sexually desirable body. It is a body that is permeated by sexual desire and lust, a body that can be said to have a dominant position in relation to the person's I/self. And it is the sexual experience that makes up the ground for the construction of the psychoanalytic libido concept. I will discuss this in the form of the following four points: the bodily character of sexual experience, the intrinsic character of sexual experience, the now-character of sexual experience and sexual experience's gravitation towards the unbounded.[6]

### The bodily character of sexual experience

In line with Merleau-Ponty's thinking of the lived body as an incarnate subject, I would like to discuss the fundamental position of the bodily experience as a fusion between the 'I' and the body. This original experience of a fusion between the 'I' and the body, as we have seen, can break down in ill health or injury. In the everyday life-world experience, the body was described first of all as a peripheral and anonymous presence, but it was also said that it could become more thematized and objectified. When it comes to sexual experiences, first of all we have a bodily experience, where the body assumes a very thematic character and can be described as dominant with respect to the person's I/self. It concerns strong bodily sensations of, for example, one's skin, genitals, heartbeat, breathing, feelings of dizziness and weakness of one's knees. Although the body in the sexual experience becomes dominant, however, this does not prevent the

---

[6] The tracing out of these four mentioned characteristics was primarily based on interviews about people's experiences of sexual lust or desire and carried out by means of the so-called EPP-method (empirical phenomenological psychological method) (Karlsson 1993).

sexually excited person from having fantasies that are important in the constitution of the sexual experience. We can detect a dialectic relation between ongoing bodily experiences and fantasies/images that makes the sexual experience and excitement stronger.[7] What is interesting to note is that those fantasies and images, in principle, are also about bodily experiences and sensations. These fantasies have their roots in partial drives and in polymorphous-perverse sexuality, which were described in the previous chapter. In the pleasure preceding the sexual act, fantasies and images are about, for example, caressing, touching, listening to and smelling the other person.[8]

In sexuality, one is tied to the other through bodies striving towards fusion. There is a wish to erase boundaries and separation – such traits that constitute reality. There is something profoundly ungraspable in the sexual experience that is due, to a large extent, to its bodily character, and to the two points discussed below, namely, its now-character and the sexual experience's gravitation towards the unbounded. Merleau-Ponty (1962/1945: 157) draws our attention to the difficulty with which the sexual character can be grasped:

> There is an erotic 'comprehension' not of the order of understanding, since understanding subsumes an experience, once perceived, under some idea, while desire comprehends blindly by linking body to body.

---

[7] Abraham (2002: 336) stresses the importance of fantasies in orgasm: 'Whatever the case, while the receptiveness of the erogenous zones undoubtedly plays an essential role in triggering orgasm, fantasy plays a role in terms of erotic sensibility and libidinal energy, a role more important and determinant than that of the body. Like a container, it envelops the whole orgasmic spiral, whatever its point of departure, whatever the circumstances and conditions prior to orgasm.'

[8] Reeder (2000: 93) writes: 'Masturbation fantasies, erotic day dreams and ideas (not rarely totally private and kept secret) that sometimes are necessary in order to carry through an ordinary sexual intercourse often rest on structures of meaning from the "deeper" layers – and therefore carry the traits of polymorphous-perverse infantile sexuality. The fact that they are contradictory to the reigning order of hetero-genital ideal leads them easily to be treated as shameful and kept secret or disguised in order to appear as innocent features of the hetero-genital project.'

The break with everyday life-world experience is obvious. Under normal circumstances, in everyday life-world experience, the body is present anonymously on the periphery of experience, whereas the sexual experience is first and foremost a bodily experience. The body occupies the person, both when it comes to strengthening the feeling of the body and body parts, and concerning a feeling of boundlessness, where bodilyness and its materiality ceases, as, for instance, in the feeling of dizziness, feeling weak at the knees, fainting experiences. It is interesting to note that when pleasure and desire are strongest and at the moment of orgasm, then the experience becomes one of dissolution.

There are certain similarities between the everyday life-world experience in ill health and the sexual experience, namely, the thematic character of the body, but in other respects the differences are essential in nature. The thematic, objectified body in ill health and in injury is experienced as hindering or restricting, whereas the body in sexual experience is the driving force that frenetically impels the experience forward. We are reminded of Freud's impersonal id. Furthermore, we can see that the objectifying body in ill health or injury and the body in the sexual experience show themselves in opposite ways: in ill health/injury, we have a centripetal movement towards the body, while the sexual experience displays a centrifugal movement away from a bodily and material centre. But even in this centrifugal movement, it is still the body that is distinct. Another way of describing this difference is that in ill health/injury the body has a non-transcendent character, while the body in the sexual excitement/experience is, rather, hyper-transcendent.

Let us look at *the concept of libido and its relation to the bodily character of sexual experience.* The sexual experience has a very manifest bodily character, which is reflected in the libido concept. The body in this case, of course, is an erogenous body, a body that feels pleasure. Freud's sexual theory of development is a description of a development that advances from one part of the body to another: oral, anal, phallic-genital. But also, as Freud (1905b) pointed out in *Three essays*, the whole body and all its parts can assume an erogenous significance.

The characteristics of the drive structure – object, aim, source and pressure – all refer to bodily processes. Genetically speaking, the first *object* is the breast and the sucking of the breast is, for Freud, the prototype for all future sexual satisfactions. The *aim* denotes the way in which satisfaction is carried out. If we remain with the sucking of the breast, then the sucking itself is the aim of the drive. The *source* is that part of the body or limb that is currently affected by satisfaction; in our example it is the mouth or the labial zone. Finally we have the *pressure* – that is, the energy of the drive – which in Freud's exposition is least thematically connected to the body, but which I would maintain has its origin in bodily felt forces.

In the previous chapter I argued that the pressure of the drive is the most obvious constructing element in Freud's theory of the drives. Here we are concerned with a psychic energy that makes the plastic character of the drive, its free motion, understandable. This figure of thought of an energy, a flow, can also be experienced in the strongest sexual experiences, namely, in the dissolving, centrifugal movement away from the bodily and material centre. The pressure of the libido, as this idealization and radicalization of the experienced sexual centrifugal movement, will be dealt with later under the concept of libido and sexual experience's gravitation towards the unbounded.

### The intrinsic character of sexual experience

The everyday life-world experience is characterized by an instrumentality – actions that are carried out with the aim of achieving a specific goal. We took note of Heidegger's hermeneutic-existential structure of understanding, where objects, or, more accurately, equipment, are there for us to use in an activity, whose accomplishment is to satisfy wishes/desires/needs. Equipment offers possibilities for me in the world, and is part of a whole structure that points to an activity, which receives its significance in a subject's 'for-the-sake-of-which'. The piece of equipment as an object for my perception and actions is lived through in a non-thematic way. I do not stop at the equipment, but I am ahead of myself, perhaps in the realization of the goal of my activity. The sexual experience breaks with this structure, both concerning the non-thematic character of the object, which I have already discussed, as well as its instrumental character, the dimension that will be taken up now.

Firstly, I will say a few words about life-world experiences in ill health or injury which also break with the normal instrumental character of life-world experiences. In a way, this was already pointed out when I called attention to how the body was experienced as hindering and restricting to the person. We can talk here about how this experience is not instrumental, but shows itself in its negativity with respect to an experienced instrumentality in the life-world. The sexual experience is neither instrumental nor a part of any structure that is carried out for a special purpose.[9] Nor should sexual experience be described in terms of a negative relation to the instrumentality of the normal everyday life-world experience. The character of the sexual experience is best described as *intrinsic*. Sexuality is carried out for its own pleasure. It is an expression of pleasure. The sexual experience as an expression of pleasure is not motivated by a more fundamental forcing drive. The sexual activity is in itself pleasurable and its sole motivation is to satisfy lust. We can refer here to Schopenhauer's idea that the will, which can be said to be the counterpart of Freud's drive, cannot be based on any other principle or law, and in that sense it is groundless.[10]

[9] Freud can sometimes describe sexuality in its reproductive function for man – the sexual intercourse between man and woman – as aiming at the preservation of the species. This possible function, however, is not based on the sexual experience itself, whereas here the focus is on the sexual experience itself.

[10] Let us look at how Schopenhauer describes his idea about the will, which connotes something broader than it does in everyday language (Schopenhauer 1995/1818: 38–9; italics in the original): 'the character of my volition cannot be explained from the motives, which merely determine its manifestation at a given point in time: they are merely the occasion of my will's showing itself. But the will itself lies outside the jurisdiction of the law of motivation, which determines nothing but its appearing at each point in time... it is only

Let us now look at *the concept of libido and its relation to the intrinsic character of sexual experience*. By the intrinsic character of the sexual experience is implied that the inherent character of the sexual experience is satisfaction of pleasure. Sexual experience is an experience of pleasure and the sexual wish is to satisfy lust. The idealization of sexual experience is represented by the pleasure principle. Freud's pleasure principle aims at immediate satisfaction, without taking into account the principles of reality. However, it does presuppose an unaccomplished, frustrating reality in terms of an experienced deficiency. The pleasure principle implies a discharge of drive energy, and in its most extreme form it functions according to the Nirvana principle – that is, a discharge of drive energy to the zero point. The pleasure principle is to be given the status of superior principle or function, from the vantage point of which one can explain human actions.[11]

## The now-character of sexual experience

The instrumentality of the normal everyday life-world experience implies a future-oriented experience of time. I am already ahead of myself, perhaps mentally even on my way to fulfilling the goal of my activity. At the sight of the attractive bottle of wine in the store, in my mind I am already having the meal with which this wine is to be drunk. We have also seen that the sexual experience is a body-focused, thematic and intrinsic experience. In accordance with and

the *manifestation* of the will that is subordinate to the principle of sufficient reason, and not the will itself, which in this respect is to be called *groundless*.'

[11] Even if one cannot say that the pleasure principle emanates out of or is motivated by another, more fundamental, principle, one should nevertheless point out that the pleasure principle presupposes certain pre-sexual psychic achievements, apart from the experienced deficiency. That the pleasure principle is not the only, sovereign principle that governs the concretely existent human being has received recognition, for example, in Freud's (1920) discussion in *Beyond the pleasure principle*. I have argued that the first achievement of man is an affirmation of existence (see also chapter 7), which belongs to the sphere of consciousness/self-consciousness and precedes the constitution of the unconscious governed by the pleasure principle. However, when one enters the realm of man as a desiring creature, psychoanalysis appropriates this pleasure principle in order to explain human conduct.

as a consequence of these characteristics, the sexual experience possesses a now-character. It is an experience in the now, anchored in the now.

Sexual excitement has its own unique character of an urge and a pressure towards an accomplished satisfaction. In sexual excitement there is a kind of future orientation, but not of an instrumental kind. There is no other intention than to accomplish satisfaction so that the urge and pressure will cease. The sexual fantasies connected to the pleasure that precedes the sexual act are therefore often concerned with the dissolution of the time gap between the now and the imagined, desired sexual accomplishment. Persons that experience lust, fantasize, as far as their perceptions can go, that they touch, caress the desired object, and wish/imagine, for example, for the sexual intercourse to happen *now*, and that they could blink their eyes and be in bed with the person in question. It may appear to be a subtle difference, but nevertheless there is a crucial difference, between, on the one hand, the everyday, future-oriented mode of being, when I am already ahead of myself in fulfilling 'the-sake-of-which', and, on the other hand, the fantasized/imagined and urging anticipating of the pleasure experience to abolish the future dimension, in order to transform by magic the present situation. This difference may perhaps be summarized as a difference in the movement between the now and the future; in the instrumental attitude I wish I were now already in the future situation, whereas in the experience of sexual excitement, I wish that the possible future situation were already here, now. In a way, one can perhaps say that the now-focusing of the sexual experience abolishes the course of time itself (the duration of time).

The nature of sexual excitement is to 'demand' satisfaction now, and this demand can only be compromised given a counterforce, and not by the excitement itself assuming an attitude of waiting. The excitement in itself (on its own conditions) can only assume another form by being satisfied. The sexual excitement that precedes the accomplishment of the sexual experience brings about the accomplishment of the experience by abolishing itself. The excitement 'demands' its own abolition. It is an urging of its own abolition. The excitement consists, therefore, of a peculiar mixture of something enjoyable and something frustrating, something pleasurable and something that entails feelings of unpleasure.[12] I believe the reason for Freud's perplexity in the final chapter of *Beyond the pleasure principle* (1920), when he struggles to understand the nature of the sexual act, is due to this double character of sexual excitement.

Let us now look at *the concept of the libido and its relation to the now-character of sexual experience.* We saw that the sexual experience is anchored in the now. The nature of excitement is to demand satisfaction immediately. By means of an idealized principle of pleasure, we are able to disregard the connection of the now with a specific situation and merely postulate a demand for immediate satisfaction. This character is reflected in the constructed pleasure principle's adherence to the primary process, free mobile energy, which is not hindered by any binding or bounded energy. In the primary process we postulate free energy, but in the subject's concrete reality there is no such thing as completely free energy, but free energy is an ideal non-empirical state.

*Sexual experience's gravitation towards the unbounded*
The everyday life-world experience is comprised of a structure. Actions in this sphere of life are carried out and receive their justification, their raison d'être, in a practical conclusion. In this model, an action is understandable if there is a correspondence between the person's intention/goal and the required action that realizes the

---

[12] Stoller (1979: 4) pays attention to the double quality of sexual excitement in the following way: 'It [the excitement] is a present state that carries within itself a future expectation. But what pleasure is anticipated, what danger awaited; what risks may arise and what hopes of avoiding them are built into one's subliminal awareness? Does "sexual excitement" not refer to the period of anticipation before an act; and to the sensual build-up during an act; and to the genital sensations alone; and to non-genital sensations alone; and also to a total-body erotic involvement? To me, "excitement" implies anticipation in which one alternates with extreme rapidity between expectation of danger and just about equal expectation of avoidance of danger, and in some cases, such as in erotism, of replacing danger with pleasure'.

intention/goal. One can perhaps say that the activity or action is contained by the structure and overarching aim of the action. It is part of a meaningful structure. The activity is part of something and is to be understood from the vantage point of a whole. One can talk about actions that are carried out in an optimal way. One side of this phenomenon is represented by the instrumental character of activities of the everyday life, which I described earlier on. Here we highlight the rationality of everyday activities in a containing context. When it comes to the everyday experience in ill health, the person can experience it as meaningless, in that the activities do not allow themselves to be included in a bigger, containing context. Sexual experience is also unique in regard to this dimension. It is neither experienced as meaningless nor is it to be included in a normal everyday rationality. I would like to say that sexual experience possesses a character of transcending boundaries.

Sexual experience is not an experience of 'just enough', but is rather like an invitation to the unknown, into that which points beyond experienced and known limits. It is perhaps against that background that one can understand the desire for stronger and more potent sexual experiences that make certain people experiment with the conditions for making the sexual experience stronger, to the point where it leads to death. In this unbounded character of sexuality, there is a relation to imaginations and presentiments about death. It is not by accident that in many languages orgasm is called 'the little death'. And in literature we can read about scenes and events where death and sexuality/sexual actions are mistaken for each other.

We also tie this character of sexuality, to transcend boundaries, with a pull towards the unknown. Sexual experience offers a strong contrast to the anchoring of the everyday experience in the world. As was pointed out earlier on, there is in sexuality a striving towards a fusion between bodies, a wish to erase boundaries and separation – such traits as constitute reality. Expressions used to describe sexual excitement and orgasm are frequently of the kind that indicates an estrangement from the world/reality: one feels crazy, one is thrown out into space, and so on.[13] The pull towards the unknown also appears when many strong sexual experiences of pleasure are connected to fantasies about having sex with persons that one does not know very well or at all. There may be many reasons why relatively unfamiliar people appear as desired sexual objects, but one reason is probably the attraction that the unknown has for the sexual fantasizing.[14]

Let us now look at *the concept of libido and sexual experience's gravitation towards the unbounded.* In sexual experience there is a pull towards transcending boundaries, to the unknown, and sexual experience can be said to gravitate towards the unbounded. In the construction of the libido we can postulate a libidinal death drive. 'Death drive' here does not refer to Freud's concept, but rather to Laplanche's ideas about it being the most untamed and uncivilized part of the libido. This wild character of the death drive reminds us of Freud's (1932: 73) description of the id as 'a chaos, a cauldron full of seething excitations'.

In discussing Lacan's 'the Thing' (*la chose, das Ding*) and *jouissance,* the unbounded character of desire has been pointed out. It is something unknowable, comparable to Kant's 'thing-in-itself'.[15] One may recognize an extreme variant of this transgression of boundaries in certain psychotic states. In its idealized, extreme variant with a postulated non-containing movement out into the unbounded, we

---

[13] Alizade (1999) emphasizes that orgasm, in particular for females, cannot be held within specific limits when it comes to spatial, anatomic and temporal nature.

[14] Stoller (1979: 6) points to hostility as an important element in sexual excitement, in pathological perversions as well as 'normal' sexual excitement: 'The absence of hostility leads to sexual indifference and boredom'. Stoller provides the motivation for his use of the term 'hostility' rather than 'power' in this context by stating that hostility has 'a crisper connotation of harm and suffering' (ibid.).

[15] Lacan's 'the Thing' is a difficult concept to capture, referring to a phenomenon that is difficult to capture. It can be described as that which never allows itself to be represented, that which escapes every attempt at symbolic representation (cf. Lacan 2007/1959–60; Evans 1996; Reeder, Sjöholm and Zivkovic 2000; Wright 1992).

are on an abstract, cognitive level that we cannot intuitively grasp. To think of the absolutely unbounded is quite impossible. As a little thought experiment, we can try to grasp a modern theory of the universe as constantly and forever expanding at an increasingly higher speed. To try to grasp this fact is profoundly bewildering and even generates anxiety, as free energy in an insufficiently contained context equals anxiety.

## THE LIBIDO – THE CONSTRUCTION OF SEXUALITY

As I pointed out earlier, one can say that this analysis has been carried out in two steps. As a background to these steps, a description was given of the way in which the life-world manifests itself most often – that is, the normal life-world experiences – as well as our way of being in the world in ill health. The first step in the construction of the theoretical concept of libido consisted of describing the structure of *conscious* sexual experience. And in a second step, certain traits in sexual experience were idealized. I do not claim that my analysis of sexual experiences is exhausting. The aim has been to present and discuss the characteristics of the sexual experience, on the basis of which an idealization can be carried out in order to obtain the theoretical concept of libido within psychoanalysis. We have moved from the level of *conscious* experience to the level of (psychoanalytic) theoretical construction.

The idealization of sexual experience implies a kind of radicalization of the experience – that is, the traits in the experience are stretched to the extreme, even beyond that which it is possible to grasp intuitively and experience concretely. This second step entails a theoretical, but not 'lived through' state. Let us look at a concrete illustration. Consider, for example, the pleasure principle in its most radical form, namely, the discharge of libido to the zero point in accordance with the Nirvana principle. But the zero point is impossible to reach; it has to be conceived of as an asymptotic limit. The concept of libido is an intra-psychic concept and is a theoretical construction within the frame of the psychic apparatus. This psychic apparatus does not imply an existential situation where man is situated in a space with other subjects and the world, but here we are dealing with overlapping, objectifying processes and principles, in which content, and historical and intersubjective aspects are disregarded.[16]

The psychoanalytic construction of the libido can thus be described as not being bodily or emotionally experiential. It cannot be intuited; nor can it be experienced directly. The construction has the character of something alien within the subject. This alien and impersonal force within the subject corresponds to Freud's notion 'the id', whose character was discussed in the previous chapter.

The intelligibility that is obtained by grounding the psycho-analytic concept of libido in life-world experiences fulfils an epistemological function. The epistemological value is that the scientific construction – the psychoanalytic concept of the libido – can be understood by grasping its roots in life-world experiences and by explicating the means by which this concept can be constructed. The construction is an idealized concept and in this sense does not refer to a descriptive, phenomenal entity. Concrete sexual experiences have to do with specific persons at a certain time and place, situated in a specific context. In the theoretical construction, all these unique and actual circumstances vanish. Instead, we pay attention to certain important characteristics that pertain to psychoanalysis, namely, those presented above (the bodily character of sexual experiences, the intrinsic character of sexual experience, the now-character of sexual experience, sexual experience's gravitation towards the unbounded). These descriptive experiential features are extrapolated to the extreme in the theoretical construction. The constructed character of the libido concept can be said to be the most radical level of the unconscious, and something that has never been conscious, that has never been experienced, something that is indeed not possible to experience. In this sense, it can be

---

[16] Lagache (1993/1962: 237) points out that Freud's metapsychology is to be understood as a kind of theoretical construction that encapsulates psychic life in objective processes.

compared to Freud's primal repression (*Urverdrängung*), understood here as a structural component, constituting the condition for such experiences that subsequently may be subjected to repression proper (*eigentliche Verdrängung*).

Psychoanalysis uses this constructed concept of the libido in order to explain human conduct. Psychoanalysis is an explanatory science that goes beyond pure description, in order to explain human behaviour. Here, I believe we can discern a difference between the explanatory character of psychoanalysis and the (at least when it comes to the so-called static) character of descriptive phenomenology. The theoretical construction of the unconscious allows for a position outside of the ego from which subjective experiences can be explained.[17]

## SUMMARY

In this chapter I have tried to justify the concept of libido in psychoanalysis on the basis of sexual experiences in the life-world. The chapter began with a description of our everyday way of being in the world. Here we have a practical, future-oriented and instrumental way of being, where the body complies smoothly with my activities on the fringe of my experience. As a contrast to this 'normal' experience of the life-world, we have the experience of illness and being injured. From the vantage point of these different kinds of life-world experiences, the unique structure of the sexual life-world experience is described by means of the following four characteristics: the bodily character of sexual experience, the intrinsic character of sexual experience, the now-character of sexual experience, and sexual experience's gravitation towards the unbounded.

---

[17] I also believe that it is by understanding, in one sense, the ego-alien character of sexuality that one can comprehend the fact, that at first sight is so surprising, namely, that prominent phenomenologists, who have carried out sophisticated analyses of many and important subjective experiences – for example, perceptual experiences, body experiences, time experiences, cognitive experiences – to a very small degree have focused their searchlight on such a central phenomenon for man as sexuality.

The sexual life-world experience is not synonymous with the psychoanalytic libido or sexual drive. In this chapter, the idea is presented that the libido/sexual drive constitutes a radicalization of the four mentioned characteristics in experienced sexuality. Thus, the psychoanalytic libido/sexual drive is not an experiential entity, but a theoretical construction, generated on the basis of idealizations of lived sexuality.

# 7  Beyond the pleasure principle: the affirmation of existence

Freud's essay *Beyond the pleasure principle* (1920) has gone down in history as one of the most important works in psychoanalysis, since his idea of a death drive is presented there for the first time. I have already touched on the concept of the death drive in preceding chapters, and, in accordance with Laplanche's original interpretation, paid attention to the death drive as the most untamed and uncivilized in the libido – as the bottom layer of the libido.

My intention in this chapter is not to go on discussing the death drive as a part of the libido; here, rather, I would like to enlighten another interpretation that Freud's essay awakens. This interpretation has to do with pre-sexual conditions of the unconscious, as discussed in chapter 4. I thus want to underline this thought by means of Freud's ideas presented in *Beyond the pleasure principle*. I mentioned several psychoanalysts in chapter 4, whose ideas imply that the Freudian unconscious, ruled by the pleasure principle, presupposes another kind of psychical process.

Freud's concept of the death drive has given rise to much controversy and to many different interpretations. It is in fact already possible to discern two diametrically opposite meanings of this concept in his essay. I will in this chapter argue that both these meanings are relevant in describing psychical life, although only one of them actually qualifies as the concept 'death drive'.

*Beyond the pleasure principle* was written in order to try to understand some everyday as well as clinical phenomena, which could not be explained by the so-called pleasure principle. Freud postulated something beyond the pleasure principle (a more adequate expression would have been 'prior to' the pleasure principle), which initially seemed to have to do with a binding energy. I will preserve

this idea and attempt to develop it within the context of a phenomenological analysis of time, which deviates from Freud's attempt to
ground the death drive in biology. The temporalization of the subject involves a very basic affirmation of existence, in that the subject experiences something constant, something that can be said to
possess the quality of a gestalt. I propose that that which is beyond
the pleasure principle – this binding of energy – should be understood as the opposite of the idea of a primordial death drive striving
towards the inorganic, towards death. Instead, as I have said, we are
concerned here with an affirmation of existence. This represents the
first discernible meaning of the death drive in Freud's essay, and it
connects especially to his ideas about the compulsion to repeat and
binding of energy. The second meaning that can be discerned in the
essay, and for which the name 'death drive' seems to be applicable,
concerns the discharge of energy.

## ON FREUD'S *BEYOND THE PLEASURE PRINCIPLE*

Freud presented his final dualistic theory of drives, one of which
was the death drive, in his essay *Beyond the pleasure principle*. This
work was written against the background of certain clinical as well
as everyday phenomena which did not fit in with Freud's conceptualization of the psychical or, as he also called it, the mental apparatus.
Before 1920, Freud had the idea that the mental apparatus was guided
entirely by the so-called 'pleasure principle' – that is, unpleasure corresponds to an increase in the quantity of excitation, and pleasure
to a diminution in the quantity of excitation in the psyche (Freud
1920: 8). As an indication of what was to come, he pointed out that
it had not been possible to justify this description of the psyche in
any psychological or philosophical theory. He found, however, some
support in Gustav Fechner's (1801–87) psychophysical works, which
indicated that the pleasure principle follows from the principle of
constancy. The principle of constancy has been ambiguously defined
as the psychical apparatus' attempt to keep the quantity of excitation as low as possible, or, at least, as constant as possible (Laplanche

and Pontalis 1985). Nevertheless, Freud found three cases which did not fit in with the idea of the pleasure principle.

Freud first referred to traumatic neuroses – that is, neurotic symptoms caused by frightening, sudden external events, which have not usually incurred any simultaneous physical wound or injury. Traumatic events are events where the sum of excitation surpasses that which the mental apparatus is able to bind. On such occasions, the mental apparatus has not been sufficiently prepared for an increase of stimuli – in other words, a sufficient readiness for anxiety preparation is lacking. Freud had seen that people who suffered from traumatic neurosis repeatedly dreamt about the situation in which the injury occurred. These dreams were of such a kind that no wish fulfilment could be traced from them, and thereby they would seem to contradict his theory that the essence of the dream is a hallucinatory wish fulfilment. Freud was influenced by these empirical experiences and came to understand this type of anxiety dream as a repetition of traumatic events, whose function was to bind energy retrospectively, thereby allowing for a certain control over the event (stimuli).

Until a certain amount of energy is bound, the pleasure principle cannot come into effect. Freud wrote that these kinds of anxiety dreams 'afford us a view of a function [that is, binding of energy] of the mental apparatus which, though it does not contradict the pleasure principle, is nevertheless independent of it and seems to be more primitive than the purpose of gaining pleasure and avoiding unpleasure' (Freud 1920: 32). This original striving – that which is beyond the pleasure principle – can thus be said to precede and be the condition for the pleasure principle, and represents the only exception to the conceptualization of dreams as wish fulfilments.

Another example of this compulsion to repeat that could not be understood from the vantage point of the pleasure principle is the 'fort-da' example, when Freud observed his grandchild playing with a wooden reel with a string tied round it, which the little boy threw out of sight, at the same time uttering 'o-o-o-o' (that is, gone), in order to pull back the reel into his view and joyfully exclaim 'da' (there). The point of this example is that the boy symbolized the *mother's disappearance* by letting the reel disappear. This was done repeatedly, despite its unpleasure.

A third example, which would call into question the universality of the pleasure principle, concerns the compulsion to repeat as found within the psychoanalytic treatment. Usually, the compulsion to repeat in psychoanalytic treatment is a good example of something that brings displeasure for the ego but pleasure to another system (repressed libido). This kind of compulsion to repeat can therefore still be understood from the vantage point of the pleasure principle. However, Freud presented cases where the compulsion to repeat did not refer to repressed pleasurable impulses, but to earlier experiences that had never been pleasurable, such as the humiliating and painful destruction of the Oedipus complex.

Freud was well aware that these examples of the compulsion to repeat could be overdetermined and thus, to a certain extent, could be explained by the pleasure principle. However, he claimed that the compulsion to repeat described in these examples proved that the pleasure principle could not be sovereign in the psyche: 'Enough is left unexplained to justify the hypothesis of a compulsion to repeat – something that seems more primitive, more elementary, more instinctual than the pleasure principle which it over-rides' (Freud 1920: 23).

So far, Freud's text has mainly offered clinical and everyday observations, which made him question the sovereign status of the pleasure principle in the mental apparatus. I believe two issues can be discerned. One issue deals with the limited scope of the pleasure principle. Something other than the pleasure principle is needed, something that is beyond it, or, better still, *prior* to it. The second issue that Freud touched on has to do with the search for a ground for the mental apparatus and the pleasure principle, a ground which he found to be missing in psychology and philosophy.

Let us see how Freud approached the subject of this something 'beyond the pleasure principle', how it became more clearly defined.

The explication of the relationship between the compulsion to repeat and the drives and their excitations brought Freud to ask: 'how is the predicate of being "instinctual" related to the compulsion to repeat?' His answer is worth quoting in extenso (Freud 1920: 36; italics in the original):

> At this point, we cannot escape a suspicion that we may have come upon a track of a universal attribute of instincts and perhaps of organic life in general which has not hitherto been clearly recognized or at least not explicitly stressed. *It seems, then, that an instinct is an urge inherent in organic life to restore an earlier state of things* which the living entity has been obliged to abandon under the pressure of external disturbing forces; that is, it is a kind of organic elasticity, or, to put it another way, the expression of the inertia inherent in organic life.

Thus, Freud asserts that not only do the drives strive for change and development, but also that they have a conservative nature, which, furthermore, supposedly applies to organic life in general. A leap in the text can be noticed when Freud places the compulsion to repeat on an equal footing, with 'an urge ... to restore an earlier state of things'. One can say that the text here undergoes an important divergence from Freud's original line of thought (cf. Lind 1991).

This 'urge ... to restore an earlier state of things' subsequently becomes described as 'the death drives', a group of drives which aim towards death. These drives can be contrasted with the life drives, also called Eros, which strive for union and make coalescence possible. Without having the opportunity to describe the final version of Freud's theory of drives in any detail, let me nevertheless point out that one can discern in the text – which seems to have the character of a paper in process – that he did not explicate the notion of death drives (*Todestrieben*), until a very laborious work had been carried out, entailing, among other things, an attempt to fit the new pair of drives together with his old sexual versus ego-drives. Roughly speaking, one can initially find that life drives correspond to sexual drives and those drives which aim towards death correspond to ego-drives. The death drives (*Todestrieben*) are, on one occasion, called 'ego or death instincts' (Freud 1920: 44; *Ich[Todes-]trieben*).

Freud wanted to find analogies with biology, and perhaps would have liked ultimately to be able to ground the death drives in biology. He was able to summarize his presentation of different biological theories of death with the following words (not without a sigh of relief, it seems): 'Thus, our expectation that biology would flatly contradict the recognition of death instincts has not been fulfilled' (Freud 1920: 49).

This wish to ground the character of the drives in biological processes implies, as far as I can understand, another metapsychological standpoint (other than his previous explication of the drives) as lying on the frontier between the mental and the physical (cf. Freud 1905b: 168, 1911: 74, 1915a: 121–2).

As stated above, Freud worked hard to comprehend the death drives, which could only be seen in coalescence with life drives, primarily in the form of sadism. Again, Freud put his faith in biology, where he seemed to find support for how original death drives were involved in life processes, which he claimed suggested the existence of the Nirvana principle and thereby death drives.[1] However, the topic was difficult and Freud was forced to make a biological-phylogenetic Odyssey via elements of mythology – which he himself recoiled from – in order to trace the origin of reproduction and the sexual drives. Even if the sexual drives were in focus in this context, the overriding aim was nevertheless to save the death drives: 'If, therefore, we are not to abandon the hypothesis of death instincts, we must suppose them to be associated from the very first with life instincts' (Freud 1920: 57).

---

[1] Freud's (1920: 55–6) explication of the Nirvana principle – the only time that expression is used in *Beyond the pleasure principle* – lacks cogency, since the description of it entails meanings that are more appropriate in describing the constancy principle: 'The dominating tendency of mental life, and perhaps of nervous life in general, is the effort to reduce, to keep constant or to remove internal tension due to stimuli (the "Nirvana principle", to borrow a term from Barbara Low) – a tendency which finds expression in the pleasure principle; and our recognition of that fact is one of our strongest reasons for believing in the existence of death instincts.'

What is most interesting for my purpose here is the fact that the death drives move further away from their original meaning – that is, the binding of energy. The original meaning of the death drives – the binding of energy/drive impulses – fades into the background in favour of a discourse which deals with psychical content, such as sexuality, aggression.

The final pages of his essay are very difficult and complex, due to Freud's introduction of some new, sketchy ideas. An important distinction that is made is the one between function and tendency. The explication of the pleasure principle is formulated in terms of it being 'a tendency operating in the service of a function whose business it is to free the mental apparatus entirely from excitation or to keep the amount of excitation in it constant or to keep it as low as possible' (Freud 1920: 62). We can recognize this idea from the initial section of the essay concerning the task of the death drives to bind energy, which is the precondition for the sovereignty of the pleasure principle. However, taken as a whole, one is forced to realize that *Beyond the pleasure principle* suffers from internal contradictions. The death drive seems to be involved both in the binding of drive impulses and in the ensuing discharge of energy that is exemplified with 'the greatest pleasure attainable by us, that of the sexual act' (ibid.).

Finally, Freud indicated the possibility of giving the concept of pleasure a more qualitative meaning, and tried to distinguish experiences of pleasure/unpleasure on the basis of primary and secondary processes. This would constitute a possible starting point for further investigations, according to Freud.

No doubt, the relationship between the pleasure principle and Eros and the death drives puzzled Freud a great deal – not only in *Beyond the pleasure principle* – and it remained an unresolved question throughout his life. In 'An outline of psycho-analysis', he wrote (Freud 1938a: 198; italics in the original):

> it remains a question of the highest theoretical importance,
> and one that has not yet been answered, when and how it is
> ever possible for the pleasure principle to be overcome. The

consideration that the pleasure principle demands a reduction, at bottom the tensions of instinctual needs (that is, *Nirvana*), leads to the still un-assessed relations between the pleasure principle and the two primal forces, Eros and the death instinct.

I have presented *Beyond the pleasure principle* in order to discuss some ideas in Freud's theory of the death drives. I will now present a brief summary of that which has been said up to now and point towards further questions I wish to discuss.

We have been able to see how Freud got an idea about the existence of something beyond the pleasure principle from certain clinical and everyday observations. It concerned different forms of compulsions to repeat, whose significance could not be explained by the pleasure principle. This something 'beyond the pleasure principle' would be temporally and logically the condition for the dominance of the pleasure principle. That which is beyond the pleasure principle was initially described as binding energy/drive impulses. After further consideration, this binding of energy was depicted as the death drives. I would maintain that the binding of energy is not appropriately described in terms of a death drive, whose aim is to extinguish life. On the contrary, I will suggest that the binding of energy is a kind of *affirmation* of existence – an idea that I will try to support by a brief consideration of the character of death.

Freud then incorporated this dimension of binding energy into a discussion about a dualistic theory of drives. He changed his earlier theory of drives on the basis of potential support from biology. Here, I think it is relevant to pose a metascientific question. Freud was trying to ground his theory of death drives on a phylogenetic and biological basis. Even if the biology of his time could only function, at best, as a ground for analogies and support, he nevertheless embraced an idea that gave biology a foundational metascientific function. I would like to raise the question of whether another approach could possibly open up other interesting dimensions. I would like to replace biology with a phenomenological approach, which pays attention to the importance of time. Such an approach, with a focus on time, could be interesting, not least because Freud himself was almost on the track of the importance of time.

The significance of the death drive shifted from being about binding energy, in line with the constancy principle, to being about a discharge of energy, in line with the Nirvana principle, exemplified, first of all, by the phenomenon of sadism. The Nirvana principle refers to the tendency of the mental apparatus to reduce the quantity of excitation to zero, or to as low a level as possible. As opposed to the constancy principle, there is no attempt to maintain homeostasis. The concept of the death drive begins to take on a new form by putting it on the same 'level' as the different drives in Freud's earlier theories of drives. The transcendent dimension – that which is beyond or that which is the condition for ... – which Freud looked for in the beginning, fades into the background; or perhaps it would be more appropriate to say that the death drives emerge in two versions. Death drives pertain not only to binding energy, but also to the release of bound energy – that is, when the dominance of the pleasure principle is established. I will briefly discuss the second discernible meaning of death drives – that is, discharge of energy. My conclusion will be that the concept 'death drives' should be limited to discharge of energy. In this context, one could discuss a number of intricate questions, such as the changed role and status that the pleasure principle has undergone. However, I will only touch on this complex of problems.

The following discussion about the death drives will be focused on its original function of binding energy, and then I will apply a phenomenological analysis of time to Freud's idea that there must be something beyond the pleasure principle, whose task is to bind energy. To introduce this 'transcendental dimension of time' implies that one goes beyond the metapsychological framework, if by metapsychology is meant a kind of theoretical construction that isolates the psychical life in terms of objective processes (cf. Lagache 1993/1962: 237).

DISCUSSION ABOUT DEATH DRIVES – BINDING OF
ENERGY – TEMPORALIZATION

In *Beyond the pleasure principle*, one can find several descriptions, although not always concordant, of the temporal dimensions of the death drives; partly as something repeating and partly as something that strives to go back to an earlier state. Even more interestingly, one can discern in Freud's thinking an idea about the importance of time in order to understand the mental apparatus. Freud mentioned that feelings of unpleasure and pleasure depend on an increase or decrease of energy within a given unit of time. Against the background of Kant's idea of time as an a priori form of intuition in consciousness, Freud allowed time to be the distinguishing factor between unconscious primary processes and the secondary processes of consciousness, where only secondary processes can apprehend time (Freud 1920: 28). My analysis of time will not be based on a Kantian idea of time, but I will take my vantage point from a phenomenological analysis of time, which is based on the subject's intentionality. Phenomenologists consider time to be one of the most fundamental constitutive dimensions in human life, and it can therefore be imagined to play a central role when it comes to the task of grounding the mental apparatus. Phenomenological analyses of time therefore represent an alternative to Freud's more naturalistic attempt to ground the mental apparatus in biology.

'Time' in the following is not that time which we can specify in terms of clock time, but rather a more fundamental and original experience of time, which is the condition for other, derived and more 'objectified' comprehensions of time, such as clock time. Merleau-Ponty (1962/1945) discussed different possible relations between time and the subject: he rejected the two mutually opposed relations – the subject is in time and time is in the subject. For Merleau-Ponty, the relationship between the subject and time was that they are both structurally identical. Time, like the subject, throws itself out of itself, transcends itself and goes beyond itself. I think one can express it in the sense that the subject, seen in its deepest sense, is a *temporalization*.

The subject and time are both open to past and future, and this openness presupposes a certain synthesizing capacity. Husserl (1964/1905) spelt this out in his explication of 'inner time consciousness'. I will exemplify this with an auditory experience. When I listen to a tone, I hear not only an isolated point or part of the tone, but a tone which endures. The capacity to hear a tone presupposes that my acts synthesize in order for an enduring object (the tone) to be apprehended. We do not only experience that which is the immediate now-phase of the tone, but also that which has just been and that which is about to come. If our experiencing would be shut-in in the now-phase, we would not be able to experience any constancy; we would not be able to hear a melody or a tone that endures for a certain period of time. Being conscious of the tone presupposes self-consciousness in the form of a synthesizing of the subjective acts, as we saw in chapter 4.

I will avoid being too technical in my presentation, but Husserl differentiates between the immediate experience of the now-phase in terms of a *primal impression*, to which belongs partly a consciousness of that which has just been (for example, a previous sequence of an enduring tone 'C' or a previous tone, such as 'D'), which Husserl calls *retention*, and partly a consciousness of that which is about to come, the so-called *protention*. Protention is a rudimentary expectation of that which is about to come, although it does not, of course, need to be explicit and determined; for the most part, it is a lived, implicit and rough expectation of that which is about to come. The inner time-consciousness, the temporalization of the subject, thus contains this fundamental structure: primal impression – retention – protention. In the primal impression is enclosed that-which-has-just-been (retention) and that-which-is-about-to-come (protention); they are all elements in an ecstatic unity. It is important not to understand these elements in each act's ecstatic unity as parts of a process; retention does not come before the primal impression, and protention does not come afterwards, but they are all differentiated elements in a unity. But what the ecstatic unity of the act succeeds in constituting is an object that can be described in terms of a process. Retention retains something that has just been, and protention announces an expectation of what is about to come.

What is important for my purpose is to show how the experience of the existence of anything depends on temporal synthesizing. All experience of existence presupposes endurance – that is, a flow of acts of consciousness that synthesize, that harmonize with one another. That which I just heard is harmonious with that which is now. It is important to realize that existence is not necessarily about the outer world, but the concept also entails an experience of an inner constancy, endurance and gestalt. I will suggest that to bind energy, to experience, to incorporate something in the mental apparatus can be said to presuppose this kind of temporalization. The binding together of, or the synthesis between, different acts of consciousness corresponds – on the object side – to a uniting of that which I would like to call the present now and that-which-has-just-been (retention), and a more or less determined idea about that-which-is-about-to-come (protention). This uniting means, in a certain sense, a binding together of presence and absence.

The synthesis of time, psychologically speaking, can be anything from the earliest experiences of the child to 'higher', more developed narratives. I am able to recall events from the past, which have been incorporated into my life. By means of memory, I can represent the sequence of events; I can enter into the event and follow different tracks, stop and dwell on different moments. This is in sharp contrast to traumatic events, where time is frozen and the storytelling has ceased. The compulsion to repeat, as Freud discovered, may perhaps be an attempt to work through and incorporate traumatic events in one's life. It is not uncommon nowadays to hear psychoanalysts claim that the incorporation of traumatic events in a narrative is an essential moment in the psychoanalytic treatment (Künstlicher 1994; Salonen 1992; Schafer 1993; Spence 1982a).

What all these phenomena (the binding of energy, temporalization, compulsion to repeat, the incorporation of traumatic events

into one's life) point to is the experience of existence. From a psychoanalytic point of view, I think it is important to bring out *the
affirmation of existence* (see chapter 4). We know from Freud's
*Interpretation of dreams* (1900) that wishes must be preceded by
and based on a real bodily-perceptual experience. A wish does not
occur in a vacuum, but only against the background of states of satisfaction which have actually taken place, to which one now wants
to return. The experience of existence thus precedes the wish fulfilment, which in the psychoanalytic language is accomplished in
terms of the pleasure principle's discharge of energy. Perhaps one
can say that this indicates that the experience of existence is the
subject's first 'achievement', before it can become desiring and wishing. This is a train of thought that I will try to develop against the
background of death. Looking at death, which is the opposite of the
experience of existence, may further support the idea that binding
energy or, in a more phenomenological language, temporalization,
can be understood as an original affirmation of existence.

Earlier on, I talked about the ecstatic unity in the form of primal impression, retention (that-which-has-just-been) and protention (that-which-is-about-to-come). Even if retention and protention
are enclosed in the primal impression, they correlate to something
which, in a certain sense, is absent. Temporalization is a binding
of something present and something absent. Given that both retention and protention correlate to something that is in a certain sense
absent, these correlates are nevertheless absent in very different
ways. Retention is that which has just been, whereas protention
entails a future horizon, which points to a final Absence. Thus protention manifests itself as a present absence, which simultaneously
bears within itself the possibility of a radically different absence –
the final Absence, death, whose essence is termination of the subject's temporalization.

Temporalization and the binding of energy, whatever this phenomenon is to be called, seem to be the absolute opposite of death.
If death is to be understood as an ultimate Absence, it should be

understood as the breach of existence, whose meaning in a way eludes all understanding. The fact that death eludes all understanding and is basically incomprehensible does not mean, of course, that it is meaningless or would lack significance. On the contrary, death in its inscrutable, existential termination has been characterized as the source of human creation (Bauman 1992), as well as giving the possibility of an authentic living (Heidegger 1980/1927). Here, it would be interesting to point out the fact that, although Freud postulated death drives, he simultaneously claimed that it was impossible to possess any knowledge about death: 'It is indeed impossible to imagine our own death; and whenever we attempt to do so we can perceive that we are in fact still present as spectators' (Freud 1915d: 289). Freud (1926) understood death anxiety in terms of castration anxiety.

Even though the meaning of death is inscrutable and incomprehensible, and the imagination of one's own death is impossible, death nevertheless manifests itself for us in one way or another. One can say that when we most often say that 'we are all going to die', death is given in a very easygoing and casual way. In these cases, it is a relatively empty signifying or intending of death. But death can show itself in a more profound way – a way, perhaps, which does not make it more determinable, but yet, I would like to claim somehow, more genuinely experienced. Death as final Absence and given as Nothingness is meant (signified) in anxiety. In order to clarify this, we may refer to Heidegger. Death shows itself most impressively in anxiety, according to Heidegger (1980/1927: 295):

> Dasein does not, proximally and for the most part, have any
> explicit or even any theoretical knowledge of the fact that it has
> been delivered over to its death, and that death thus belongs
> to Being-in-the-world. Thrownness into death reveals itself to
> Dasein in a more primordial and impressive manner in the state-
> of-mind which we have called 'anxiety'.

For Heidegger, this kind of ontological anxiety is an anxiety with no specific object. This description of anxiety resembles Freud's first theory of anxiety, concerning an unbound energy, namely, libidinal impulses that do not find an object to attach themselves to. The similarity can be said to be structural, but with completely different significations. Freud's anxiety is a psychological experience of an especially early kind. Heidegger's concept of anxiety is ontological and pertains to a self-reflective being, capable of making decisions. The ontological anxiety makes authenticity and responsibility possible, according to Heidegger.

One can consider the binding of energy as a counter-move in the confrontation with Nothingness, and a counterbalance to and suspension of this early anxiety. The counter-move consists of letting the subject's intending attach itself to an object, which soothes by providing the subject with an affirmation of the experience of existence. If my suggestion is correct, it is unfortunate to use the concept 'death drives' to describe the binding of energy, since the binding of energy seen in this way can be regarded as the subject's way of 'fighting back' Nothingness (death). For this reason it would be more adequate to use another term than death drives for the 'achievement' that I have described in terms of an affirmation of existence.

If the experience of existence is the subject's original achievement, the thought of an original, real striving towards death in the mental apparatus is unfounded. Death is certainly always a possibility, even a certain possibility, as Heidegger points out. Death is a certain possibility to which I, nevertheless, would *not* like to ascribe the status of a real, original human striving. Freud (1920: 45) himself was not unfamiliar with the idea that a primordial death drive serves to soothe and maintain an illusion: 'It may be, however, that this belief in the internal necessity of dying is only another of those illusions which we have created "um die Schwere des Daseins zu ertragen"' (the German-phrased ending is a quote from Schiller and translates as 'to bear the burden of existence').

The experience of existence must be the subject's first, original striving, and that which is 'beyond' the pleasure principle. Whatever name should be given to this striving can always be discussed. Here,

I want to remind the reader that in connection with the discussion about the 'affirmation of existence' in chapter 4, I stressed that the joy of life that the experience of existence can fill us with should be differentiated from the pleasure that has to do with the functioning of the pleasure principle (immediate discharge of energy), from both a psychoanalytic-economic and a phenomenological standpoint.

I mentioned earlier that I think one can discern two versions of the death drive in *Beyond the pleasure principle*. So far I have concentrated on the one that has to do with the binding of energy, which is the side in psychical life that deals with affirming existence. The other version of the death drive would then be about the other side of the psyche, and here I think that the notion 'death drive' is applicable, as long as one does not take it in a biological, organic sense, but rather in a metaphorical sense, as it has been described earlier. Here we are concerned with the opposite of binding, namely, discharging. This is a movement towards the dissolution, towards a zero point in accordance with the Nirvana principle. Furthermore, concerning the synthesis of time, I would like to emphasize the dissolution of the synthesizing, where the integration of temporal ecstasies breaks down further and further. However, the discharge of the libido never reaches zero. The zero point is an asymptotic border and temporalization never completely ceases within the framework of the biological, organic life. Binding energy and the synthesis of time are not either/or phenomena, but relative concepts designating more or less (cf. Holt 1989: 106).

FURTHER REFLECTIONS ON THE RELATIONSHIP
BETWEEN CONSCIOUSNESS AND THE UNCONSCIOUS
In chapter 4, when I discussed the conceptualization of the psychical in psychoanalysis, we took note of these two opposing tendencies in psychical life: on the one hand, binding of energy/synthesis of time/affirmation of existence, and on the other hand, discharge of energy/dissolution of the synthesis of time/the libido. I argued that the unconscious can only arise given certain pre-sexual conditions

under which a bodily ego develops continuity, coherence and whole-ness. This is the level in psychical (conscious) life that has to func-tion in a sufficient, adequate way in order for sexuality not to be too traumatizing (cf. Anzieu 1989: 39, 104; Winnicott 1965/1962: 57). However, at this point I would like to problematize and modulate the discussion, and avoid simplifying too much the relationship between consciousness/the ego and the unconscious/sexuality.

From the point of view of Winnicott's ideas about ego-needs and id-needs, it may be of interest to discuss the dialectical relation-ship that governs the ego and sexuality. Winnicott (1965/1960b: 141) writes:

> In the area that I am examining the instincts are not yet clearly defined as internal to the infant. The instincts can be as much external as can a clap of thunder or hit. The infant's ego is building up strength and in consequence is getting towards a state in which id-demands will be felt as part of the self, and not as environmental. When this development occurs, then id-satisfaction becomes a very important strengthener of the ego, or of the True Self; but id-excitements can be traumatic when the ego is not able to include them, and not yet able to contain the risks involved and the frustrations experienced up to the point when id-satisfaction becomes a fact.

Winnicott's way of formulating the relationship between ego-needs and id-needs has great similarities with the way that I have discussed the relationship between the sphere of consciousness/self-conscious-ness and the unconscious. The interesting thing is that the id/id-excitement/sexuality/pleasure principle can constitute a threat and also offer support for the ego. It becomes a threat if the ego does not possess the required containing capability; however, if the ego pos-sesses a sufficient containing capability, it can be strengthened.

Let me apply this idea to the conceptual apparatus that I have used: the dissolving character of sexuality/the pleasure prin-ciple risks acquiring psychotic qualities if the ego is not sufficiently contained. The first human achievement, tied to identity/individuality/the ego, is an affirmation of existence, which I argued is beyond (or rather prior to) the pleasure principle. Sexuality and the pleasure principle, under certain circumstances, can acquire an annihilating character (as in psychotic states). But sexuality not only contains a risk of annihilation, but also a possibility of strengthening the experience of existence.

This circumstance can only be made intelligible if we avoid closing existence into a bipolar system, where a state either exists or does not exist. As I have pointed out, the affirmation of existence is not an either/or phenomenon, but a more-or-less phenomenon. Not least, the psychoanalytic experience testifies that existence can be experienced with different intensity. And the dissolving character of sexuality can thus offer a deepened and intensified affirmation of existence. Thus, I think that once again we have taken part of the transforming power of affirmation.

SUMMARY

The point of departure of this chapter is Freud's essay *Beyond the pleasure principle*, in which he struggles with everyday and clinical experiences that do not lend themselves to being understood in accordance with the pleasure principle. Freud postulated something beyond the pleasure principle that eventually came to be named 'death drives'. Freud's death drives later on gave rise to different interpretations and much controversy. I argue that in Freud's essay one can discern two opposing meanings of the death drives, and that both these meanings are relevant in describing psychic life, but that only one of the meanings qualifies for the name 'death drives'.

*Beyond the pleasure principle* was written in order to understand everyday and clinical phenomena that Freud did not succeed in making intelligible from the vantage point of the pleasure principle. That which puzzled Freud a great deal was that these phenomena were repeated, in spite of the fact that they did not offer pleasure to any of the person's different systems. Freud postulated something beyond the pleasure principle, which initially seemed to have to do with binding of energy. This is the idea that I preserve and discuss against the background of phenomenological reflections on time. This binding of energy, or the subject's temporalization, makes an experience of existence possible. My suggestion is that that which is beyond the pleasure principle, this binding of energy, is to be understood as the opposite of the idea of an original death drive that strives towards death. On the contrary, that which is beyond the pleasure principle reflects a striving towards existence, which can be said to correspond to Freud's first and, in the essay, initial meaning of death drive. The second meaning qualifies for the name 'death drive' given that death drive here is understood in accordance with Laplanche's interpretation, as a part of the libido. Here death drive has to do with a discharge of energy or, in different terminology, dissolution of time.

The chapter ends with the threads from chapter 4 being picked up again, and elaborates on the relationship between the pre-sexual conditions for the unconscious and sexuality/the libido, which is the core of the unconscious.

# 8　The question of truth claims in psychoanalysis

In this book I have conceived of psychoanalysis as a science and not merely as a method of treatment. To conceive of psychoanalysis as a science implies that the psychoanalytic project is about searching for truth. The psychoanalytic project of acquiring knowledge of oneself is the same as knowing the truth of oneself. It may appear a pretentious claim, but one should not understand it as if psychoanalysis has a monopoly of what truth about man and human existence is. Instead, psychoanalysis is one of several possible approaches in investigating man and human existential conditions. The unique and special task of psychoanalysis is to bring about knowledge of the unconscious, as well as obscure levels of consciousness, as I have stressed earlier on, in particular in chapter 4. In this chapter, my aim, first of all, is to discuss the psychoanalytic concept of truth and truth claims with respect to the unconscious.

The scientific status of psychoanalysis continues to be a controversial issue in an ever-present debate, and the disagreements between psychoanalysts are significant. One of the reasons that psychoanalysis as a science struggles with difficult epistemological problems is that its subject matter – the unconscious – is constituted in terms of negativity. What other science investigates something that is defined by the prefix un-?[1] The fact that our subject matter presents itself as extraordinarily complex and difficult, does not, of course, render the need for clarification less urgent and compelling.

I will address the discussion about the concept of truth in psychoanalysis by taking my vantage point, in particular, from the

---

[1] The only similar discipline, in this sense, may be 'negative theology', which claims that an understanding of God can only be reached by stating what God is *not*.

concepts 'construction' and 'reconstruction', as well as 'historical truth' and 'narrative truth'. They are important concepts, but ones which, unfortunately, have been treated in a confusing way in the psychoanalytic literature (cf. Wetzler 1985).

This chapter is divided into two parts. Part 1 consists of a historical background concerning the question of truth claims in psychoanalysis. I begin by discussing Freud's ideas in terms of construction, reconstruction and historical truth. Thereafter I concentrate on what can be called 'the narrative tradition' in psychoanalysis, which presents itself as a clear alternative to Freud's point of view. Although I consider that the narrative tradition has contributed to a greater epistemological awareness in psychoanalysis, its ultimate view of the psychoanalytic project is, in my eyes, unsatisfactory. I disagree with this tradition's polarization between reconstruction versus construction, as well as its treatment of historical and narrative truth. A third voice in my historical account is Bion, who, at least implicitly, seems to hold a view that synthesizes construction and reconstruction. To the extent that one can apply historical and narrative truth to Bion's ideas, they do not seem to contradict each other. I finish part 1 by presenting a riddle that is to be solved in part 2 of this chapter. This riddle is as follows: the psychoanalytic interpretation is based on the unconscious as a theoretical construction, while at the same time this construction should enable the analysand to validate and reconstruct his life story – that is, with his conscious experience reconstruct his past in terms of the unconscious.

# Part 1: Historical Background

## ON FREUD'S VIEW

If we go back to the dawn of psychoanalysis, we see that Freud's initial idea was that a reconstruction of the subject's past would reveal a historical truth. This revelation of truth would have a curative effect on the analysand and liberate him/her from his/her suffering and symptoms. In his and Breuer's work on hysteria, the cure consisted of filling in the memory gaps that the patient/analysand suffered from (Breuer and Freud 1893–95). Along with this idea of reconstruction as the revelation of a historical truth was the epistemological position of *realism* – that is, the truth concerned a world of actual events, whose status was independent of the current psychoanalytic situation. Thus, the beginning of psychoanalysis presents us with a rather clear-cut and unequivocal picture: historical truth, reconstruction and actual events. The sequel to this beginning is anything but unequivocal.

As early as 1897, in a letter to Fliess (Freud 1954/1897: letter 69), we note that Freud gives up the idea of historical actuality of past events in his abandonment of the seduction theory. The analysand's trauma was henceforth not reducible to being a victim of someone else's action, but was constituted by his own inner life, in terms of phantasies and wishes. The fact that the reconstruction of the past presupposes, for instance, unconscious phantasies, wishes, feelings and instinctual derivates, calls for constructions. Freud had to handle both of these seemingly contradictory concepts – reconstruction and construction. However, for Freud, they were in no way contradictory. The term 'construction', as used by Freud, never signified an epistemological concept that was linked to an idea of narrative truth, in opposition to historical truth, as was the case for the narrative tradition developed later on within the psychoanalytic movement.

Freud himself never gave up the idea that psychoanalysis deals with reconstruction, just as his conviction was also that psychoanalysis concerns historical truths. The revelation of historical truth came about by means of reconstructing the analysand's past. Construction was hardly an epistemological concept – understood as an alternative to reconstruction. Rather, it was a methodological term, describing the work of the analyst in reconstructing the analysand's past. Thus, construction resembles, to a certain extent, interpretation, the difference being that the interpretation 'applies to something that one does to some single element of the material ... it is "construction" when one lays before the subject of analysis a piece of early history that he has forgotten' (Freud 1937: 260). A construction can be seen as a more elaborate account of a process of events, feelings, wishes, and so on, from the past. Reconstruction signifies the end result of the analyst's and the analysand's work, while construction has a more methodological, instrumental function, describing the analyst's work, and is only a 'preliminary labour' (Freud 1937: 260). Construction is necessary because the material that is produced by the analysand in the transference relationship with the analyst is so fragmented that it is out of reach for the analysand's memory. The construction is always a reconstruction of a past: 'his work of construction, or, if it is preferred, of reconstruction' (Freud 1937: 259). Construction becomes an essential ingredient in the reconstructing aim of psychoanalysis.

Let us look at what is perhaps Freud's most famous reconstruction of an analysand's historical past, namely, the Wolf Man's observation of the primal scene when he was about a year and a half. The fact that this analysand has been called the Wolf Man has to do with irrational fear of wolves and a wolf dream he had at the age of 4 years. He was in treatment with Freud, and related this wolf dream in his psychoanalysis when he was 23 years old. The dream is thus dreamt when he turns 4, and is about how the window in his bedroom suddenly opened of its own accord and there were six or seven wolves sitting on the walnut tree in front of the window. The wolves are white, but have big tails like foxes. He feels great anxiety, and is afraid of being eaten by the wolves; he screams and wakes up. There are more details in the dream, but this description suffices for my purpose. The interesting thing in this context is not the dream itself, but the fact that it is on the basis of this dream, and the Wolf Man's associations with the dream, that Freud reconstructs this historical event – the primal scene – that the Wolf Man supposedly observed at the age of one and a half. In this reconstruction, we simultaneously get a good description of an analyst's construction (Freud 1918: 37; italics in the original):

He had been sleeping in his cot, then, in his parents' bedroom, and woke up, perhaps because of his rising fever, in the afternoon, possibly at five o'clock, the hour which was later marked out by depression. It harmonizes with our assumption that it was a hot summer's day, if we suppose that his parents had retired, half undressed, for an afternoon *siesta*. When he woke up, he witnessed coitus *a tergo* [sexual intercourse from behind], three times repeated; he was able to see his mother's genitals as well as his father's organ; and he understood the process as well as its significance.

As I said, Freud did not polarize between reconstruction and construction, and neither of those concepts invalidated the value of historical truth. In the above quote, the reconstruction/construction concerns an actual historical truth, which deserves a couple of remarks of interest in this context. Even if Freud's account is actual and historically situated, it is nevertheless based on a deferred action (*Nachträglichkeit*) and on something as unreal as a dream (Laplanche 1992). And not only that, but the dream is dreamt at the age of 4 – that is, two and a half years after the alleged observation of the primal scene – and the Wolf Man relates his dream to Freud in his analysis when he is 23 years old. When it comes to criticism of the sources, one can certainly have opinions about the value of Freud's historical reconstruction.

To be fair, it should be said that Freud showed a vacillating attitude to the question of whether the Wolf Man had actually experienced the primal scene in reality. No doubt, Freud puts much emphasis on showing in detail that it took place and how it actually happened. Surprisingly, at the same time, he expresses that its reality character can be put in doubt and that it does not matter whether it actually happened or not. One possibility is that the child observed copulation between animals, which was then displaced on to his parents (Freud 1918: 57). Later on he concludes (p. 60): 'I intend on this occasion to close the discussion of the reality of the primal scene with a *non liquet*' (*non liquet* = it is not clear). And in another passage (p. 97) of this case study, we learn that 'the answer to this question [whether it was a phantasy or an experience of a real event] is not in fact a matter of very great importance'. However, it seems that the fact that Freud allowed the primal scene experience the status of pure phantasy took place against the background that he could assign the reality character of it to 'an inherited endowment, a phylogenetic heritage' (p. 97).[2] The child 'fills in the gaps in individual truth with prehistoric truth; he replaces occurrences in his own life by occurrences in the life of his ancestors' (p. 97).

In brief, Freud's epistemological position can be described as a strong inclination to embrace some kind of realistic position. Psychic reality was understood in a rather objectivistic manner. A development can be seen from the initial opinion that the unconscious contained the repression of actual events towards a loosening up of the reality character of the events in an ontogenetic context, preserved, however, within a phylogenetic framework. A third realistic position that he holds – although of a less naïve character – is that the unconscious is the true psychical reality and the world of consciousness is a distorted world. He makes the analogy to natural science and concludes that the natural scientific description/construction of the world is the real world, whereas the perceived world is not really the real world. The reality character is here placed on that which is 'behind' the experienced/perceived.

To conclude, the phenomenon of construction does not threaten a realistic epistemology in Freud's thinking; nor does it challenge an idea of reconstructing historical truths. Even if his development meant that the 'actuality' of past events were de-emphasized, they were still conceived of as real within a realistic epistemology – for instance, in his ideas of a phylogenetic heritage.

## ON THE POST-FREUDIAN DEVELOPMENT

Wetzler (1985) puts special emphasis on the development of ego-psychology in explaining the diffusion of the idea of reconstruction.

---

[2] By 'phylogenetic heritage' is meant characteristics that are handed down from generation to generation in the history of mankind, and implies that real events for earlier generations are handed down as phantasies in the person's subjective life.

In brief, he accounts for two trends that changed the status of the process of reconstruction (Wetzler 1985: 191): 'One, that past external realities, reactions, later overlays and impulse derivatives increasingly became the focus. Secondly, that generic ego states became the subject matter since reconstructions were approximates at best'. Kris (1956: 77) pointed out that these 'complex patterns' that psychoanalysis deals with, and the facts that are imbued with meaning, furthermore undergo meaning transformations: 'Not only were the events loaded with meaning when they occurred; each later stage of the conflict pattern may endow part of the events, or of their elaboration with added meaning'.

The gradual diffusion of the idea of reconstruction was followed by a rejection of the idea of reconstruction by representatives of the narrative tradition (for example, Bellin 1984; Schafer 1976, 1979, 1980; Spence 1982a, 1982b, 1983; Viderman 1979).[3] Narrative truth took the place of historical truth. A polarization occurred between, on the one hand, historical truth and reconstruction, and, on the other hand, narrative truth and construction (cf. Spence 1982a, 1982b). The term 'construction' has thus gained an epistemological significance, and thereby the idea of epistemological realism is rejected – that is, the idea that the interpretation/construction as a kind of image reflects the original event/situation completely independent of the present psychoanalytic situation and the psychoanalytic theories. Within the narrative tradition, construction signifies the adoption of a perspective, an implication it never had for Freud.

An important characteristic of the narrative tradition is the view that the narrative in itself can have a truth value. One does not attempt to find a correspondence between assertions/interpretations/narratives and historical facts/events. Narrative truth means

---

[3] The differences that exist between the representatives in the narrative tradition cannot be discussed further in this context. I will restrict myself to discussing certain positions that have been connected to this tradition. In particular, I will discuss some of the writings of Spence, who is, perhaps, the foremost representative of the narrative tradition.

that a story's different threads fit together and make up a meaningful whole. Coherence between parts replaces the traditional idea of
truth, which is about correspondence between statements and facts.
The making of a coherent narrative is a construction and life is not
limited to one type of construction, but can be captured by many
different constructed narratives. Thus, in this tradition, 'truth' is a
relative concept. The narrative tradition represents an alternative to
a more positivistic coloured position within psychoanalysis, where
truth would be about reconstructions of certain objective historical
facts.

The narrative position implies a rejection of the idea that
there are historical facts in themselves. A reconstruction of the past
entails the-past-as-it-is-seen-from-the-present. The understanding of
the past is always conditioned by the present perspective, with its
wishes, conflicts, projects, and so on. 'The historical truth' in this
sense is never known, which, according to Spence (1983: 469), is the
reason why the analyst has to make as convincing a story as possible
with the facts at his/her disposal. Another aspect of that narrative
approach is that it makes us sensitive to the transference in the here-
and-now situation, which is of such great importance for the psychoanalytic treatment.

There is good reason to be thankful for the narrative tradition's challenge of a traditional concept of truth that many still
want to apply to psychoanalysis. The narrative tradition challenges
our ingrained everyday understanding of truth to such an extent
that we may become deaf to their position. Wetzler (1985) exempli-
fies this; he presents the position of the narrative tradition in a fair
manner, but is unable to recognize narration as a legitimate epistemological concept describing the nature of truth. For Wetzler,
truth seems inherently to mean correspondence, since he points out
that 'It is clear that stories or narrative accounts which are epistemologically consistent and clinically useful are not necessarily
veridical ... Narratives must be constrained by the actual historical
circumstances' (Wetzler 1985: 195). Consequently, in the sequel of

his article, 'narrative accounts', 'narratives' and 'narrative format' replace the term 'narrative truth'. Narrative consistency seems, at best, to be a good indication of truth, perhaps a necessary indication, but not a criterion for truth.

It is striking how difficult it is to step outside the position of truth as a correspondence. The narrative tradition should be credited for having shown the possibility of another concept of truth germane to psychoanalysis, which implies a rejection of a realistic epistemological standpoint and instead brings forth the psychoanalyst's and the analysand's constructing parts of what is true in psychoanalysis. They have succeeded in bringing the notion of 'construction' to an epistemological level, and have thus developed the concept of truth in psychoanalysis. Later on I will preserve the idea of the logic of the narrative as a necessary feature in defining truth in psychoanalysis. Such a feature does not have to do with a correspondence between an assertion and a fact, but with a creation of psychic material in order to obtain coherence and wholeness.

However, I have serious objections to some of the standpoints embraced by well-known narrative psychoanalysts. In the course of this chapter, it will be clear that I am dissatisfied with what I consider to be the fundamental polarization between narrative versus historical truth and construction versus reconstruction. In part 2 I will attempt to harmonize these concepts.

One point of criticism against the narrative tradition concerns its treatment of the historical dimension in psychoanalysis. It is right, I think, in rejecting the objectivistic and realistic concept of the possibility of historical truths. But there is a clear tendency in the narrative tradition to downplay the historical dimension. It is unfortunate that the historical dimension and the here-and-now transference become separated, since the phenomenon of transference is precisely one of the avenues which allows us to acquire knowledge about the analysand's unconscious relationship to his/her past.

The narrative tradition makes us sensitive to the importance of the here-and-now, but it is hard to conceive of psychoanalysis without the historical dimension, without recognizing some kind of historical determination of the psychoanalytic subject/analysand (cf. Ch. Hanly 1990; M.F. Hanly 1996). The psychoanalytic project is inherently connected to an investigation of the analysand's past experiences. The rejection of historical truth seems to be based on an objectivistic idea of history and is hardly valid for any sense of history in psychoanalysis. A quote like the following, from Spence (1983: 469), illustrates the neglect of the historical dimension:

> If interpretations depend on being compelling, persuasive, and possibly predictive, they can be effective without being historically true; and, indeed, the main thrust of our argument has been to show that their historical truth may be their least significant dimension.

It is odd to see, in this same article, how Spence tries to illustrate his position by a clinical example in which the analysand refers to several past memories. Half a page later, Spence (1983: 472) writes: 'the patient is always speaking in the present – if not always in the present tense ... part of the force of the narrative being constructed comes from its here-and-now fit'. Reading the quote one can ask if this 'here-and-now fit' does not get its force from, among other things, the analysand's past experiences. Is it not the case that the 'here-and-now fit' is partly conditioned by what the analysand brings with him/her to the ongoing psychoanalytic situation? Is there not a risk that Spence's position threatens to deprive the subject of his/her history? The force of history comes out in every analysis, where the analysand in his/her free association and storytelling constantly refers back to previous experiences – a force also visible in Spence's own example.

A look at Spence's critique of Freud for his description of the fundamental rule reveals the implausibility of his ideas. Spence (1983: 460–1) is critical of Freud's description of free association as an image of the analysand as a train passenger, whose task it is to report everything he sees through the window. Spence corrects this idea of free association by commenting that the analysand is doing

much more than passively describing the passing scene. The analys-
and is actively constructing a narrative out of pieces of his/her life.
This may be correct, but it is not an exhaustive description of free
association, which exhibits itself at its best when it precisely breaks
with all kinds of coherent storytelling. Who has not been witness to
the situation in which free association shows itself most remarkably
as that thought, image, feeling, and so on, which seemingly out of
nowhere suddenly pops into the mind of the analysand, breaking
with the previous chain of thoughts? Free association shows itself
as the breaking of a coherent storytelling. And it is the analysand's
history that is breaking in. It is quite another point that the meaning of that which is freely associated cannot be traced unless one can
contextualize it in a narrative. But such a contextualization occurs
after the spontaneous association.

Neglecting the historical dimension in psychoanalysis seems
to me to be based on an objectivistic idea of history. Is there any
other way to conceive of the historical dimension and its legitimacy
in psychoanalysis? Perhaps Gadamer's (1985/1960) ideas can shed
light on this question. His reflections on what the conditions are for
understanding highlight the importance of our historical situated-
ness and that our understanding is necessarily historical. History
in this primordial sense is not something that lies behind or above
us as objective facts, but rather that which guides us and leads our
understanding. Our understanding of history is already historical.
The historical dimension that a psychoanalytic project would shed
light on must pertain to our past experiences that lie embedded in
our capacity to understand our present. Let me put off a further discussion of this issue until part 2, when I will try to work out an
alternative to the alleged antithesis between historical truth versus
narrative truth and reconstruction versus construction.

## ON BION'S TRANSFORMATIONS

If the narrative tradition left us with an antithetical relationship
between reconstruction versus construction and historical versus narrative truth, I will now take up Wilfred Bion's (1965) work

*Transformations*, which contains a very interesting position with regard to the topic here, although he never explicitly talks about or uses the concepts construction, reconstruction, narrative and historical truth. I believe, however, that some of the ideas presented in the above-mentioned work imply a position on the question of the relationship between construction and reconstruction, which I will use as a point of departure for part 2 of this chapter. Bion's ideas that the psychoanalytic process consists of a chain of *invariant* transformations implies, in my view, a mutual connectedness between reconstruction and construction. Each transformation, by means of the alpha-function, brings that which is transformed to another level, and does this in such a way that something remains the same in that transformation. For example, the unsymbolized somatic pain is transformed into a feeling of being abandoned and vulnerable (something that is psychically experienced). Something remains the same on those two levels. However, it would be misleading to conceive of his idea of invariance as a pure reconstruction, since he openly recognizes the dependence of the transformation on a perspective. When it comes to the domain of psychoanalysis, there are many different schools (Freudians, Kleinians, and so on), and many different theories (Oedipus theory, the theory of projective identification and splitting, and so on) that all make their own invariant transformation from their particular perspective. Bion (1965: 4) states, for example: 'Any interpretation belongs to the class of statements embodying invariants under one psycho-analytic theory; thus an interpretation could be comprehensible because of its embodiment of "invariants under the theory of the Oedipus situation".' And another example (Bion 1965: 5):

> Kleinian transformation, associated with certain Kleinian theories, would have different invariants from the invariants in a classical Freudian transformation. Since the invariants would be different so the meaning conveyed would be different even if the material transformed (the analytic experience or realization) could be conceived as being the same in both instances.

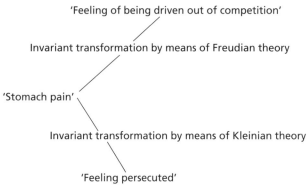

FIGURE 8.1 Illustration of Bion's ideas about the invariant transformations

Bion's ideas may be illustrated by means of figure 8.1.

Let us suppose that we have an analysand who often suffers from stomach pain. This state of affairs can, eventually, with the assistance of interpretations, be transformed into a feeling of being driven out of competition, from – let us suppose – the vantage point of a Freudian theory. Here we have a transformation from one state of affairs to another (from 'stomach pain' to a 'feeling of being driven out of competition'), at the same time as we have something invariant, identical in both these states of affairs. Bion's idea is thus that there is something in the analysand's feeling of being driven out of competition that was also represented in the analysand's stomach pain. And this transformation to feeling driven out of competition presupposes a psychoanalytic theory – for example, a Freudian theory in our example. Furthermore, one can imagine that this stomach pain is transformed into something else by means of another psychoanalytic theory. In our example, the stomach pain is transformed into feeling persecuted by means of a Kleinian theory. And still, there is something that is identical in these two different states of affairs: to have stomach pain and to feel persecuted.

Bion's position is interesting because it preserves something of the idea of reconstruction – that is, that which is interpreted in the psychoanalytic process reflects or reconstructs an earlier state of affairs. His position would be that there is an interpretation (transformation) of something that remains the same/identical/invariant from a certain psychoanalytic theoretical perspective. As such, his position does not entail a naïve realistic idea that the transformed is simply a copy of that which has been transformed. A constructing element is recognized, since different perspectives address the same material. Two different interpretations may both justifiably claim that the interpretations about the 'same' material are true.

To understand the terms 'construction' and 'reconstruction' in light of Bion's transformations shows that they are not as antithetic as they have been conceived of by Spence, for instance. Furthermore, it is not a question of holding construction as a necessary step in a psychoanalytic reconstruction of one's past, as Freud would have it. The transformed reconstruction presupposes the construction, presupposes the holding of a specific analytic perspective. Such a position abolishes the dichotomy between construction and reconstruction. The key to understanding such a position, I believe, is to acknowledge that the unconscious can only be captured by means of constructions. In part 2 of this chapter I will try to justify the synthesis of construction and reconstruction, as well as of historical and narrative truth. The riddle involved in my position could be expressed in the following way: the psychoanalytic interpretation is based on the unconscious as a theoretical construction, while at the same time this construction should enable the analysand to validate and reconstruct her life story – that is, with her conscious experience reconstruct her past in terms of the unconscious.

# Part 2: Sketching a Solution

## ON THE CONSTRUCTED CHARACTER OF THE UNCONSCIOUS

In order to try to solve the above-mentioned riddle, several steps have to be taken. The first issue to examine is how the unconscious is to be understood – an examination that will be carried out against the background of consciousness. The epistemological priority of

consciousness in relationship to the unconscious has been emphasized before, in particular in chapter 4. In principle, I will repeat
this point of view, but this time from a somewhat different point
of departure. Our experience of our lives and ourselves begins with
our conscious experience, but consciousness has not received the
interest it deserves from psychoanalysts. In Freud's struggle against
philosophy, one can even discern a kind of condescending attitude
towards an interest in consciousness. As early as in *The interpretation of dreams* (1900: 613) Freud even seems to want to deprive consciousness of a psychical existence by claiming: 'The unconscious
is the true psychical reality', and at the end of his life he wrote
(Freud 1938a: 158): 'the psychical is the unconscious itself'.[4] Because
he regards the unconscious as the truly psychical, consciousness is
only a quality, although he can also recognize its importance: 'It
[the quality of being conscious] remains the one light which illuminates our path and leads us through the darkness of mental life ...
our scientific work in psychology will consist in translating unconscious processes into conscious ones, and thus filling in the gaps in
conscious perceptions' (Freud 1938b: 286). Whatever the form of its
existence and character, psychoanalytic practice cannot do without
consciousness. One never reaches the unconscious directly, but as it
can be traced in conscious and preconscious material.

Let us begin by looking at the word 'consciousness', whose
root is the Latin *con*, meaning 'together with', and *scire*, meaning 'to
know'. This 'knowing together with ...' has been transformed in the

---

[4] This idea of the unconscious as the truly psychical should probably be understood as reflecting a realistic standpoint concerning the notion of the unconscious, as I pointed out earlier on. With regard to the descriptions yielded by
(natural) sciences, Freud places psychoanalysis on a par with (other) natural
sciences. Freud (1938b) makes the analogy between natural scientific descriptions (according to me, constructions) of the perceived world – as real descriptions of the world – and the psychoanalytic descriptions (constructions) of the
unconscious as descriptions of the psyche. Here, as elsewhere, Freud understands
psychoanalysis as a natural science. However, Freud vacillates between talking
about the real world sometimes as the perceived world and sometimes as the
world as it is described/constructed by natural science.

course of history. Originally it meant a sharing with anyone. During the Middle Ages the knowledge that was shared became limited to sharing with some people, but not others. Finally, the meaning was restricted to oneself, a knowledge that one shared with oneself (Humphrey 1992).

Thus, consciousness signifies awareness or knowing that entails a kind of ego. To be conscious is to be with one's knowledge. The ego need not be explicit about its knowing, but implicitly it is at least *with* it. Consciousness involves a being that is with its knowing. Thus, not only is consciousness a characteristic of someone(ego)-who-is-knowing, but within the field of consciousness we also find a knowing of ourselves: a self-consciousness. This capacity to be self-conscious is of importance in psychoanalytic treatment, as was pointed out in chapter 4, and to which I will return at the end of this chapter.

If consciousness involves a being who is with its knowing, we can now trace a first important trait of the unconscious: its negativity. The unconscious does not entail awareness or knowing. Nothing is with it (such as an ego). In consciousness, 'to be aware' implies 'to be with the awareness'. In the unconscious there is nothing (no one) with a knowing. Knowing should be understood here in a very broad sense, including all sorts of conscious psychical processes. Thus, the unconscious can be said to be something alien to a first-person perspective, something estranged from the ego's subjective intending.

The negativity of the unconscious is noticeable through defects in consciousness. Freud assumed that the unconscious 'is *necessary* because the data of consciousness have a very large number of gaps in them' (Freud 1915a: 166; italics in the original). It is due to these gaps and omissions that we need a constructed theory. We cannot disclose psychical unconscious meaning by simply recollecting past conscious acts. The stream of conscious acts (including the preconscious) can be recovered (recalled) by simple reflections on the ego's subjective intending. Reflection means that we go back over that which has been (consciously or preconsciously) lived, in order to illuminate its

meaning. When it comes to psychoanalysis and its search for unconscious material, we can see that this reflective path, belonging to consciousness and the preconscious, is insufficient. Indeed, reflection is
still an important part of the psychoanalytic process, but the unconscious cannot be recalled by means of reflection. The unconscious
breaks precisely with the subjective intending, which is reflected in
the psychoanalytic method – the free association – in which the ego's
control is abandoned (to a greater or lesser extent).

The unconscious, constituted as a break with consciousness,
calls for a metapsychology. Psychoanalytic theory becomes a mixed
discourse of meaning language and, for example, language of energies and forces (Ricoeur 1970). Psychoanalysis becomes an explanatory science, which aims at explaining the symptom. We want to
be able to explain the mechanisms by which the symptom and the
suffering can exist. Psychoanalysis goes beyond a mere descriptive
hermeneutic science because it entails an explanatory moment
(Habermas 1972; Lesche 1981).

Although the unconscious emerges as a break with consciousness and presents itself as negativity with respect to consciousness/
self-consciousness, this does not prevent us from ascribing certain
characteristics and structures to the unconscious. We fill the 'un' in
the unconscious with something. There exist different levels of theoretical constructs, such as metapsychological theories, models of
mind and various clinical theories. Today, there is no longer just one
psychoanalysis, but many, such as Freudian, Kleinian, post-Klein-
ian, Lacanian, self-psychology (cf. Wallerstein 1992).

The constructed character of the unconscious is, in the course
of the analytic process, to be appropriated as part of a reconstruction
of the analysand's life story.

## THE INTEGRATION OF CONSTRUCTION,
## RECONSTRUCTION, AND HISTORICAL AND
## NARRATIVE TRUTH

The psychoanalytic process, whose aim is to disclose a person's unconscious, is made up of the analysand's and analyst's material – not

least the analysand's free associations – produced during the psychoanalytic sessions. One may ask: what is the nature of the truth claims of psychoanalytic interpretations and how do they relate to the notions of construction and reconstruction, and historical and narrative truth? I will deal with this question in the following three steps: (1) To begin with, I will attempt to integrate construction and reconstruction, which leads me to coin the expression a 'constructed reconstruction'; (2) thereafter I will try to show that the constructed reconstruction should possess the character of a narrative – that is, of wholeness/meaningfulness/a good gestalt; (3) finally, it remains to discuss how this meaningfully constructed reconstruction can be said to say something true about the analysand's past, about his/her history. This integration is only described in the form of three steps because of pedagogical reasons. These steps should not be viewed as describing a process or chronology, but have to be understood as three dimensions that are integrated.

*Integration of construction and reconstruction: a constructed reconstruction*

There are several possible ways to describe the point of departure for the psychoanalytic process. It begins with a person seeking help for his suffering and wanting to do something about it. One can say that the person does not succeed in reconstructing his life, due to imperfections, distortions and gaps in his conscious life. The person feels his suffering, but does not understand why he suffers or the meaning of his suffering. The person suffers from a distorted self-understanding, and he does not possess a narrative understanding that can be completed in a good gestalt or be formed in a coherent way. These imperfections within the sphere of consciousness make psychoanalysis see the need of an unconscious. Thus, we need an understanding of the unconscious, which is something beyond the horizon opened up by conscious experience. One will not be able to fill in the gaps of conscious life simply by reflecting on the ego's experiencing. Instead, one abandons the sphere of the ego's conscious life in the psychoanalytic process, by means of free associating. We attempt to release the control of the ego's conscious intentions in order to take part in ego-alien ideas, thoughts and feelings that suddenly turn up in our consciousness.

The next thing is to fill in the gaps – the unconscious – by means of a constructed perspective, the specific nature of which cannot be discussed here. But as I pointed out, today there are many different constructions and conceptualizations of the unconscious. To fill in the gaps in consciousness by means of a constructed perspective should not be conceived as an autonomous step in the psychoanalytic process. We must understand it rather as an analytic step (in a logical sense), where the dialogue in the psychoanalytic process is coloured by the psychoanalytic perspective, an analytic step that constitutes the ground for reoccurring reconstructions – thus, a reconstruction that now takes place from the vantage point of the analysand's unconscious. In practice, the psychoanalytic process and the dialogue between analyst and analysand will scrutinize the different reconstructions that are deconstructed or modified, thereby opening up new horizons that, in turn, enable new reconstructions of the analysand's history and a new understanding of his life.

This new psychoanalytic reconstruction is thus carried out from the perspective of the constructed unconscious. There is no reason to oppose construction and reconstruction. On the contrary, the reconstruction of the analysand's life story can only be legitimized from the constructed perspective. A Freudian dream interpretation is a good example of how an elaborate theoretical construction is needed in order to trace out the unconscious meaning of the dream. By means of this constructed perspective, the analysand is able to reconstruct her life in a new way. The term 'construction' has taken on epistemological significance, and is not to be confused with the methodological meaning that the term 'construction' had for Freud. We recognize that psychoanalytic understanding (of the unconscious) is based on a constructed perspective. Psychoanalytic understanding has to do with *constructed reconstructions*.

## The narrative logic of the constructed reconstruction

The constructed reconstruction possesses the character of a narrative. The basis of the term 'narrative' is the idea of wholeness, of a good gestalt. The terms 'wholeness' and 'a good gestalt' can be viewed as making up different sides of one and the same phenomenon. It is obvious that this idea is the condition upon which the whole psychoanalytic project rests – the search for meaning. The psychoanalytic project, to attempt to find a new – that is, constructed – reconstruction of the analysand's life, is conditioned by the structure of narrative, of a narrative logic. In other words, the psychoanalytic project is guided by the principle of the potentiality of being meaningful/of wholeness/of forming a good gestalt.

The validity of a potential constructed perspective is inherently dependent on its narrativity. The logic of a narrative is made up of a coherent forming. This is not the place, however, to evaluate different possible narratives for psychoanalysis. The validation of a specific perspective is a complex and difficult task that entails both an empirical and a metascientific level. The empirical level deals with how well the psychoanalytic (empirical) material can be understood from the vantage point of the specific theory/theories that are to be validated. The metascientific level concerns the validity in, for example, philosophical/ontological implications in the psychoanalytic theories in question.

## The historical validity of the constructed reconstruction

What is there to say about historical truth and the psychoanalytic revelation of the unconscious? Does the idea of a historical truth allow itself to be included in the psychoanalytic project? Yes, I believe so. However, 'historical truth' should not be understood as a truth that simply copies or mirrors a past actuality. Yet the psychoanalytic project deals with a historical dimension. The analysand is always brought back to his past in order to understand the present situation. This is not something that we have to impose on the analysand, but the connections to the analysand's history come

spontaneously and easily in his free associations, reflections and storytelling. The analysand's past that is revealed in the psychoanalytic
process is not an actual reconstruction of an event seen from a third-
person 'objective' position. Since the psychoanalytic investigation
entails a constructed perspective from outside the ego's conscious
intending, we are here dealing with a perspective that is neither a
third-person perspective nor, in any pure sense, what I called earlier
on a first-person perspective. The psychoanalytic perspective situ-
ates itself within the subject, but as that which is estranged from the
ego's conscious intending. One can say that psychoanalysis concerns
itself with the other thing (*das Andere*) within oneself. (Here I have
chosen to comply with Laplanche's terminology and to talk about
the other thing [*das Andere*] – that is, something thing-like, reified
and not about the other person [*der Andere*]; see chapter 4.)

The question to pose at this point is whether the analysand's
past experiences of the past correspond to her ongoing understanding of the past. The difficulty in answering this question lies in the
fact that there is no Godlike position from which we could answer
the question. We cannot lift ourselves out of the present situation in
order to get an overview of both the past and the present at the same
time. We must answer this question from our present perspective,
with the past at a distance. Nevertheless, I would like to address this
issue by first rejecting two possible positions, which, in a certain
sense, constitute each other's opposite.

On the one hand, we have a position that, for lack of a better
term, I call *relativistic*. I call this position relativistic because historical truth claims are either downplayed or completely rejected. In
other words, according to this view, the present understanding of the
past is of no use or significance in telling us about the past as-it-was-
experienced-in-the-past. Such a relativistic position with respect to
psychoanalysis can be seen, I believe, in two versions, one of which
is the idea that the historical dimension is of little relevance to psychoanalysis. Such a viewpoint was briefly discussed and rejected in
part 1 of this chapter, when dealing with the narrative tradition in

psychoanalysis. Another type of relativism is a general relativistic position where no criterion whatsoever is available for epistemological evaluation with respect to interpretations. This type of position is entailed in positivism, in which science is restricted to observing facts. Furthermore, I believe that such a position is also entailed in the sceptic's position – the sceptic who rejects the concept of truth altogether. The sceptic's position has been discussed throughout the history of philosophy. Let me simply reiterate one common argument against a fundamental epistemological relativism, namely, that the statement 'there is no truth' is self-contradictory.

On the other hand, the opposite view of relativism is the idea of an *absolute* position, where a correct understanding of one's historical past would correspond in an exact way with the historical past. Correct understanding precludes here the possibility of understanding in many different ways, and the only correct way is the same at any point in time. I would argue against such an absolute position, which I believe treats the relationship between the present and the past as a relationship between facts, and, as such, cannot be applicable to a psychoanalytic project interested in meaning. In the psychoanalytic project of investigating the meaning of the analysand's past, there is an ongoing transformation of how one can understand and look on one's past experiences. And the fact that one's understanding today is based on a reflective self-understanding different from the self-understanding from the past changes in some way the phenomenon that is investigated.

My position will be to defend the idea that psychoanalytic insights concerning the analysand's past do reflect the past and are valid historically, but that these insights are not reflections (mirrors) of an objective, actual past. In order to understand my position, I need to introduce the concept 'horizon'. All experiences imply an unclosed horizon. Experience is never a finished and closed entity, but depends on a certain openness that can be filled in, in different ways. This pertains to the adult's experiences as well as to the child's and the infant's experiences. The indeterminacy and difficulty in understanding one's situation is particularly prevalent at the beginning of life. The existence of 'deferred action' (*Nachträglichkeit*) may well serve as an illustration of the unfinished character of experiences.

The notion of 'horizon' makes it possible to see man as an ever open and meaning-imbuing (sense-making) being. One's existence reveals at every moment an open and unclosed horizon, both to one's past and to one's future. The significance of what was will be determined from the present perspective, whose significance in turn depends on its relation to one's past and future. These three dimensions of time – the present, the past and the future – are interwoven with one another.

The connection between the-past-as-it-was-experienced-in-the-past and the-past-as-understood-from-the-present can, I suggest, be understood in terms of Gadamer's (1985/1960) expression 'fusion of horizons'. I borrow his model of understanding only to apply it to this psychoanalytic context. Truth arises when one's present horizon fuses with the past horizon opened up in this dialogue between present and past. In figure 8.2 I try to illustrate that the experience in the past entails certain possible meanings that can be actualized or understood in the present psychoanalytic situation. I have marked that by means, for instance, of a certain psychoanalytic theory (theory #1), a certain meaning is actualized/understood, and with another theory (theory #2), another meaning is understood/actualized. We are reminded here about Bion's ideas that were discussed earlier.

The merit of the position outlined here is supported by clinical experiences that I believe all of us have encountered many times. It allows for the fact that the 'same' material of the past permits itself to be understood in different ways in the course of the analytic process, as well as with different psychoanalytic theories. However, it is not a question of a total relativism, since any present reconstruction of the past will not do. This notion of horizon prevents us from considering the relationship between the past and the present as a fixed one-to-one correspondence. Although legitimate reconstructions of the past can be counted in pluralis, not just any reconstruction will do.

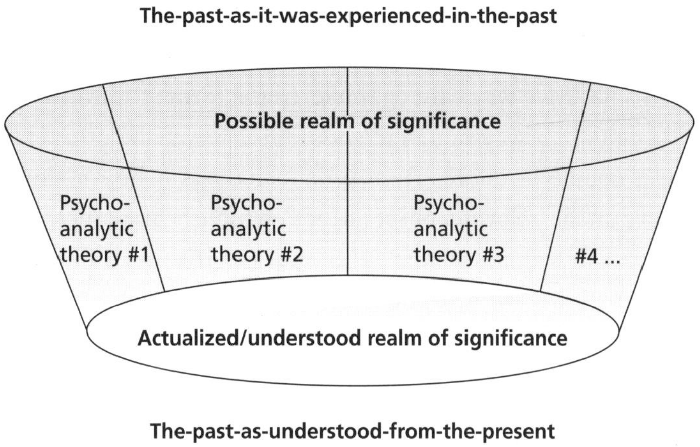

The-past-as-it-was-experienced-in-the-past

Possible realm of significance

| Psycho-analytic theory #1 | Psycho-analytic theory #2 | Psycho-analytic theory #3 | #4 ... |

Actualized/understood realm of significance

The-past-as-understood-from-the-present

FIGURE 8.2 Illustration of the fusion of horizons that occurs in the psychoanalytic process between 'the-past-as-it-was-experienced-in-the-past' and 'the-past-as-understood-from-the-present'

Given that my position is valid, the concepts construction–reconstruction, and narrative truth–historical truth are not antithetical concepts. Quite the opposite, in order to explicate the psychoanalytic truth claims, one must integrate and synthesize them. Psychoanalysis reconstructs historical truths, even though it is not a question of an actual history, but a historical truth based on a constructed perspective. What now remains is to apply this integration to the analysand. We must avoid restricting this discussion about truth claims to the psychoanalyst's account of the analysand. The synthesis between reconstruction and construction, historical and narrative truth has to be useful to the analysand herself. In the next, final section of this chapter I will therefore say something about the nature of the analysand's validation of psychoanalytic insights.

CONSCIOUSNESS/SELF-CONSCIOUSNESS AND THE
INTEGRATION OF RECONSTRUCTION, CONSTRUCTION,
AND HISTORICAL AND NARRATIVE TRUTH

I will begin this section with some general remarks about the overall function of self-consciousness in grasping truth and distorted self-understanding in our lives. Our self-consciousness has always at least an implicit relation to truth, although perhaps only experienced in a negative way – for example, in the form of suffering – that something is in a way not as it 'should' be. It may be of interest to look at a couple of quotes from psychoanalysts, who, in this context, have made relevant observations, which bear witness to the significance of self-consciousness in order to live in truth. In Freud (1938a: 201–2), we can read the following:

> Even in a state so far removed from the reality of the external world as one of hallucinatory confusion (amentia), one learns from patients after their recovery that at the time in some corner of their mind (as they put it) there was a normal person hidden, who, like a detached spectator, watched the hubbub of illness go past him.

And in Bion (1987: 46) we find the following:

> I do not think ... that the ego is ever wholly withdrawn from reality ... On this fact, that the ego retains contact with reality, depends the existence of a non-psychotic personality parallel with, but obscured by, the psychotic personality.

As stated, I believe that these quotes reflect something that one could express as the overall psychic function of self-consciousness. Freud's and Bion's discussion concerns the analysand's relationship to reality. The quotes illustrate well the importance of a perspective from within, a first-person perspective, in order to understand the human being's relationship to the world. By understanding the relationship subject/analysand – the world from a first-person perspective, a perspective from within – we can account for the capability of self-consciousness to 'realize' the subject's own distortion and incapacity to constitutionally harmonize an intersubjective reality.

This capability of self-consciousness to 'realize' the subject's own distortion should *not* be understood as if the subject in its wholeness certainly is incapable of explicitly embracing the truth,

but as if truth in one way or another were stored within conscious-
ness/self-consciousness. I would say it is rather a dormant and potential awareness – originating from self-consciousness – in the sense
that one (the subject) is about to carry out something irrationally and
distortedly. This awareness is given from within – that the stream
of acts of consciousness is not harmoniously synthesizing. Thus, it
is not a question of being aware of what there actually is, but rather
of what there is not. This being the case is the reason why the psychoanalytic process, in principle, does not use any external norms
or criteria in order to validate its understanding. The psychoanalytic
criterion of truth is a question of – in the analysand's experiencing –
an inner coherence that evolves laboriously and meanderingly during the psychoanalytic process.

Let us turn to the specific complex of problems that have been
in focus in this chapter. I have argued that the psychoanalytic concept of truth entails an integration of reconstruction, construction,
historical and narrative truth, and that this integration must take
place within the analysand himself. In other words, what is presupposed in this being, whose task it is to understand himself, to gain
insight/knowledge of his own unconscious? He needs to be of such
a nature that this whole 'epistemological edifice' can be contained
within himself. The theoretical, constructed unconscious is an
objectification of certain psychical processes. In the clinical situation we nevertheless encounter a 'whole person' – that is, the conscious as well as the unconscious, with whom our psychoanalysis
is to be carried out. Our theoretical attitude has brought about a
certain division of the subject, but in the clinical situation we deal
with the whole person. The unconscious is thus embedded within a
larger framework of the psychoanalytic subject.

Here, I want to point out the necessary function of conscious-
ness/self-consciousness for the analysand (subject), in order to
investigate her unconscious (as being experienced as a part of herself). I want to suggest that the functioning of consciousness/self-
consciousness is the condition for the analysand to be able to validate

the truth of the psychoanalytic process, and thereby to be able to encompass the integration of the psychoanalytic narrative.

Consciousness/self-consciousness enables the subject to hold a variety of perspectives. The subject can entertain a variety of meanings regarding the past. That which once was an estranged part within oneself is appropriated into one's subjective intending and stream of consciousness. That which was illogical, absurd and meaningless has become transformed and reaffirmed as something meaningful. This inherent meaning-imbuing capacity of consciousness/self-consciousness involves the capacity to symbolize, to see possibilities and to be able to adopt a perspective. Consciousness/self-consciousness is the unique capacity belonging to human beings which enables man to imbue existence with possibilities. We know from Gestalt psychology research with animals that animals are not able to perceive possible worlds. They are stimuli-bound and react to situations in a one-sided manner. For example, chimpanzees can learn to use a box as a seat; however, they could not use the same box as something to stand on in order to reach something outside of their cage. Thus, for the chimpanzees, the box can never be perceived as one object with several uses. They cannot see the box in terms of possibilities.

Human beings, on the other hand, possess this specific capacity to imbue the world with possible meanings. Things in the world are not understood in a stimuli context, but present themselves as possibilities. In a similar way, we may consider the relationship between one's present situation and one's history. Because one may exercise self-conscious reflection, one can also treat oneself and one's own past experiences in light of possibilities, possible meanings. One can pick up one's past experiences as sources of meanings and possibilities, and see their efficacy in one's life today. In a way, this is nothing new for psychoanalysts, who appreciate the necessity and function of a symbolizing capacity for psychical growth. What I want to suggest here is simply that this symbolizing function does not need to be characterized in technical terms – for example, Bion's

THE QUESTION OF TRUTH CLAIMS IN PSYCHOANALYSIS 189

alpha-function – in order to gain intelligibility. I believe that psycho- [
analysis needs more research concerning the role of consciousness/
self-consciousness in the psychoanalytic project, which in no way
implies a depreciation of the importance of the unconscious.

SUMMARY
The controversial question of psychoanalytic truth claims is discussed in this chapter. The point of departure for this discussion
is the two conceptual pairs of reconstruction–construction and historical–narrative truth. The chapter is divided into two parts. Part 1
consists of a historical background concerning the concept of truth
in psychoanalysis. Three psychoanalytic positions are presented and
discussed: Freud's views, ideas within the narrative tradition and,
finally, Bion's ideas about invariant transformations. These three
voices represent different points of view. Freud embraced the idea
that the task of psychoanalysis was to reconstruct historical truths.
The narrative tradition pleads that the task of psychoanalysis is to
construct persuasive narrative accounts that obtain the status of
truth. Finally, Bion's ideas implying that construction and reconstruction are not incompatible are discussed.

In part 2, I argue that these conceptual pairs – reconstruction–
construction and historical–narrative truth – are not incompatible,
but have to be integrated in order to capture adequately the concept
of truth in psychoanalysis. The integration of these concepts is carried out in terms of three steps:

(1) An integration of construction and reconstruction is proposed. The
    psychoanalytic understanding of the unconscious is based on a con-
    structed perspective, which is why one can say that psychoanalytic
    understanding has to do with constructed reconstructions.
(2) The constructed reconstruction possesses the logic of a narrative –
    that is, its logic is wholeness/meaningfulness/a good gestalt. This is
    the narrative moment in the concept of truth.
(3) The meaningfully constructed reconstruction can claim to say
    something valid about the analysand's history, given that one does

not understand history objectivistically. Instead, the historical validity is conceptualized in terms of Gadamer's 'fusion of horizons', between 'the-past-as-it-was-experienced-in-the-past' and 'the-past-as-understood-from-the-present'.

The chapter ends by pointing out the function of consciousness/self-consciousness for the psychoanalytic project of acquiring knowledge about one's unconscious.

# Concluding remarks

The purpose of this work has been to discuss the domain and conditions of psychoanalysis. Phenomenological reflections and ideas have been of help, and phenomenological conceptions, such as life-world experiences and the intentionality of consciousness have played an important role in this book.

In chapters 2 and 3 we have the phenomenological view of the life-world, scientific activity and intentionality of consciousness that amounts to the claim that recent attempts to build a so-called 'neuropsychoanalysis' are revealed as unfounded.

Consciousness cannot be neglected in either the psychoanalytic investigation or the attempts to understand theoretically the essential character of psychoanalysis. I argued that consciousness has an epistemological priority in relation to the unconscious. This is an idea that, at least implicitly, is found among many psychoanalysts, including Freud, who admitted, among other things, that: 'Now all our knowledge is invariably bound up with consciousness. We can come to know even the *Ucs.* only by making it conscious' (Freud 1923: 19). One could also express it in the way that the unconscious can only be understood from the vantage point of consciousness and its intentional character. However, the epistemological priority of consciousness in relation to the unconscious does not mean that the unconscious is similar to consciousness. The difference between consciousness and the unconscious has, quite to the contrary, been thoroughly stressed.

I claimed earlier on that psychoanalysis is a human science, but of a special kind. In psychoanalytic experience, the human being is not synonymous with what I have called the 'ego's conscious intending'. Psychoanalysis concerns itself with a suffering that cannot be understood from the vantage point of the conscious experience. Suffering can be experienced very explicitly, but we cannot understand in any depth why the person suffers, and nor does it seem as if the suffering has any point or meaning. When the suffering cannot be understood from the vantage point of conscious experiences, it is then that psychoanalysis with its unconscious becomes interesting.

The unconscious appears as something unfamiliar and contradictory in relation to the conscious intending. The unconscious, together with the concept 'meaning', is most likely the most important concept in psychoanalysis. The unconscious is the distinguishing mark of psychoanalysis, its 'shibboleth' said Freud.[1] Despite the fact that one can hardly exaggerate the importance of the unconscious for psychoanalysis, the concept still suffers from vagueness and obscurity to an unsatisfactorily high degree. The unconscious can be said to be an 'operative' concept, in the sense that much work remains before we reach a thematic and clear determination of it. This concept is indispensable for psychoanalysts and plays an important function both in everyday practice and in theoretical discussions among colleagues, even though psychoanalysts describe it very differently, and even in one and the same psychoanalyst one can find incompatible ways in the conceptualization of the unconscious. Certainly it is a gigantic and important task for psychoanalysis to clarify as far as possible the psychoanalytic concept, 'the unconscious'.

Basically, I have followed a Freudian line in this work in the sense that it is the libido/the sexual drive that constitutes the core of the unconscious. Freud was very clear about making a radical distinction between the unconscious and consciousness. I believe it is important to maintain this clear and radical difference, and not dilute the significance of the unconscious by making it into a

[1] 'Shibboleth' stems from a story in the Bible (Judges 12:6) in which the men of Gilead judged whether people would be allowed to cross the river Jordan; if they were revealed to be Ephraimite, by their pronunciation of the word 'Shibboleth', they were seized and killed.

second (unconscious) consciousness. It is important to pay attention to the unconscious in its most radical form and which breaks
radically with the intentionality of consciousness, which I have
described by means of the terms 'continuity', 'coherence' and
'wholeness'.

The unconscious in its most radical form thus breaks with
the way that consciousness functions. The different psychoanalytic
descriptions of the unconscious that I have presented bring forth its
dissolving character. My analysis of the unconscious in its most radical form leads to its formulation as a theoretical and constructed
concept. The theoretical construction has its basis in the sexual
life-world experience. But as a theoretical construction, in terms of
libido/sexual drive, it is something that cannot be experienced. My
analysis has been limited to trying to grasp this most radical level
of the unconscious. In a way, this level can be seen as the bottom
layer of the unconscious, in the form of something repressed that has
never been conscious. In this sense, it reminds us of Freud's idea of
primal repression (*Urverdrängung*).

The unconscious can be said to lie on the frontier between the
ego's conscious intending and a rudimentary body-ego experiencing.
We saw that Freud (1920) realized that the unconscious, ruled by
the pleasure principle, presupposes another kind of psychical process. This is a common idea among psychoanalysts, although its
implications are unclear. We run into neglected problems within
psychoanalysis, self-consciousness and the concept of existence.
The affirming potentiality of self-consciousness is of great importance in clinical practice. The whole psychoanalytic process should
be characterized by an affirming attitude, even though this attitude
receives its specific significance in dealing with traumatic experiences and so-called early disturbances. The existential experience
and self-consciousness have not, in this book, been illuminated primarily from the perspective of clinical psychoanalysis. Rather, what
has been in the forefront here has been their theoretical relevance for
understanding the domain of psychoanalysis.

# References

Abraham, G. (2002). The psychodynamics of orgasm. *International journal of psychoanalysis*, 83: 325–38.

Alizade, A.M. (1999). *Feminine sensuality*. London: Karnac Books.

Alvarez, A. (1992). *Live company*. London: Routledge.

Andersson, O. (1962). *Studies in the prehistory of psychoanalysis*. Stockholm: Norstedts.

Anzieu, D. (1986). *Freud's self-analysis*. London: The Hogarth Press.

——— (1989). *The skin ego*. New Haven: Yale University Press.

——— (1995). *Le moi-peau*. Paris: Dumond.

Bauman, Z. (1992). *Mortality, immortality and other life strategies*. Oxford: Blackwell Publishers.

Bellin, E.H. (1984). The psychoanalytic narrative: On the transformational axis between writing and speech. *Psychoanalysis and contemporary thought*, 7: 3–42.

Bermúdez, J.L. (2000). *The paradox of self-consciousness*. Cambridge: The MIT Press.

Bernet, R. (1996). The unconscious between representation and drive: Freud, Husserl, and Schopenhauer. In J.J. Drummond and J.G. Hart (eds.). *The truthful and the good*. Dordrecht: Kluwer Academic Publishers.

Biemel, W. (1971). Réflexions à propos des recherches husserliennes de la Lebenswelt. *Tijdschrift voor Filosofie*, 33: 659–83.

Binswanger, L. (1975). *Being-in-the-world. Selected papers of Ludwig Binswanger*. London: Souvenir Press.

Bion, W. (1965). *Transformations*. London: Karnac Books.

——— (1987). *Second thoughts. Selected papers on psycho-analysis*. London: Maresfield Library.

——— (1988). Notes on memory and desire. In E. Bott Spillius (ed.). *Melanie Klein today. Developments in theory and practice. Volume 2: Mainly practice*. London: Routledge.

Boss, M. (1979). *Existential foundations of medicine and psychology*. New York: Aronson.

Brentano, F. (1973/1874). *Psychologie vom Empirischen Standpunkte. Erster Band.* Leipzig: Verlag von Duncker & Humblot. (English translation: *Psychology from an empirical standpoint.* London: Routledge & Kegan Paul, 1973.)

Breuer, J. and Freud, S. (1893–95). *Studies on hysteria. The standard edition of the complete psychological works of Sigmund Freud,* 2.

Bullington, J. (1998). Merleau-Ponty and Freud: Phenomenology and meta-psychology. Paper presented at The Nordic Network for Philosophy, Medicine and Mental Health, 4th Annual Meeting in Tromsö, 8–9 October 1998.

(1999). *The mysterious life of the body: A new look at psychosomatics.* Stockholm: Almqvist & Wiksell International.

(2004). En 'alternativ' syn på kroppen, inspirerad av Merleau-Pontys filosofi [An 'alternative' view of the body, inspired by Merleau-Ponty's philosophy]. In M. Eklöf (ed.). *Perspektiv på komplementär medicin* [Perspectives of complementary medicine]. Lund: Studenlitteratur.

and Karlsson, G. (1997). Body experiences of persons who are congenitally blind: A phenomenological-psychological study. *Journal of visual impairment and blindness,* 91: 151–62.

Carr, D. (1977). Husserl's problematic concept of the life-world. In F. Elliston and P. McCormick (eds.). *Husserl: Exposition and Appraisals.* University of Notre Dame Press.

Changeux, J.-P. and Ricoeur, P. (2000). *What makes us think? A neuroscientist and a philosopher argue about ethics, human nature, and the brain.* Princeton University Press.

Churchland, P. M. (1984). *Matter and consciousness. A contemporary introduction to the philosophy of mind.* Cambridge: MIT Press/Bradford.

Churchland, P. S. (1986). *Neurophilosophy: Toward a unified science of the mind–brain.* Cambridge: MIT Press/Bradford.

Cohen, A. (2002). Franz Brentano, Freud's philosophical mentor. In G. Van de Vijer and F. Geerardyn (eds.). *The pre-psychoanalytic writings of Sigmund Freud.* London: Karnac Books.

Dreyfus, H. (1975). The priority of *the* world to *my* world: Heidegger's answer to Husserl (and) Sartre. *Man and world,* 8: 121–30.

Edgcumbe, R. (1990). The development of Freud's instinct theory, 1894–1939. In H. Nagera (ed.). *Basic psychoanalytic concepts on the theory of instincts.* London: Karnac Books.

Enckell, H. (2002). *Metaphor and the psychodynamic functions of the mind.* Kuopio University Publications D. Medical Sciences 265. Doctoral thesis at the Department of Psychiatry, University of Kuopio.

Etchegoyen, R.H. (1991). *The fundamentals of psychoanalytic technique.* London: Karnac Books.

Evans, D. (1996). *An introductory dictionary of Lacanian psychoanalysis.* London: Routledge.

Ey, H. (1978). *Consciousness. A phenomenological study of being conscious and becoming conscious.* Bloomington: Indiana University Press.

Federn, P. (1952). *Ego psychology and the psychoses.* New York: Aronson.

Fletcher, J. (1999). Introduction: Psychoanalysis and the question of the other. In J. Laplanche. *Essays on otherness.* London: Routledge.

Freud, S. (1888). Hysteria. *The standard edition of the complete psychological works of Sigmund Freud,* 1.

(1893a). On the psychical mechanism of hysterical phenomena. *The standard edition of the complete psychological works of Sigmund Freud,* 3.

(1893b). Some points for a comparative study of organic and hysterical motor paralyses. *The standard edition of the complete psychological works of Sigmund Freud,* 1.

(1894). The neuro-psychoses of defence. *The standard edition of the complete psychological works of Sigmund Freud,* 3.

(1895). On the grounds for detaching a particular syndrome from neurasthenia under the description 'anxiety neurosis'. *The standard edition of the complete psychological works of Sigmund Freud,* 3.

(1896). Heredity and aetiology of the neurosis. *The standard edition of the complete psychological works of Sigmund Freud,* 3.

(1900). *The interpretation of dreams. The standard edition of the complete psychological works of Sigmund Freud,* 4 and 5.

(1905a). *Jokes and their relation to the unconscious. The standard edition of the complete psychological works of Sigmund Freud,* 8.

(1905b). *Three essays on the theory of sexuality. The standard edition of the complete psychological works of Sigmund Freud,* 7.

(1909). *Analysis of a phobia in a five-year-old boy. The standard edition of the complete psychological works of Sigmund Freud,* 10.

(1910). The psycho-analytic view of psychogenic disturbance of vision. *The standard edition of the complete psychological works of Sigmund Freud,* 11.

(1911). Psycho-analytic notes on an autobiographical account of a case of paranoia (dementia paranoides). *The standard edition of the complete psychological works of Sigmund Freud,* 12.

(1912). A note on the unconscious in psychoanalysis. *The standard edition of the complete psychological works of Sigmund Freud,* 12.

(1914). On narcissism: An introduction. *The standard edition of the complete psychological works of Sigmund Freud,* 14.

(1915a). The unconscious. *The standard edition of the complete psychological works of Sigmund Freud*, 14.

(1915b). Repression. *The standard edition of the complete psychological works of Sigmund Freud*, 14.

(1915c). Instincts and their vicissitudes. *The standard edition of the complete psychological works of Sigmund Freud*, 14.

(1915d). Thoughts for the times on war and death. *The standard edition of the complete psychological works of Sigmund Freud*, 14.

(1916–17). Introductory lectures on psychoanalysis. *The standard edition of the complete psychological works of Sigmund Freud*, 16.

(1918). From the history of an infantile neurosis. *The standard edition of the complete psychological works of Sigmund Freud*, 17.

(1920). Beyond the pleasure principle. *The standard edition of the complete psychological works of Sigmund Freud*, 18.

(1923). The ego and the id. *The standard edition of the complete psychological works of Sigmund Freud*, 19.

(1925). An autobiographical study. *The standard edition of the complete psychological works of Sigmund Freud*, 20.

(1926). Inhibitions, symptoms and anxiety. *The standard edition of the complete psychological works of Sigmund Freud*, 20.

(1930). Civilization and its discontents. *The standard edition of the complete psychological works of Sigmund Freud*, 21.

(1932). New introductory lectures on psycho-analysis. *The standard edition of the complete psychological works of Sigmund Freud*, 22.

(1937). Constructions in analysis. *The standard edition of the complete psychological works of Sigmund Freud*, 23.

(1938a). An outline of psycho-analysis. *The standard edition of the complete psychological works of Sigmund Freud*, 23.

(1938b) Some elementary lessons. *The standard edition of the complete psychological works of Sigmund Freud*, 23.

(1950/1895). *Project for a scientific psychology. The standard edition of the complete psychological works of Sigmund Freud*, 1.

(1954/1897). *The origins of psycho-analysis: Letters to Wilhelm Fliess, drafts and notes. 1887–1902.* M. Bonaparte, A. Freud and E. Kris (eds.). New York: Basic Books.

(1995/1887–1904). *The complete letters of Sigmund Freud to Wilhelm Fliess 1887–1904.* Cambridge, Mass.: The Belknap Press of Harvard University Press.

Gadamer, H.-G. (1985/1960). *Truth and method.* New York: Crossroad.

Geerardyn, F. (1997). *Freud's project. On the roots of psychoanalysis.* London: Rebus Press.

Green, A. (1996). Has sexuality anything to do with psychoanalysis? *International journal of psychoanalysis*, 76: 871–83.

(2003). *The chains of Eros. The sexual in psychoanalysis.* London: Karnac Books.

Grünbaum, A. (1984). *The foundations of psychoanalysis: A philosophical critique.* Berkeley: University of California Press.

Gurwitsch, A. (1964). *The field of consciousness.* Pittsburgh: Duquesne University Press.

Habermas, J. (1972). *Knowledge and human interests.* Boston: Beacon Press.

Halling, S. (1997). Truth in the context of relationship: The researcher as witness. Paper presented at Phenomenology and Narrative Psychology. The Fourteenth Annual Symposium of the Simon Silverman Phenomenology Center. Duquesne University, Pittsburgh, USA.

Hanly, Ch. (1990). The concept of truth in psychoanalysis. *International journal of psychoanalysis*, 71: 375–83.

Hanly, M. F. (1996). 'Narrative', now and then: A critical realist approach. *International journal of psychoanalysis*, 77: 445–57.

Heidegger, M. (1980/1927). *Being and time.* Oxford: Basil Blackwell.

(2001). *Zollikon seminars. Protocols – Conversations – Letters.* Medard Boss (ed.). Evanston, Ill.: Northwestern University Press.

Holt, R. (1989). *Freud reappraised.* New York: The Guilford Press.

Humphrey, N. (1992). *A history of the mind.* London: Chatto & Windus.

Husserl, E. (1956/1923–24). *Erste Philosophie. Erster Teil. Kritische Ideengeschichte.* Den Haag: Martinus Nijhoff.

(1959/1923–24). *Erste Philosophie. Zweiter Teil. Theorie der phänomenologischen Reduktion.* Den Haag: Martinus Nijhoff.

(1962/1913). *Ideas. General introduction to pure phenomenology*, vol. I. New York: Collier Books.

(1964/1905). *The phenomenology of internal time-consciousness.* Bloomington: Indiana University Press.

(1965/1910–11). Philosophy as rigorous science. In E. Husserl. *Phenomenology and the crisis of philosophy.* New York: Harper Row.

(1968/1928). Amsterdam Vorträge: Phänomenologische Psychologie. In E. Husserl. *Phänomenologische Psychologie.* Den Haag: Martinus Nijhoff.

(1970/1900–1). *Logical investigations.* New York: Humanities Press.

(1970/1936a). *The crisis of European sciences and transcendental phenomenology.* Evanston, Ill.: Northwestern University Press.

(1970/1936b). Fink's appendix on the problem of the 'unconscious'. In E. Husserl. *The crisis of European sciences and transcendental phenomenology.* Evanston, Ill.: Northwestern University Press.

(1970/1936c). The origin of geometry. In E. Husserl. *The crisis of European sciences and transcendental phenomenology*. Evanston, Ill.: Northwestern University Press.

(1977/1925). *Phenomenological psychology*. The Hague: Martinus Nijhoff.

(1980/1912). *Ideas pertaining to a pure phenomenology and to a phenomenological philosophy. Third book. Phenomenology and the foundations of the sciences*. The Hague: Martinus Nijhoff.

(1981/1927). Phenomenology. (Husserl's article for the *Encyclopaedia Britannica*. Revised translation by R.E. Palmer). In P. McCormick and F. Elliston (eds.). *Husserl: Shorter works*. University of Notre Dame Press.

(2000/1918). *Ideas pertaining to a pure phenomenology and to a phenomenological philosophy. Second book. Studies in the phenomenology of constitution*. The Hague: Martinus Nijhoff.

Igra, L. (1998). Inledning [Introduction]. In *Samlade skrifter av Sigmund Freud [The collected works of Sigmund Freud]*, vol. V. Stockholm: Natur och Kultur.

James, W. (1890). *The principle of psychology*. London: Macmillan and Company.

Johansson, P.M. (1997). Förord [Preface]. In P. Robinson. *Freud och hans kritiker [Freud and his critics]*. Göteborg: Daidalos.

Kaplan, S. (2002). Children in the Holocaust. Dealing with affects and memory images in trauma and generational linking. Doctoral dissertation at the Department of Education, Stockholm University.

Kaplan-Solms, K. and Solms, M. (2000). *Clinical studies in neuro-psychoanalysis. Introduction to a depth neuropsychology*. London: Karnac Books.

Karlsson, G. (1992). The grounding of psychological research in a phenomenological epistemology. *Theory & psychology*, 2: 403–29.

(1993). *Psychological qualitative research from a phenomenological perspective*. Stockholm: Almqvist & Wiksell International.

(1998). Beyond the pleasure principle: The affirmation of existence. *Scandinavian psychoanalytic review*, 21: 37–52.

(2000). The question of truth claims in psychoanalysis. *Scandinavian psychoanalytic review*, 23: 3–24.

(2004). The conceptualisation of the psychical in psychoanalysis. *International journal of psychoanalysis*, 85: 381–400.

Kielhofner, G., Tham, K., Baz, T. and Hutson, J. (2002). Performance capacity and lived body. In G. Kielhofner (ed.). *Model of human occupation*. Baltimore: Lipincott Williams & Wilkins.

Killingmo, B. (1989). Conflict and deficit: Implications for technique. *International journal of psychoanalysis*, 70: 65–79.

Kris, E. (1956). The recovery of childhood memories in psychoanalysis. *Psychoanalytic study of the child*, 11: 54–88.

Künstlicher, R. (1994). 'Nachträglichkeit': The intermediary of an unassimilated impression and experience. *Scandinavian psychoanalytic review*, 17: 101–18.

Lacan, J. (2007/1959–60). *Ethics of psychoanalysis*. London: Taylor & Francis Ltd.

Lagache, D. (1993/1962). The conception of man in the psychoanalytic experience. In D. Lagache. *The work of Daniel Lagache. Selected writings*. London: Karnac Books.

Landgrebe, L. (1966). The world concept. In L. Landgrebe. *Major problems in contemporary European philosophy*. New York: Ungar.

—— (1981). The problem of a transcendental science, of the a priori of the life-world. In P. Welton (ed.). *The phenomenology of Edmund Husserl. Six essays*. Ithaca: Cornell University Press.

Laplanche, J. (1979). Une métapsychologie à l'épreuve de l'angoisse. *Psychanalyse à l'Université*, 4: 709–36.

—— (1986). La pulsion de mort dans la théorie de la pulsion sexuelle. In A. Green, P. Ikonen, J. Laplanche, E. Rechardt, H. Segal and D. Widlöcher (eds.). *La pulsion de mort*. Paris: Presses Universitaires de France.

—— (1989). *New foundations for psychoanalysis*. Cambridge: Basil Blackwell.

—— (1992). Interpretation between determinism and hermeneutics: A restatement of the problem. *International journal of psychoanalysis*, 73: 429–45.

—— (1999a). *The unconscious and the id*. London: Rebus Press.

—— (1999b). *Essays on otherness*. London: Routledge.

—— and Pontalis, J.-B. (1985). *The language of psychoanalysis*. London: The Hogarth Press.

Laub, D. and Auerhahn, N.C. (1993). Knowing and not knowing massive psychiatric trauma: Forms of traumatic memory. *International journal of psychoanalysis*, 74: 287–302.

Lerner, M. (1999). *Psykosomatik. Kroppens och själens dialektik [Psychosomatics. The dialectic of body and soul]*. Stockholm: Natur och Kultur.

Lesche, C. (1981). The relation between metapsychology and psychoanalytic practice. *Scandinavian psychoanalytic review*, 4: 59–74.

Lind, L. (1991). Thanatos: The drive without a name. The development of the concept of the death drive in Freud's writings. *Scandinavian psychoanalytic review*, 14: 60–80.

Matte-Blanco, I. (1988). *Thinking, feeling, and being. Clinical reflections on the fundamental antinomy of human beings and world*. London: Routledge.

Matthis, I. (1997). *Den tänkande kroppen. Studier i det hysteriska symptomet* *[The thinking body. Studies in the hysteric symptom].* Stockholm: Natur och Kultur.

May, U. (1999). Freud's early clinical theory (1894–1896): Outline and context. *International journal of psychoanalysis,* 80: 769–81.

McCall, R. (1983). *Phenomenological psychology.* London: The University of Wisconsin Press.

McDougall, J. (1989). *A psychoanalytic approach to psychosomatic illness.* London: W. W. Norton & Company Inc.

Merleau-Ponty, M. (1962/1945). *The phenomenology of perception.* New Jersey: The Humanities Press.

——— (1963/1942). *The structure of behavior.* Boston: Beacon Press.

——— (1982–83). Phenomenology and psychoanalysis: Preface to Hesnard's L'oeuvre de Freud. *Review of existential psychology and psychiatry,* 18: 67–72.

Monti, M. R. (2005). New interpretative styles: Progress or contamination? Psychoanalysis and phenomenological psychopathology. *International journal of psychoanalysis,* 86: 1011–32.

Norman, J. (2001). The psychoanalyst and the baby: A new look at work with infants. *International journal of psychoanalysis,* 82: 83–100.

Ogden, T. H. (1992). *The primitive edge of experience.* London: Karnac Books.

Olds, D. and Cooper, A. M. (1997). Dialogue with other sciences: Opportunities for mutual gain. *International journal of psychoanalysis,* 78: 219–25.

Pally, R. and Olds, D. (1998). Consciousness: A neuroscience perspective. *International journal of psychoanalysis,* 79: 971–89.

Pontalis, J.-B. (1982–83). The problem of the unconscious in Merleau-Ponty's thought. *Review of existential psychology & psychiatry,* 18: 83–96.

Popper, K. (1959). *The logic of scientific discovery.* London: Routledge and Kegan Paul.

——— (1972). *Conjectures and refutations.* London: Routledge and Kegan Paul.

Pöstényi, A. (1996). Hitom lusprincipen. Dröm, trauma, dödsdrift [On this side of the pleasure principle. Dream, trauma, death drive]. *Divan,* 3: 4–15.

Reeder, J. (2000). The real thing. Objektrelationens etiska bräcklighet [The real thing. The ethical fragility of the object relation]. In J. Reeder, C. Sjöholm and Z. Zivkovic (eds.). *Tingets imperium. Tre läsningar av Jacques Lacans Psykoanalysens etik [The empire of the thing. Three readings of Jacques Lacan's Ethics of psychoanalysis].* Stockholm: Natur och Kultur.

Reeder, J., Sjöholm, C. and Zivkovic, Z. (2000). *Tingets imperium. Tre läsningar av Jacques Lacans Psykoanalysens etik [The empire of the thing. Three readings of Jacques Lacan's Ethics of psychoanalysis].* Stockholm: Natur och Kultur.

Ricoeur, P. (1970). *Freud and philosophy: An essay on interpretation.* New Haven, Conn.: Yale University Press.

(1977). The question of proof in Freud's psychoanalytic writings. *Journal of the American Psychoanalytic Association*, 25: 835–71. (Also published in P. Ricoeur (1981). *Hermeneutics and the human sciences.* Cambridge University Press.)

Salonen, S. (1992). The reconstruction of psychic trauma. *Scandinavian psychoanalytic review*, 15: 89–103.

Sandler, J. and Sandler, A.-M. (1983). The 'second censorship', the 'three box model' and some technical implications. *International journal of psychoanalysis*, 64: 413–25.

Sartre, J.-P. (1948). *The emotions: Outline of a theory.* New Jersey: Citadel Press.

(1956/1942). *Being and nothingness. A phenomenological essay on ontology.* New York: Simon & Schuster.

Schafer, R. (1976). *A new language for psychoanalysis.* New York: Yale University Press.

(1979). The appreciative analytic attitude and the construction of multiple histories. *Psychoanalysis and contemporary thought*, 2: 3–24.

(1980). Narration in the psychoanalytic dialogue. *Critical inquiry*, 7: 29–53.

(1993). *The analytic attitude.* London: Karnac Books.

Schopenhauer, A. (1995/1818). *The world as will and idea.* London: Everyman.

Schütz, A. (1962). On multiple realities. In A. Schütz. *Collected Papers vol. 1: The problem of social reality.* The Hague: Martinus Nijhoff.

Sokolowski, R. (2000). *Introduction to phenomenology.* Cambridge University Press.

Solms, M. (1997). What is consciousness? *Journal of the American Psychoanalytic Association*, 45: 681–703.

and Turnbull, O. (2002). *The brain and the inner world.* New York: Other Press.

Spence, D. P. (1982a). *Narrative truth and historical truth. Meaning and interpretation in psychoanalysis.* New York: W. W. Norton & Company Inc.

(1982b). Narrative truth and theoretical truth. *Psychoanalytic quarterly*, 51: 43–69.

(1983). Narrative persuasion. *Psychoanalysis and contemporary thought*, 6: 457–81.

Spiegelberg, H. (1967). The relevance of phenomenological philosophy for psychology. In E. N. Lee and M. Mandelbaum (eds.). *Phenomenology and existentialism.* Baltimore: The Johns Hopkins Press.

(1972). *Phenomenology in psychology and psychiatry: A historical introduction.* Evanston, Ill.: Northwestern University Press.

(1982). *The phenomenological movement. A historical introduction.* The Hague: Martinus Nijhoff.

Stein, R. (1998a). The enigmatic dimension of sexual experience: The 'otherness' of sexuality and primal seduction. *Psychoanalytic quarterly,* 67: 594–625.

(1998b). The poignant, the excessive and the enigmatic in sexuality. *International journal of psychoanalysis,* 79: 253–68.

(2008). The otherness of sexuality: Excess. *Journal of the American Psychoanalytic Association,* 56: 43–71.

Steinbock, A.J. (1995). *Home and beyond. Generative phenomenology after Husserl.* Evanston, Ill.: Northwestern University Press.

Stoller, R.J. (1979). *Sexual excitement. Dynamics of erotic life.* London: Maresfield Library.

Strachey, J. (1957). Editor's note to S. Freud's 'Instincts and their vicissitudes' (1915). *The standard edition of the complete psychological works of Sigmund Freud,* 14: 111–16.

(1962). Editor's note to S. Freud's 'On the grounds for detaching a particular syndrome from neurasthenia under the description "anxiety neurosis"' (1895). *The standard edition of the complete psychological works of Sigmund Freud,* 3: 87–9.

Svenaeus, F. (2001). *The hermeneutics of medicine and the phenomenology of health: Steps towards a philosophy of medical practice.* Dordrecht: Kluwer Academic Publishers.

Toombs, K. (1992). *The meaning of illness. A phenomenological account of the different perspectives of physician and patient.* Dordrecht: Kluwer Academic Publishers.

Viderman, S. (1979). The analytic space: Meaning and problems. *Psychoanalytic quarterly,* 48: 257–91.

Wallerstein, R.S. (1983). Reality and its attributes as psychoanalytic concepts: An historical overview. *International review of psychoanalysis,* 10: 125–44.

(1985). The concept of psychic reality: Its meaning and value. *Journal of the American Psychoanalytic Association,* 33: 555–69.

(1992). One psychoanalysis or many. In R.S. Wallerstein (ed.). *The common ground of psychoanalysis.* London: Jason Aronson.

Wetzler, S. (1985). The historical truth of psychoanalytic reconstructions. *International review of psychoanalysis,* 12: 187–97.

Winnicott, D.W. (1965/1960a). The theory of the parent–infant relationship. In D.W. Winnicott. *The maturational processes and the facilitating environment.* London: The Hogarth Press.

(1965/1960b). Ego distortion in terms of true and false self. In D.W. Winnicott. *The maturational processes and the facilitating environment.* London: The Hogarth Press.

(1965/1962). Ego integration in child development. In D.W. Winnicott. *The maturational processes and the facilitating environment.* London: The Hogarth Press.

(1965/1963). Psychiatric disorder in terms of infantile maturational processes. In D.W. Winnicott. *The maturational processes and the facilitating environment.* London: The Hogarth Press.

Wright, E. (1992). *Feminism and psychoanalysis. A critical dictionary.* Oxford: Blackwell Publishers.

Zahavi, D. (1999). *Self-awareness and alterity. A phenomenological investigation.* Evanston, Ill.: Northwestern University Press.

(2003). *Husserl's phenomenology.* California: Stanford University Press.

# Index